# THE
# TAYLOR
# YEARS

Cricket books by Ken Piesse

*Great Triumphs in Test Cricket* (1979)
*Prahran Cricket Club Centenary History* (1979)
*Cricket Digest Annual* (ed.) (1980)
*Cricket Year Annual* (ed.) (1980–83)
*Calypso Summers* (with Jim Main) (1981)
*The Great Australian Book of Cricket Stories* (1982)
*The Golden Age of Australian Cricket* (ed.) (1982)
*Duel for Glory: England Tours of Australia 1861–1982*
(with Jim Main) (1982)
*Donald Bradman* (*Famous Australians* series) (1983)
*Cartoonists at the Cricket* (ed.) (1983)
*The A to Z of Cricket* (1983)
*Bradman & the Bush* (with Ian Ferguson) (1986)
*Great Australian Cricket Stories* (1988)
*Hooked on Cricket* (with Max Walker) (1988)
*Match Drawn* (ed.) (1988)
*Simply the Best: The Allan Border Story* (1993)
*Warne: Sultan of Spin* (1995)
*Cricket Skills & Secrets* (1995–99)
*One Day Magic* (1996)
*The Big Australian Cricket Book* (1996)
*Wildmen of Cricket Vol. 1* (with Brian Hansen) (1998)
*TJ Over the Top* (with Terry Jenner) (1999)

# THE
# TAYLOR
# YEARS

## AUSTRALIAN
## CRICKET
## 1994–99

### KEN PIESSE

VIKING

The author and publisher would like to thank the following for permission to include material: *Steve Waugh's West Indian Tour Diary* by Steve Waugh © 1995, published by HarperCollins Publishers; *The Sunday Age*; *Inside Edge* magazine.

Viking
Penguin Books Australia Ltd
487 Maroondah Highway, PO Box 257
Ringwood, Victoria 3134, Australia
Penguin Books Ltd
Harmondsworth, Middlesex, England
Penguin Putnam Inc.
375 Hudson Street, New York, New York 10014, USA
Penguin Books Canada Limited
10 Alcorn Avenue, Toronto, Ontario, Canada M4V 3B2
Penguin Books (N.Z.) Ltd
Cnr Rosedale and Airborne Roads, Albany, Auckland, New Zealand
Penguin Books (South Africa) (Pty) Ltd
5 Watkins Street, Denver Ext 4, 2094, South Africa
Penguin Books India (P) Ltd
11, Community Centre, Panchsheel Park, New Delhi 110 017, India

First published by Penguin Books Australia Ltd 1999

1 3 5 7 9 10 8 6 4 2

Copyright © Ken Piesse 1999

Cover design by Anitra Blackford, Penguin Design Studio
Text design by Penguin Design Studio
Typeset in 11/15 Fairfield by Midland Typesetters, Maryborough, Victoria
Printed and bound in Australia by Australian Print Group, Maryborough, Victoria

National Library of Australia
Cataloguing-in-Publication data:

Piesse, Ken.
The Taylor years: Australian cricket 1994–99.

Bibliography.
Includes index.
ISBN 0 670 88829 X.

1. Taylor, Mark, 1964–. 2. Cricket – Australia. 3. Cricket captains – Australia. 4. Cricket players – Australia – Biography. 5. Test matches (Cricket). I. Title.

796.358650994

www.penguin.com.au

# CONTENTS

Acknowledgements    VII
Foreword by Ian Healy    IX
FIRST BALL    I

ONE
THE SCOOP OF THE CENTURY    6

TWO
A YOUNG CAPTAIN EMERGES    12

THREE
SUCCEEDING A LEGEND    19

FOUR
PAKISTAN '94    24

FIVE
CHASING THE TITLE    38

SIX
A WINNING COMBINATION    46

SEVEN
DEFENDING THE ASHES    57

EIGHT
THE PROUDEST MOMENT    63

NINE

JUSTICE IN THE GAME    80

TEN

THE ULTIMATE BOILOVER    94

ELEVEN

A WAKE-UP CALL    102

TWELVE

SUMMER OF SPEED AND SPITE    106

THIRTEEN

SPEAKING OF SUCCESSORS    117

FOURTEEN

HITTING THE WALL    129

FIFTEEN

CRUSADING FOR THEIR MATES    137

SIXTEEN

AMBUSHED, TORTURED AND TRAMPLED    151

SEVENTEEN

CHASING THE DON    160

EIGHTEEN

A PROUD FAREWELL    174

NINETEEN

AUSTRALIAN OF THE YEAR    188

FINAL OVER    198
Taylor Tributes    203
Statistics    208
Further Reading    232
Index    234

# ACKNOWLEDGEMENTS

I'M ONE OF THE FORTUNATE ones who happen to love their job. Sitting through five days of riveting cricket in Barbados and Antigua in 1999 and sharing the highs and lows with 2000 Australians who had also made the big trip was a position of privilege and a springboard to the publication of this book.

It has been a glorious decade for Australian cricket, in which the interest in the game and the national team has snowballed. Australia's status as Test and one-day world champions is well deserved.

My particular thanks to Ian Healy for contributing the foreword and to Ken Williams for his expert statistical appraisals.

Many others, on tour, in conversations and interviews throughout the period have also participated. In particular, my thanks to Wendy and Shane Aston, David Boon, Wayne Carey, Greg Chappell, Kevin Chevell, Alan Crompton, Kevin Dale, Ross Dundas, Craig Dunshea, Jack Edwards, Ric Finlay/TCPro, Damien Fleming, John Fordham, Brian Freedman, Graham Gooch, Graham Halbish, Austin Hughes, Terry Jenner, Len King, Bill Lawry, Stuart MacGill, Neil Marks, Geoff Marsh, Tim May, Glenn McGrath, Bob Merriman, Bob Parish, Peter Philpott, Rod Pilon, Denis Rogers, Michael Slater, Peter Taylor, Tony & Judy Taylor, Ross Turner and Steve and Mark Waugh.

I'd also like to thank Robert Sessions, Katie Purvis, Peter Ascot and everyone at Penguin for their confidence in the project.

# FOREWORD
# BY IAN HEALY

GREG CHAPPELL ONCE SAID you pay the price for success in advance. Nothing could be truer when it comes to the unprecedented record of the Australian cricket team in the 90s. Having built the foundation under Allan Border, whose leadership in the toughest possible climate should never be underrated, we became the world's best under Mark Taylor and as we approach the year 2000, remain No. 1 under Steve Waugh.

The balance of a world-championship team is crucial and the core players of the side have a hard edge and have performed when needed. I don't know if many of the other sides train like Australia; we rarely see them. But the work ethic and the effort is very important and it does pay off. There are no short cuts taken and no substitute for hard work.

It's the Australian way and one which should always be – though it may pay us to keep an eye on other sides and what is coming through, especially the South Africans. A little spying to see how they are working wouldn't go astray!

It has been a demanding and highly challenging era . . . times I'll always regard as the greatest of my life. To be part of one of the most successful Australian teams of all time is a position of privilege. Under Mark, our wins in Jamaica in '95 and Johannesburg and Port Elizabeth in '97 were nothing short of sensational.

The Windies, unbeaten at home for 20 years, had evened the series on one of the greenest wickets we'd ever seen at Port-of-Spain, setting up a last-man-standing showdown at Jamaica. The Waugh partnership really took us out of their reach and then our bowlers did the rest. Stephen's 200 remains the best innings I've seen in Test cricket. Sachin Tendulkar and Brian Lara have also played some gems, but Stephen's was the one which had most impact on me. He was peppered by the short stuff and had to jump and weave for most of the 10 hours he batted. It was a magnificent feat of endurance and without it, we could never have won as comprehensively. We partied like world champions should and seeing Stephen, still in all his playing gear including his baggy green, with that Charlie Chaplin walk of his trying to find a door which matched his room key that night remains an enduring memory, as does Justin Langer proudly draping himself in an Australian flag all night.

At Port Elizabeth, having started the series with such impact at Johannesburg, the South Africans were really coming at us and looking to square the series 1–1. The wicket was doing plenty and they'd established a 184-run lead with all 10 second innings wickets in hand. With three days still to play, a result was assured. It wasn't going to be a draw. That night we met and re-emphasised what we needed to do. None of us could have imagined what was to happen the next day. We took 10 for 85 and they set us 270 to win – and we finished up getting them through a great century from Mark Waugh, at the time the best I'd ever seen from Mark. My winning six capped it off nicely for me. It was a great atmosphere afterwards and prelude to another absolutely outstanding party!

I was Mark's deputy captain in that period and for that I'm very proud. The vice-captaincy role probably suited me the best, especially in an era when Australia's attack was so heavily biased towards spin. For wicketkeepers, Test match cricket is so much harder than one-dayers, especially when the team is under pressure and the batsmen are getting on top. The 'keeper needs to be right on his mettle and work as hard as he can on his job, and that isn't easy on flat wickets with spin bowlers operating for long periods. Shane Warne's genius helped put me on the map and for that I'm thankful, but it was still bloody hard work! And I wouldn't mind a dollar for every time I said, 'Bowled, Shane!'

I was always genuinely thrilled to be given any leadership role and the opportunity to captain the team on the Sri Lanka and South African one-day tours in 1996–97 remains a big highlight for me. Our team was very powerful, very united and very switched on, which had a lot to do with Mark's handling of players and his open lines of communication. He was constantly setting us challenges, seeing just how far we could go.

There were some that got away from us, but not many and that's to Mark's great credit. He always wanted us to play our natural games and to enjoy it along the way.

There were some difficult periods for him as a batsman and I have no doubt that the captaincy sapped his energy. But throughout all of those 50 Tests as captain, he gave great confidence to the rest of the side and had an evenness and confidence in all situations.

People have often asked me could we have been as good if Mark *hadn't* been captain. I would never say that anyone else would have done the job that Mark did, but what we may have lost in his captaincy, we would have picked up in his batting.

What really made our era was our consistent performances and our depth, which for years has undoubtedly been the best in the world. The players were not only very, very good in Australia, they were champions everywhere else, too. Mark's captaincy was the icing on the cake.

The side's dynamic has been great for the last seven or eight years. If Allan Border missed out, then one of the Waughs or Greg Blewett would put their hands up and throw in a big one when it was most needed. 'Slats' (Michael Slater) has also been good like that.

The bowlers have worked off each other and while we have been heavily dependent on Shane Warne and Glenn McGrath in recent times, the input of Merv Hughes and Craig McDermott in the early years should never be forgotten. Tim May had a good combination going with Shane for a time. Others such as Paul Reiffel, Damien Fleming, 'Dizzy' Gillespie, Michael Kasprowicz and Michael Bevan have also had their big moments.

Because we had these guys to back each other up and Warnie in such superb form, we were able to cope without McGrath for almost a year. When Warnie struggled to come up again after his shoulder operation, 'Pigeon' (McGrath) and 'Magilla' (Stewie MacGill) put their hands up. Batsmen rarely had any room to move.

It seems we have always been able to change players smoothly, which says something about our system and the good job Rod Marsh is doing down at the Cricket Academy.

Our planning and homework has also played a part. Team meetings have varied of late from either being the night before or two nights before a game. Not everyone can absorb a whole heap of information immediately before performing and I believe the earlier you get that information in your head the better. The coach will open the meetings with his say and then hand over to the captain to run it. Mark always liked to let as many people as possible have their say before setting our plans in concrete.

Mark was observant and always thinking. His strategies were second to none. We nutted out the Poms pretty well, how to bowl to them and where we felt we could get each of them out. The focus would then be on the bowlers to get the field working for them. We also had pretty good success with Brian Lara – up until the '99 series, anyway!

Mark certainly controlled the team but never knocked back anybody else's opinion because he knew even if they were 12th or 13th they still have a lot of cricket experience to offer and this should be tapped into.

Over the years we had many lighter moments, beers and bar room chats. On the field, we were pretty well focused on our immediate jobs, though we'd occasionally toss something around about what might have happened the previous night.

Mark's reflexes at slip were remarkable. He covered for me a couple of times when I didn't move particularly well for catches. Going to his left or his right was never a problem. He was very supple and would get to the low ones, one hand or two. Once, in Sydney, he caught Carl Hooper soccer-style, having kicked the ball up with his feet and finished on his back with the ball in his grip! His old PE teacher at Wagga would have been rapt in that one! 'Bevo' certainly was. Talk about a bonus for a bowler!

More than 50 of Mark's catches came off Warnie, which must be some sort of record. Fifteen of those would have been screamers; ones in which I've just looked around to see him emerging with the ball. If you have good basics the screamers will happen and no one, not even 'Junior' (Mark Waugh) has taken as many as Mark.

Mark's most noticeable on-field habit was his gum chewing, which as his old mate Neil Marks loves to say, clearly resembles a cow. Standing next to him so often, I always found it audible. On tense afternoons, it could be downright loud!

Still, it was his way of helping himself to keep it together and invariably it worked.

Mark's winning strike-rate, as documented in Ken Piesse's excellent book, is right up there with some of the very best captains of them all. Ken says our teams under Mark stand tall as the best of all time, outside Don Bradman's '48 side to England. It's difficult to compare eras, but no one has gone undefeated in nine series in a row like us. No matter where history eventually places us, it's a record everyone who had an involvement is very proud of. May this book recapture some of the magic memories of what will always be regarded as one of Australian cricket's finest eras. It was a pleasure to be a part of it.

*Ian Healy*
BRISBANE, AUGUST 1999

# FIRST BALL

THE INVINCIBLES ASIDE, Mark Taylor's Australians have every claim to be Australia's all-time outstanding cricket team. Their success rate in the Cyberspace era against all comers was simply phenomenal. No team, not even the Greats of '48, could boast nine consecutive series without defeat.

Under Taylor, Australia embarked on an extraordinary run of success, winning 52 per cent of its matches and ranking as the game's undisputed world champion.

With the Waugh twins, Shane Warne, Ian Healy and Glenn McGrath, the side boasted a group of Australia's all-time finest, whose impact will remain indelible for generations.

Great men have invariably been in charge of the most celebrated cricket teams and in Taylor, Australia not only had an outstanding opening batsman and slipsman, but a consummate ambassador who, from his opening days in office, stamped his imprimatur with flair and dignity.

Until Taylor inherited Australian sport's most coveted position in May 1994, the Australian cricket team had been unable to deliver the ultimate knockout blow against the long-running champions, the West Indies. Determining to be proactive and imaginative, Taylor changed the entire philosophy against the Windies. The fear factor was forgotten as the West Indian tailenders were bounced and intimidated, the Australians laughing at the fun of it all. Not only were the Windies beaten for the first time in the Caribbean for more than 20 years, Australia was to defeat Pakistan on the subcontinent for the first time for 39 years.

In 50 Tests as captain, Taylor challenged and surpassed the records of the game's finest post-war leaders. He led with skill, polish and imagination, setting his players fresh goals and encouraging them to aspire to new levels. He also brought a rare sanctity and boy-next-door feel to the position, his ambassadorial skills reinforcing the very fibre of the greatest of games.

So good was he that in 1999, Australian cricket authorities were prepared to break a golden rule and pick him first, followed by the 10 next best players, just to keep him involved. Some of the longest-serving administrators even rated him the very best captain since Don Bradman.

Having survived the worst form lapse of any Australian captain in history, Taylor's renaissance in England in '97 and particularly in Pakistan in '98 saw him rival team-mate Shane Warne and tennis ace Pat Rafter as the most popular sportsman in the country.

Throughout his reign, Taylor retained the perspective that Test cricket, as serious as it often could be, was still a game and should be enjoyed accordingly. Just days after what proved to be his farewell Test match in Sydney in January, he joined his club-mates at Northern District for a Saturday–Sunday fixture at Waitara Oval. He was as happy to be back with them as they were to see him.

When naming him the Australian of the Year in 1999, the Australia Day Council said: 'Cricket fans, or not, we admire his strength and the reflection in his character of the best of what is Australian.'

Optimistic and approachable, Taylor never put himself on a pedestal. He revelled in feedback and was always ready for a chat. Occasionally, he'd also get angry, but invariably it would only be passing. He ran the team his way, happily shouldering sole responsibility for decisions, his eye always on the win.

He could also be firm and opinionated when necessary, especially in his dealings over contracts and conditions with the Board. But they held him in highest possible esteem, thankful, even during the prolonged pay dispute in 1997–98, for his involvement. His approval meant everything when it came to dealing with a group of rebellious players, who, as a last resort, had threatened to boycott the opening four one-day games of the summer.

A reflection of his calm leadership and sporting philosophies was illustrated in the marked improvement of Australia's on-field behaviour. Only three players, fast bowlers Jo Angel and McGrath and wicketkeeper Healy, so contravened the spirit of the game as to warrant official rebuke. The dressing room was happier, more relaxed and focused with the banning of Walkmans and mobile phones. Players were encouraged to play their natural games and back themselves.

Some say Australia's success was all to do with timing and Taylor's sheer good fortune in having access to world-class strike bowlers like McGrath and Warne. But even they had their off days, and that's when Taylor truly showed his worth, improvising with a Ricky Ponting or a Greg Blewett or facilitating a radical fielding change which could see two and three fieldsmen at short midwicket, all in the name of trying to activate something.

While others like Border could be overly dour and, as a result, failed to win as many series as they should have, Taylor's philosophies from the first ball of a game centred squarely on victory. He refused to let a game meander, always believing he and his Australians had a duty to uphold the game's best traditions and play in as entertaining and as positive a fashion as possible.

The Waugh twins and Healy were magnificent lieutenants, as good as anyone in a crisis. Together with David Boon and Craig McDermott in the early days, and later Warne, McGrath and Greg Blewett, they had a central involvement in some unforgettable wins. When one failed, another would fire and invariably at the right time.

For years, Taylor was the cornerstone for a star-studded top order. He didn't always look pretty, but he was effective and his crease occupations paved the way for others to succeed, invariably when the conditions were easier.

At his peak he was the leading opening batsman in the world. While records were but an incidental, his tally of 19 Test centuries, including 100s at all six of Australia's Test grounds, has been surpassed by only the absolute elite.

As a slips fielder, he had no superior, not even the exquisitely gifted

Mark Waugh. Ian Healy aside, he took more catches than anyone in Australia's team in his five years at the helm.

Captaincy matters sometimes clouded his batting focus. After missing out a couple of times in his early days as Border's deputy, team-mates advised him to go back and read the batting hints he contributed to *Cricketer* magazine!

His game was built around a rock-like defence, a hook and a pull shot and when fully set, a full-faced drive which would race past extra cover to reach even the longest square boundary.

His special gift, just like a Warne leg-break or a Mark Waugh cover drive, was his determination and ability to soak up pressure and stay cool, even when it seemed everything else was falling apart around him. 'He's a stronger man than you or me,' team coach Geoff Marsh once said.

The records of every Australian side, bar the Bradman-led Ashes trip in 1948, pale against the feats of Taylor and Co.

The closest, in terms of the champions they fielded and their win–loss records, are:

- Joe Darling's 1901–02 side which came from behind to win the Ashes 4–1. It included the immortal Victor Trumper, the champion of the Golden Age;
- Warwick Armstrong's 1921 Australians who won seven Ashes Tests and drew the other two for the calendar year. Their famous opening attack of Jack Gregory and Ted McDonald is among the most feted in history;
- and Ian and Greg Chappell's champion teams of the early to mid-70s, featuring an even more intimidating set of matchwinners in Dennis Lillee and Jeff Thomson.

However, in an era which has never been more competitive, with teams like Pakistan and Sri Lanka becoming world beaters and even Test cricket minnows Zimbabwe warranting a tour and a historic first Test match against a full-strength Australian XI, the Taylor-led sides of the 90s will stand ahead – and deservedly so – of even the finest of those Australian cricket combinations.

And to think that Taylor's original appointment wasn't even unanimous! Those Australian Cricket Board delegates who did vote against him at an airport motel in Melbourne in mid-May, 1994, are mighty glad they were wrong.

# ONE

---

# THE
## SCOOP OF THE
## CENTURY

*Could Tubby be on the first plane to Sydney
tomorrow for the press conference?*

---

MARK TAYLOR WAS SITTING in his best suit at the Moree airport in
north-west New South Wales, waiting for the 8 a.m. plane to Sydney,
when a farmer in check shirt and overalls approached, keen to talk
cricket.

Farmer: 'You're Mark Taylor, aren't you?'

Taylor: 'That's correct.'

Farmer: 'Allan Border retired last week, didn't he? And you're vice-
captain. I reckon you're off to Sydney because you're the next captain.'

Taylor: 'Mate, if you can work all that out, you've got a four-hour
exclusive, because no one else in Australia is going to find out until
midday.'

It was 19 May 1994, just a week after Allan Border's muddied
retirement, in which he broadsided authorities, claiming he'd been
pushed into announcing his decision prematurely – all because of the
Australian Cricket Board's desire to release their squad for the
springtime tour to Pakistan, still four months away.

As Border's deputy-captain for 24 of the previous 26 Tests, Taylor, at 28, was heir apparent to Australian sport's No. 1 job. He'd captained New South Wales for two years with notable aggression and common sense. He'd also led an Australian 'B' team to Zimbabwe on the eve of the 1991–92 season. Not only was he respected for his skills as a world-class opening batsman and first slipsman, he was also a fine team player and diplomat. He was used to acting as a go-between for the rest of the side and the sometimes-feisty Border, once dubbed Captain Grumpy' after an infamous press conference. While Border was unashamedly a player's man and warred with the Board over discipline and fines, Taylor was the absolute professional off and on the field, and a keen listener with a sympathetic ear.

Just weeks earlier, at Stellenbosch in South Africa, it had been Taylor who counselled an angry Shane Warne, saying Warne was not acting like the Shane Warne all the players liked and respected. There'd been provocation at the Bullring during the first Test in Johannesburg, but all cricketers felt the heat at some stage in their career. The way they handled it was important. Cricketers had to be aware of their responsibilities on and off the field.

Weeks earlier, at Northern Transvaal, in the opening first-class fixture of the tour, he'd admonished opening partner Michael Slater for a reckless shot, saying he had to learn to be less impetuous and set himself to make big scores consistently.

To assist the selection process, the team's senior playing quartet of Taylor, Ian Healy, Steve Waugh and David Boon had all been interviewed, formally and individually, by the 14 directors of the Australian Cricket Board. Questions about how they saw the team and how they saw the immediate future were important factors in the first captaincy vote for 10 years.

All the directors had previously been briefed about the candidates, but for some it was the first opportunity to truly form their own opinion. Each of the interviews went for at least 15 minutes, some longer.

A complication for the directors in formulating a decision was that the youngest of the candidates, Healy and Waugh, while outstanding players and frontline choices at both levels of the game, had only had limited leadership experience.

Healy had been a Sheffield Shield captain since 1992–93 and thrown himself into his responsibilities with enthusiasm and purpose. However, he'd missed large chunks of the domestic season because of his international duties. History was also against his appointment. Only one wicketkeeper had led Australia in 100 years and that was as a fill-in (Barry Jarman for one Ashes Test in 1968, after touring captain Bill Lawry broke a finger). Steve Waugh had captained NSW only twice, when coming back from an injury, but had been very impressive.

At 33, Boon was the oldest of the quartet. He was only 18 months away from his international retirement and was considered by most as an outsider, despite having first been made Australia's vice-captain in 1986–87, at the age of 25. He'd played more Tests (89) than Taylor (54), Waugh (65) and Healy (62).

The five-man national selection committee endorsed Taylor, NSW captain since 1992–93.

The Board members met at a Tullamarine motel, chosen for its proximity to Melbourne airport, and while Board minutes do not disclose the fine details, it's understood when chairman Alan Crompton called for an initial vote, Taylor received 10 votes, Healy 2, Boon 2 and Waugh 0. In a split decision, Healy, four years Boon's junior, was made vice-captain.

'Extensive reports on all the candidates were provided,' said the ACB's Denis Rogers, then a Tasmanian delegate. 'We had a chance to interview them all. It was obvious Mark had the depth of character and quality of personality to cope with the job.'

The Taylors were staying at 'Glen Eden', an 8000-acre farm in Gurley owned by old friend and Northern District team-mate, ex-Australian spin bowler Peter Taylor, when the telephone rang. It was Ian McDonald, the Australian Cricket Board's media manager, who'd just returned to Sydney from a directors' meeting in Melbourne.

McDonald was calling from his mobile and for security reasons didn't want to talk for too long. The directors had earlier that day ratified Taylor as captain. Ian Healy was to be his deputy. Could

Tubby be on the first plane to Sydney tomorrow for the press conference?

Taylor allowed himself two glasses of champagne before packing himself off to bed. He wanted to be fully rested. The next day he was to face the media as Australia's 39th Test captain.

As part of the elaborate plan to keep Taylor's appointment secret, McDonald had arranged a ticket to be at the Moree airport in the name of 'Peter Taylor'. He didn't want to alert even airport staff at a tiny country outpost of the ACB's plans. Australia hadn't had a new Test captain for 10 years. The story mustn't get out just yet.

Taylor must have looked quite a sight sitting in his suit high up in the cabin of Peter Taylor's favourite old truck, complete with its dirty steel seats, bumping the 35 kilometres into the town's airport.

Hours later, Taylor was beckoned through a side door at the New South Wales Cricket Association's offices in Druitt St, Sydney, as ACB chairman Alan Crompton made the announcement.

Dozens of media men were present. In addition to the television news reporters, there was a live cross to Channel Nine's *Midday Show* and later an appearance on *A Current Affair*. Taylor hadn't been prepared for all the fuss, or the hard line of many of the questions.

Several in the team had become frustrated and lost their cool months earlier in South Africa, but there was no room in his game plan for further player misbehaviour or sledging. He didn't intend to turn the Australian team into pussycats. But no longer would there be an excuse for the media to label his side as 'Ugly Australians'.

Central in his objectives, Taylor said, was not only to defeat Pakistan for the first time in 35 years on the subcontinent, but to gain a little revenge on Border's behalf next time Australia toured the Caribbean.

He returned to Moree on the night plane, where he was met by his wife Judi and the Taylors, who had organised a booking at a local restaurant, Cascades. A huge seafood platter was prepared and on being asked for the bill, the owners insisted that everything was on the house. It was enough for them to have Australia's new captain there for a night. Returning that night to 27 messages, all received in a three-hour period, Taylor realised that his life was never to be quite the same again.

From day one in office, Taylor addressed the issues with refreshing openness. Far from being in 'the second-most important job in Australia behind only the Prime Minister', as Channel 9's Ray Martin termed it that night, Taylor saw himself as being a sportsman first and foremost who was playing for the enjoyment. Once it became a chore, he'd quit.

He did admit, however, that the pressure on his post was so immense that there were sure to be occasions when he, too, might not always be able to set the right example. 'There'll be a Captain Grumpy come out of me at certain stages, for sure,' he said.

TAYLOR WAS INHERITING an accomplished, star-studded team which had, but for an erroneous umpiring decision, all but won the unofficial Test world championship 15 months earlier in Adelaide. Umpire Darrell Hair gave Australian No. 11 Craig McDermott out, when replays showed Courtney Walsh's head-high bouncer had touched his helmet rather than his gloves on the way through to wicketkeeper Junior Murray.

In a gripping ending, McDermott and Tim May had lifted Australia to within one run of a tie, with a brave 40-run stand for the last wicket after the top order had disintegrated. Earlier in Walsh's 19th over, had McDermott's attempted pull shot not been brilliantly stopped by Desmond Haynes at short leg, the Australians would certainly have won, giving Allan Border his finest moment in cricket.

'I thought it definitely hit the glove. I had as good a view as Darrell did at the time,' said Hair's co-umpire Len King. 'He looked over to me as we were walking off and I said: "Good decision." Allan Border even came into the room later and had a drink with Darrell and I. He said "Billy" [McDermott] was disappointed and felt he could have been given the benefit of the doubt, but he didn't make an issue out of it. It was only later that I saw a replay from a different angle which showed it could have tipped the helmet.'

Instead of Australia leading the Frank Worrell Trophy 2–0 with one

Test to play, it was 1–1. Four days later it was 1–2, thanks to Curtly Ambrose's demolition of the top order on a Perth green-top.

Australia was bowled out well before tea on the first day for just 119. In the most intimidating spell of fast bowling since Frank 'Typhoon' Tyson in Melbourne and Sydney almost 40 years earlier, Ambrose took 7/1 from 32 balls. The game, Border's 75th in a row as captain, lasted just eight sessions. Ambrose was man of the match and man of the series. It was the closest Border came to a series victory against the long-time world champions.

Asked about Taylor's appointment, Border said, 'He was always the best candidate. He has done a good job when called upon to captain the side in the past and will do so again.'

Taylor's father, Tony, was also in no doubt of his son's ability to accept the new challenges. 'I'm sure he can handle it and that he'll make a very good captain,' he told Tony Squires in the *Sydney Morning Herald*. 'To be captain of the highest-profile sporting team in the country, with a world profile, is a big responsibility. There'll be a lot of weight on him. [But] he's quite a disciplinarian in his own way, and there needs to be some firming up in that area.'

Mark Taylor knew he had a quality side, despite Border's retirement, Boon being on the brink of retirement and battle-scarred Merv Hughes having played his last Test.

Apart from Ambrose, Craig McDermott was the outstanding strike bowler in the world, while Shane Warne was rapidly developing into a master spinner. There was also a raw-boned kid from the New South Wales bush, Glenn McGrath, who looked good. He'd become the first to emerge from the Australian Cricket Academy into the Test team in the same season.

There was little hint, however, that on retirement five years later, Taylor would be feted as one of the all-time great Australian leaders and his team compared favourably with the greatest side of all time, Don Bradman's Invincibles.

# TWO

---

# A

# YOUNG CAPTAIN
# EMERGES

*'"Okay Matt, go over and do some fielding."*
*Clearly he could play – and from that day on*
*I never again forgot his name!'*

---

IT WAS MARK TAYLOR'S seventh birthday and the backyard Test was
in full swing at West Wyalong when a family friend, Rod Pilon,
happened to venture outside for a look.

'One of my boys, Tony, is the same age as Mark and they were
very friendly at school,' Pilon recalls. 'The kids were all playing cricket
out in the backyard. Normally at that age, they tend to take a cross-
batted swipe at the ball and don't go within six inches of it. When
Mark was batting, he was playing straight bat shots, real shots. It was
obvious he was a natural. I went and got [my wife] Laurie. "Come
out and watch young Mark," I said to her. "This kid will play for
Australia one day."'

Mark's father, Tony, was a bank manager whose work commitments
saw him move semi-regularly in the southern Riverina area and back
again to the city. His mother, Judy, was a church elder and totally
involved in her family.

Taylor was born at Leeton, second-in-line behind his sister Tina and ahead of the youngest, Lisa. The Taylors lived briefly in Dareton and West Wyalong before shifting to Wagga Wagga when Mark was eight. Like most country kids, he was keen on all sports and particularly promising at Australian football and cricket.

Tony Taylor was a typical sports-loving Australian father, good enough to play first-grade rugby in Newcastle and happy to take his coat off after work, roll up his sleeves and get involved in some backyard cricket with his son. He calculates he must have bowled to Mark in the backyard car park for 'days on end'.

'I reckon my right arm is stretched from the amount of balls I bowled to him!' he said. 'He was very determined. He never used to let me have too many bats. Occasionally I'd check him on something and he'd pick up his bat and ball and go inside. Ten minutes later he'd be back again, saying he'd got over it and was ready to go again.

'As long as he had a ball next to him, he was happy. He would play anything. He got his first plastic bat and ball one Christmas when he was about 4 and he could play straight by the time he was 6 or 7. He was never a big hitter of the ball. His whole game was based on defence. The same day he made his first century in the under 14s at Lake Albert [in Wagga], he scored 60 or 70 in the afternoon in the third-grade side.

'I used to say I taught him everything he knows and dined out on that for years until one night in front of four million on *Burke's Backyard*, Mark said I was a Z-grade change bowler. That changed everything.'

Tony imbued a competitive edge, but without the demands some parents insist on enforcing. As an emerging young sportsman, Taylor cannot remember his father raising his voice even once at a cricket or football match. He preached the enjoyment angle, and if Mark wasn't enjoying a particular sport, he'd recommend Mark go and do something else.

Tony admits he wasn't even the first to pick up just how talented a young cricketer Mark was. 'While we were living in West Wyalong in the late 60s and early 70s, two very good mates, Ellis Lees and Rod Pilon, told me that Mark would play for Australia one day. Both had played a lot of cricket. They've proved to be pretty good judges.'

Another who rated the young Taylor particularly highly was his junior coach at Lake Albert, Bernie O'Connor.

When Mark was 14, the Taylors moved to the city, and Mark attended Chatswood High where soon he was to become head prefect. In winter he played football with Pennant Hills Australian Rules Club and in summer, cricket with Lindfield in the Sydney shires competition. So impressive was he that Lindfield's president Ken Walker rang his counterpart, Austin Hughes, at nearby Northern District to alert him to Taylor's potential. 'We have a young guy down here too good to be playing shires,' he said. 'He should be up with you playing grade cricket.'

The next summer, just weeks before his 17th birthday, Taylor debuted with Northern District's third XI, having shown immediate poise batting in the No. 1 net against the club's first grade pacemen. He also seemed exceptionally proficient as a close-to-the-wicket catcher.

'Mark came up and introduced himself to me,' said Neil Marks, an ex-NSW Shield player, who had just taken over as chairman of selectors at Northern District.

'I remembered who he was and how he'd come highly recommended and said, "Okay Matt, go over and do some fielding".'

'"It's Mark. Mark Taylor," he said, looking me in the eye, before joining the others for some slippers. Clearly he could play – and from that day on I never again forgot his name!'

In one of his debut matches, an all-day game at Asquith Oval, he received a stern lecture from Marks, standing in as thirds captain, having arrived only minutes before start of play. His sister, Lisa, was learning to drive and with Tony Taylor navigating and Mark sitting in the back seat, the Taylors lost their way, ending up hopelessly lost down near Berowra.

'I didn't say anything to him at the time, as he was about to open the innings, but at the end of the day I tore strips off him,' said Marks. 'He copped it sweet. Years later he told me what had happened and how he thought I was a big-headed old bastard who was trying to bounce everybody just to show how important I was!'

The following year saw a maiden century with the thirds and 500 runs and a place in the seconds' premiership XI. He also played first grade and from the start of the 1983–84 season was a first XI regular.

Austin Hughes said Taylor was keen, polite and involved from his first days at the club. 'The captain of the thirds, John Blazey, was an ex-first grade player and very knowledgeable. He said to Neil Marks and I that we should come up and have look at this young kid. He's going to be pretty good.

'We did, and he made runs. And not only could be bat, he was a great catcher in the slips and always respectful and humble in his own way. He didn't big-note or anything like that. He'd just go along with the rest of the boys.

'We appointed him captain of the first XI at a young age (22, in 1987–88), and once he got into the leadership role, he proved himself very capable of being a fine leader of men. He played in two consecutive premierships with us. Peter Taylor was also in that side.'

In a game against Mosman in 1985–86, Taylor was on the verge of his first double century in any form of cricket when he relayed a message back to his captain Ross Turner in the pavilion saying a declaration was in order. 'Gaining a result was always more important to him than individual records,' said Turner. 'Mark was always totally unselfish. The team always came first.'

Turner, now based at Lord's as the International Cricket Council's development manager, was most influential in nurturing Taylor's leadership style. He was an excellent communicator, rarely raised his voice and consistently encouraged a high level of performance.

'Mark's first season in first grade was remarkable, not so much for amassing big scores, but for the temperament exhibited and his ability to adjust to the circumstance as required,' Turner said. 'In the very first one-dayer he played, he batted No. 7 against North Sydney and didn't get a bat until the final three overs. One could be forgiven at age 18 for placing personal ambition above the team, but typical of the person he is, Mark did the opposite, played in cavalier fashion and finished with a brisk 15 not out.

'Later that year against Bankstown-Canterbury, which was a powerful team with players such as the Waugh twins, Lenny Pascoe, Bob Vidler and Rod Bower, Mark hit the winning runs, courtesy of two 6s in a row from the fiery Pascoe on a very lively pitch at Epping Oval. It was a fabulous effort.'

Neil Marks said Taylor's ability to focus on the next ball was outstanding. 'He didn't seem to worry about the ball that had been. That was his big attribute. He refused to store any negative thoughts.'

Peter Taylor believed it was 'almost inevitable' Mark would be a success at first class level. 'There was a maturity about his play,' he says. 'Nothing seemed to faze him. He was such a good concentrator.'

Taylor was one of those most responsible for Peter Taylor's own Sheffield Shield selection after taking a series of spectacular catches at club level. 'One year I won the [club] best and fairest and Mark must have taken something like 20 catches at slip,' Peter Taylor said. 'Some were absolutely outstanding. For a spinner to have a good fielding side around him at grade level means everything. I have a lot to thank him for.'

In his formative years, Taylor juggled a surveying course at the University of New South Wales around his cricket commitments. Even then, his sport was a priority as he deferred one of his surveying examinations when it clashed with a NSW international against the touring New Zealanders.

He'd first played with NSW in the opening game of the 1985–86 season, when regular openers Steve Smith and John Dyson opted to play in South Africa with the Australian rebel team. Opening with another rookie, Bankstown-Canterbury's Mark Waugh, against Tasmania at the ramshackle Tasmanian Cricket Association Ground in Hobart, he made 12 and 56 not out. 'These two fellas [Taylor and Waugh] will play for Australia one day,' Marks told Sydney cricket writer Phil Wilkins.

Centuries soon afterwards against South Australia, home and away, confirmed Taylor's talent. As a slipsman, one pearler to dismiss WA's Chris Matthews in an early game in Perth was proof that the Blues had unearthed a fieldsman with extraordinarily good reflexes. In March

1986 he played in NSW's title-winning team. In those days he answered to the nickname 'Stodgy', in reference to his limited array of shots, the best of which included a flick off his pads and his square cut. Only when well set would he generally allow himself the luxury of an off-drive or a pull shot. However, he displayed enormous discipline and poise and seemed to relish the challenge of opening up, even against the genuine pacemen on greenish club wickets. He was never fussed by what had been. The next ball always counted.

In 1986–87, he thought he'd been named for Australia for the New Year Test match when a Sydney television reporter rang, waking the Taylor household before dawn, and asked if he was the 'Taylor' named to play. Taylor had played the entire Sheffield Shield season and scored a career-best 186 in the final match before Christmas. He made arrangements to do the interview before a double-check found that his Northern District team-mate Peter Taylor, who'd played only once with NSW all summer, was in fact the chosen one.

As NSW's acting captain for the first time in the 1989–90 Sheffield Shield final in Sydney, Taylor scored 127 and 100 to spearhead NSW's 40th Shield, by an emphatic 345 runs. He'd been told of his appointment only 20 minutes before the start of play when Geoff Lawson was ruled out with injury.

NSW did not have a designated vice-captain that season, and Taylor's appointment, after a hurried set of phone-calls, was endorsed by Marks and by team coach Steve Rixon.

'Henry [Lawson] told us he was 85 per cent,' Marks said, 'but for such an important game, we thought it was too great a risk to take. We went with Mark.

'He was doing some slips catching practice when I approached him. "I want you to do two things today, Mark," I said. "Score a 100 . . . and win the toss." '

Taylor had made twin 100s just 12 months previously, against Western Australia in Perth, being the first to reach 1000 runs for the season. Marks, a stalwart of NSW cricket, said his second-innings 152 in that game was superlative, as good as he'd seen from Taylor to that time.

In 1989, Marks was one of the most prophetic in rating Taylor's leadership capabilities. In an interview with journalist and commentator Frank Crook for *Talking Cricket with Frank Crook,* he was asked who he believed should succeed Allan Border. 'The two outstanding candidates are Steve Waugh and Mark Taylor, both from NSW,' he said, 'and Geoff Lawson, who's captain of NSW and did a superb job last year. The next captain of NSW could well be the next captain of Australia.'

It took four years, but he was spot on.

# THREE

## SUCCEEDING
## A LEGEND

*'It's done with a heavy heart,' Border said.*
*'It's like a part of me has died.'*

SOUTH AFRICA, 1994, was Allan Border's final tour. At 38, he knew
he wasn't the player he had been, but he'd never been keen on
declarations. 'It's done with a heavy heart,' Border said on his
retirement. 'It's like a part of me has died.'

His hunger for the game after 17 years as Australia's most-celebrated
international player was dimming. He'd delayed an announcement,
hoping to avoid at least some of the fuss and headlines. But he'd
confided to Taylor during one of the farewell functions in South Africa
that he was in his last days as a player. If he was to continue, it would
be purely at domestic level, to help Queensland win a Sheffield Shield.

When considering a successor, Taylor deserved to be favourite. He'd
performed with distinction on two Ashes tours, particularly on his first
trip in 1989 when he displayed career-best touch, making 839 runs in
a Bradman-like set of performances. His captaincy of the NSW team
had been positive and at times daring. He'd also been Border's deputy
since 1992 and replaced him as captain for the three Australasia Cup

games in Sharjah, the final commitments of the extended 1993–94 summer.

However, just over 12 months previously at the conclusion of the 1992–93 West Indian tour, he'd been omitted from the XI for the fifth Test in Perth to decide cricket's new world champion. And he'd several times been dropped from the one-day side – including three internationals in a row in mid-series in South Africa – at the hands of his fellow tour selectors Ian Healy and Steve Waugh. It was an invidious position for the most senior players having to make judgements on each other and one which continues today, despite some concessions, when Australia tours overseas.

Taylor's time as a leader had been brief, but given his experiences, especially at Sydney grade level under Ross Turner, he exuded a calm confidence and an undoubted authority which was important in winning support, on and off the field.

As much as he admired Border for his approach and enthusiasm, he didn't necessarily agree at all times with the way games under Border tended to meander. Border's farewell Test, for example, finished in a tame draw, despite its status as the series decider. South Africa may have batted into a third day for just 422, but the Australians, sent into bat on day one, had established the guidelines, taking seven and a half hours at the head of the match for just 269. It was a virtual 'non-match' – one Taylor had no wish ever to be a part of again. He believed five days was more than enough in which to obtain a result. He wanted to lift the image of Test cricket and help it prosper once again.

EVER SINCE THE INFAMOUS Sid Barnes affair when, for reasons other than cricket, the then Australian Board of Control refused to ratify the selection of the controversial New South Welshman for the third Test against the West Indies in 1951–52, a clause remains in Australian Cricket Board regulations that the Board has the ultimate right to approve each member of a selected Australian XI. To avoid any mid-season blow-ups, the Board now approves its list of players for selection prior to the start of each season.

As a top-notch, established batsman, slip fielder and one of the six

Sheffield Shield captains, Taylor seemed ideally suited to immediate responsibility. He liked to play positive, result-oriented cricket. He also had excellent communication skills and an endearing affability.

Having decided on Taylor ahead of Ian Healy, the Australian Cricket Board stressed that Taylor's appointment was for both the Test and one-day teams, thereby avoiding the embarrassment of having to name separate leaders for different competitions. Just months earlier, Taylor had been omitted from the World Series finals, despite having captained the team in the absence of the injured Border only days before during an international in Perth.

At the team's first training camp in Adelaide in August, on the eve of the subcontinent tours of Sri Lanka and Pakistan, Taylor outlined the way he intended to lead and told of his expectations. He'd welcome input into team tactics from senior and junior members of the team alike, but the ultimate call would always be his. He knew he was inheriting a top-notch, ambitious side, already one of the very best in the world, which focused around players of the calibre of Healy, the Waugh twins, David Boon and Craig McDermott. The infrastructure behind the team was also at a new sophisticated level, as was the development of the next set of Test and one-day cricketers working under Rod Marsh and Richard Done at the AIS Australian Cricket Academy in Adelaide.

It was a settled, confident team, one which was extremely well-drilled by coach and ex-captain Bob Simpson. 'Simmo' had proved to be a true lieutenant for Border, shouldering many of the responsibilities, including media, which allowed Border to concentrate almost purely on training and playing. It had been a good mix and Australia's performances since regaining the Ashes under Border in England in 1989 indicated a new consistency.

The team's one-day performances had also lifted. On home wickets, they were exceptionally hard to beat. Since surprising host nations India and Pakistan and winning the World Cup in 1987–88, the only team to consistently outplay the Aussies in the triangular World Series Cup was the West Indies, which won the title in 1988–89 and 1992–93.

## AUSTRALIA'S TEST RESURRECTION

| Year | Opponent | P | W | L | D | Series result |
|------|----------|---|---|---|---|---------------|
| 1989 (away) | England | 6 | 4 | 0 | 2 | Australia 4–0 |
| 1989–90 | New Zealand | 1 | 0 | 0 | 1 | No result |
| | Sri Lanka | 2 | 1 | 0 | 1 | Australia 1–0 |
| | Pakistan | 3 | 1 | 0 | 2 | Australia 1–0 |
| 1989–90 (a) | New Zealand | 1 | 0 | 1 | 0 | New Zealand 1–0 |
| 1990–91 | England | 5 | 3 | 0 | 2 | Australia 3–0 |
| 1990–91 (a) | West Indies | 5 | 1 | 2 | 2 | West Indies 2–1 |
| 1991–92 | India | 5 | 4 | 0 | 1 | Australia 4–0 |
| 1992–93 (a) | Sri Lanka | 3 | 1 | 0 | 2 | Australia 1–0 |
| 1992–93 | West Indies | 5 | 1 | 2 | 2 | West Indies 2–1 |
| 1992–93 (a) | New Zealand | 3 | 1 | 1 | 1 | Series drawn |
| 1993 (a) | England | 6 | 4 | 1 | 1 | Australia 4–1 |
| 1993–94 | New Zealand | 3 | 2 | 0 | 1 | Australia 2–0 |
| | South Africa | 3 | 1 | 1 | 1 | Series drawn |
| 1993–94 (a) | South Africa | 3 | 1 | 1 | 1 | Series drawn |

The continuing development of the nation's best young players via the Cricket Academy was proving a boon with Shane Warne and Glenn McGrath the first two to emerge into Test cricket. Both had played fewer than 10 games at Sheffield Shield level. Their fast-tracking was seen as undeniable proof of the Academy's growing importance as a direct stepping-stone for players entering Test and one-day international cricket.

Taylor had definite plans for Warne, whom he regarded as his jewel in the crown. Rather than use him as a stock bowler, as had been Border's habit, he wanted to attack with him, in shortish spells with batsmen ringed by close-in fieldsmen. If 'fill-in' overs were needed at any stage, that would be the job of the medium-pacers, not his star leggie.

The season before becoming Australia's 39th captain, Mark Taylor and Michael Slater were being slow handclapped by sections of crowd in Perth for not showing sufficient urgency in mid-match against New Zealand.

Taylor, who made 64 and 142 not out for the match, returned to the rooms cursing and swearing about 'bloody WACA crowds' before Steve Waugh chipped in and said, 'Actually mate, that was us . . . we started the chant.'

# FOUR

## PAKISTAN '94

*'I don't think you understand.*
*Our pride is at stake. Everything is at stake.*
*We can't lose this first Test.'*

NO AUSTRALIAN TEAM had ever been set a more demanding schedule as that approaching Mark Taylor's first Test as captain at Karachi in 1994. The side was due to play 12 Tests and up to two dozen one-day games in a gruelling nine-month period, the majority offshore. A short tour of Sri Lanka, three Tests in Pakistan and a full Ashes series back home was to be followed by the Frank Worrell Trophy series in the Caribbean for Test cricket's unofficial world championship.

Pakistan on its home wickets was a particular challenge, especially after the upsets of 1988 when Australia's elite players, claiming umpiring bias and frustrated at dodgy pitches, voted to come home with two Tests still to be played.

Any divisions between the two Boards, however, were soon repaired with the reciprocal agreement for each team to visit each other every four years. With its array of attractive, world-class players, headed by the feared fast bowling duo of Wasim Akram and Waqar Younis and dashing batsmen Saeed Anwar and Saleem Malik, patching relations with Pakistan made economic sense.

From a world ratings perspective, the Australian team also had to prove it could consistently perform out of its comfort zone and win offshore. Allan Border had inspired fresh momentum, but the team still showed a disturbing vulnerability overseas.

No Australian side had won a Test in the Islamic republic in 35 years and no overseas team a series there in 25 years.

To help the Australian squad better cope with the conditions and culture, and to defuse any potential controversies, a suggested list of responses to ticklish questions was issued to each player by an ACB-employed Sydney public relations firm at a pre-season camp in Adelaide. The topics were wide-ranging, from umpiring standards through to racism and conditions in the Third World.

Public speaking and nutritional tips were also given, the overriding message for squad members being to remain positive and enthusiastic. Players were encouraged to rehearse and use responses and phrases such as:

- 'Harsh conditions are part of international cricket.'
- 'Weather conditions during a hot Australian summer are just as challenging for touring teams.'
- 'Conditions in Pakistan are very comfortable: five-star accommodation, hotel-prepared food at the grounds and bottled water.'
- 'Irrespective of who or where we play, our job is to focus on playing cricket to the best of our ability.'

Leading into the tour and during time off at Coffs Harbour where his wife Judi's family have a banana plantation, Taylor worked hard at his fitness, losing two kilograms in bodyweight and noticeably increasing his aerobic endurance. He also worked diligently at his skills, Judi being one of several standing by a bowling machine, feeding her husband dozens of balls in preparation for the expected onslaught from Wasim and Waqar.

From the opening days of the tour, when he made double figures only once in his first seven innings on the subcontinent, Taylor remained in buoyant spirits. However, at Karachi, he lobbed a tame return catch to Wasim for a fourth-ball duck in the first innings and was caught behind seventh ball from Waqar in the second. He became the first captain in 1296 Tests to make a pair on his debut, and joined Joe Darling (1902), Richie Benaud (1961) and Allan Border (1992–93) as the only Australian captains to be dismissed for no score in each innings of a Test match. Taylor knew he had to work harder on his own game in the nets, rather than concentrating as much on the form of others.

It was his most forgettable performance in 55 Test matches. He'd been so focused on other things, he'd hardly remembered to watch the ball. It was the rudest possible reminder that he was supposed to get runs, too.

However, thanks to steely contributions from Steve Waugh and debutant Michael Bevan in the first innings, and David Boon and Mark Waugh in the second, Australia worked itself into a winning position, setting Pakistan 314 to win on a wearing wicket.

Unbeaten in 30 Tests at the National Stadium, the Pakistanis started the chase in forthright fashion with 90 for the first wicket and 63 for the second before a Shane Warne-inspired collapse saw the home team slump from 1/153 to 9/258, still 56 runs from victory.

However, 'The Multan Monolith', Inzamam-ul-Haq, batting at No. 8 and No. 11 Mushtaq Ahmed could not be separated, despite a huge lbw shout against Inzamam from Jo Angel, who had replaced the injured Craig McDermott in the XI on the morning of the match.

The winning runs for Pakistan came in bizarre circumstances via a difficult low-down stumping chance to Ian Healy from the bowling of Warne. Healy initially thought the skidding leg-break, which had dipped late, was going to bowl Inzamam. But it missed everything, including Healy's gloves and pads and careered away to the boundary for four byes. In the confusion umpire Dickie Bird initially indicated leg-byes before later changing his ruling to byes.

As he watched the ball disappear toward third man, Healy knelt on one knee and bowed his head before kicking the stumps in frustration. He blamed himself for the loss, saying the missed chance, as difficult as it was, would always remain his career low point.

The Pakistanis showed unrestrained delight at winning such an epic encounter. Mushtaq fell to his knees kissing the pitch and thanking Allah. The crowd remained in their positions repeatedly chanting 'Allah-o-Akbar' (God is great). It was the first time Pakistan had ever chased 300 in a fourth innings of a Test and won.

With 58 not out, Inzamam had made one of his most important contributions since his spectacular showings in the 1991–92 World Cup in Australasia. Mushtaq, who was to make a pair in the next Test, finished 20 not out.

With eight wickets for the game, Warne had again been Australia's key bowler, carrying his superlative form from 1993–94 (when he was the International Cricketer of the Year) into his maiden tour of Pakistan.

Glenn McGrath had injured a hamstring and was unable to bowl in the second innings, while Tim May was also restricted with a neck injury. Had McGrath been fit to bowl on day four, Taylor felt Australia would have won comfortably.

THERE ARE FEW character-building sports which compare with cricket. Despite his double disappointment with the bat and the agony of so narrowly losing his maiden Test as captain, Taylor was genuinely proud of how his players had fought. The prolonged silence in the rooms in Karachi showed how keenly his players felt the defeat.

As a batsman, Taylor knew he could only improve, and with Craig McDermott having recovered from an ingrown toenail in time for the second Test just three days later in Rawalpindi, he was confident Australia could square the series.

The spirit in the team was undeniable. Steve Waugh and Gavin Robertson produced a weekly newsletter, titled *The No Whinge, No Wine Tour*, in which they conducted interviews, ran player profiles and generally poked fun at anybody and everybody. Tim May and Damien Fleming armed themselves with a video recorder and conducted a street-talk segment, in which they asked puzzled locals who was going to win the big one back in Melbourne on Saturday, North Melbourne or Hawthorn!

The facial hair growth competition was also hilarious. For the only time in his career Taylor grew a beard, and Steve Waugh a moustache and goatee. Those who refused, or couldn't meet certain specifications, were all fined.

After being sent in to bat at Rawalpindi, a 176-run opening stand between Taylor and Michael Slater and some resolute middle-order contributions from the Waugh twins, Michael Bevan and Ian Healy allowed Australia to declare late on the second day at 9/521.

Slater should have been caught at point at 2, while Taylor survived a chillingly-close lbw appeal against Waqar having made just 1.

The courage of Steve Waugh and others amidst the second-day onslaught from Wasim and Waqar was the innings highlight. Both had left the field for lengthy periods on the opening day and were restricted from bowling until after noon on the second, courtesy of a newly implemented ruling from the International Cricket Council.

Wasim, in particular, bowled at high pace with the second new ball, but it was Waqar who made the breakthrough with Waugh on the verge of a richly deserved century.

Fending a rearing bouncer from his face, Waugh watched in horror as it landed on his calf before trickling from his heel onto the stumps with sufficient force to dislodge the leg bail. He'd made 98.

Waugh said afterwards he'd never faced a faster burst of bowling. There were several incidents in mid innings where Waugh pulled away from his crease and asked umpire Karl Liebenberg to intervene as Pakistan's close-in fieldsmen talked freely, even when Wasim or Waqar had started their run-ups.

Playing with steely defiance and great composure despite the avalanche of short-pitched deliveries, the only time Waugh stopped to talk to anyone but his partners in mid-pitch was when he asked Wasim how was his 'bad' back, which had forced him from the field on the opening day.

'Okay,' came the reply, and on Waugh batted. At one stage he was caught off a Wasim no-ball at third man, but still remained totally focused, revelling in the battle.

Facing the media afterwards, he said: 'Have I got tired of being a target? It doesn't worry me. My record is not too bad against short-pitched bowling over the last couple of years. I don't mind taking a couple on the body as long as I can get some runs and 98 will do me every time. Certainly it was quick, short and nasty. But this is Test cricket and you don't expect any favours out there.'

Pakistan eventually drew the match, despite being forced to follow on. Benefiting from some good fortune early in his innings, Saleem Malik made 237 in a monumental counter-attack. His concentration and composure were immense and single-handedly he saved the match.

Years before Pakistan's legendary all-rounder Imran Khan had called Malik a 'flat wicket bully', a description which does little justice to his artistry, his wristwork in finding the gaps or his sparkling footwork. His was a glorious knock and for nine hours, the tiring Australian attack could take only three wickets before debutant Fleming grabbed three wickets in consecutive deliveries in a rare moment of glory for the bowlers.

Having dismissed Aamir Malik and Inzamam-ul-Haq with the fifth and sixth deliveries of his 23rd over, he took the prize wicket of Malik with the first of his 24th with a perfectly pitched outswinger which Malik could only nibble to Ian Healy for the fourth of his five catches for the innings.

After England's Maurice Allom and New Zealand's Peter Petherick, it was only the third time a first-gamer had taken a hat-trick.

Angel hoisted Fleming onto his shoulder in delight. The Victorian had predicted at the intervening drinks break that Malik was about to become part of history, and delighted as he was to do it, it was a sombre Australian dressing room afterwards, with missed catches having again proved crucial — especially Taylor's at slip from the bowling of Angel when Malik had made just 20.

With hindsight, Taylor would not have enforced the follow-on, but at the time felt his bowlers were fresh enough to bowl the Pakistanis out a second time, having dismissed them in just 71 overs in the first innings. With a lead of 261, Australia's position appeared impregnable.

Eight catches had been missed in the opening two Tests, reviving memories of the luckless 1982 and 1988 campaigns when 35 catches were grassed.

Even the normally efficient Healy allowed 27 byes for the match, including 17 in Pakistan's prolonged second innings.

Taylor was so devastated by his two missed chances that he removed himself completely from slip. His first Test wicket (Rashid Latif) in a rare appearance at the bowling crease late in the day was little consolation.

'It was a crucial catch for sure,' said Taylor afterwards. 'If I'd taken it, they're 2/120, the captain's out and we're fired up. Player for player I think we've proved we're a better side than these blokes but we've got to make sure we do it on the scoreboard.'

Having trailed by 261, Pakistan was 2/324 at stumps on day four having effectively played Australia out of the game. Shane Warne's neck strain late in the match had robbed the attack of its normal bite.

Taylor had left the horrors of Karachi behind him, with 60 and 6 not out. His captaincy had also been thoughtful and at times passionate, his use of two fine-legs to in-form Aamir Sohail all but paying off (but for Shane Warne muffing a catch late on day three). In mid-match, he'd called his bowlers together for a pep talk while everyone else was walking off to lunch. It may have been unusual, but no one was left in any doubt as to their role in the team.

Malik was again to be Australia's nemesis in the third and final Test at Gadaffi Stadium in Lahore, scoring 75 and 143 to ensure Pakistan the series in another high-scoring draw. Both teams were weakened by withdrawals: Steve Waugh (dislocated shoulder), Fleming (shoulder) and Healy (broken thumb) being unable to play for Australia, having being injured during the one-day series scheduled in between the second and third Tests. Pakistan was unable to select either of its fast bowling champions Wasim or Waqar, who between them had taken more than 400 Test wickets. Intriguingly, both withdrew at the 11th hour, Wasim with apparent sinus and back problems and Waqar with knee and hamstring injuries. Given that it was the deciding Test in the series, it was a crippling blow for Pakistan. However, four more catches went down in the field, costing Australia 150 runs and hours of effort.

The one-day triangular series victory, highlighted by Glenn McGrath's first-ever 'five-for' in limited-over internationals, was encouraging but of little real significance, though Taylor's calmness was notable, through a riot at Gujranwalla and a hail of stones and exploding firecrackers at Peshawar. With Australia not having won a series in Pakistan for 35 years, Taylor's focus, however, was clearly on the Tests. To his frustration, the Australians had controlled much of the series, leading comfortably on the first innings in each of the three games without being able to deliver the knockout punch.

'You look back on the tour and say it was a pretty good one,' Taylor told journalists, 'but you've got to look at the result. That's what is going to be there for everyone to see in years to come and we lost 1–0.'

Having snatched the first Test, Pakistan was able to defend and play for draws at Rawalpindi and Lahore. In Taylor's eyes, it was a clear case of the better team running second. Steve Waugh agreed. 'If we'd taken our catches in the Tests we'd probably have won 3–0,' he told Mark Ray of the *Sunday Age*.

The failure of the injury-depleted attack, Shane Warne excepted, to take the big wicket at key moments had been the difference between winning and losing. The Australian public also felt cheated. They'd hardly seen a ball bowled on television. Nor was there a live ball-by-ball description.

WITH A RECORD 557 runs in three Tests at an average of 90-plus, the masterly Saleem Malik re-emerged as one of world cricket's leading batsmen.

He'd first toured Australia more than a decade earlier as a teenage starlet, and while renowned for his timing and artistry on the slower, lower wickets of the subcontinent and England, he hadn't proved to be anywhere near as effective in Australia or the West Indies.

Unfortunately for Malik, the most memorable series of his life was to be irrevocably besmirched when he was named as the central player in a bribery scandal which was to rock the cricket world.

Match fixing, especially in games on the subcontinent, had been a dressing room talking point for years. When news leaked in February 1995 that Malik had allegedly offered Shane Warne, Mark Waugh and Tim May $US200 000 to perform badly during games in Pakistan in 1994, the ramifications were enormous.

The backlash was to involve other champion Pakistani players, including Wasim Akram and Mushtaq Ahmed. And Malik was later stood down in disgrace, pending an inquiry.

The very ethics of the game were in question. No longer could cricketers claim their game to be morally superior or purer than others.

In Pakistan, Wasim's father was kidnapped for two days, allegedly by bookies' henchmen. And at a later betting inquiry in Lahore, a bookmaker gave evidence that he'd paid $US100 000 each to Malik and Mushtaq to ensure Pakistan lost a one-day match to Australia in Colombo in 1994. The monies offered easily surpassed the annual wages of even elite Pakistani players.

In evidence Warne claimed Malik had called him on the second last night of the Karachi Test and asked him to come to his room 'to discuss something very important'.

At 3/155, Pakistan needed just 159 more to force a famous victory.

'Look, we cannot lose tomorrow,' Malik is alleged to have said to Warne.

Warne: 'What do you mean you cannot lose tomorrow?'

Malik: 'I don't think you understand. Our pride is at stake. Everything is at stake. We can't lose this first Test.'

Warne: 'Well mate, our pride is at stake too. I'm sorry to tell you this, but we are going to whip your blokes tomorrow.'

Malik: 'I don't think you understand what I am asking of you. What I want is for you and Tim May to bowl wide of off stump and bowl poorly so that the match is a draw. And for that I will give you and Tim May $US200 000. I can have it in your room in half an hour.'

Warne: 'What the heck is going on here? What do you mean? What are you talking about? I don't understand.'

Malik: 'I am serious. You must get back to me.'

After telling Malik what he thought of his offer, Warne went back to his room, told May and rang Malik back, reinforcing the message that Australia was going all out to win.

In his book *My Own Story*, Warne said Malik had approached him again after the game, saying he was stupid to reject his offer as Australia had lost and he could have had the money. 'He made more approaches during the rest of the one-day series,' Warne wrote.

Warne said it was nonsensical to suggest that he'd concoct the story. 'What have we got to gain by making it up? Nothing.'

Mark Waugh was allegedly approached by Malik at a function in Rawalpindi on the eve of the one-day series. Again the lure was $US200 000. All Waugh had to do was encourage four or five of the Australians to perform poorly in a one-day game the following day. Again the offer was rejected.

Warne and May told captain Mark Taylor of the approach the following morning. Coach Bob Simpson was then informed and statements made to the Australian Cricket Board.

The fallout from the furore lasted for years, and it wasn't until Australia's following tour of Pakistan four years later that Waugh and Taylor made statements to Pakistan's match-fixing inquiry. Warne, who missed the tour with injury, later offered evidence, in Melbourne, further damning Malik's attempts to clear his name.

## PROFILE: SHANE WARNE

Shane Warne's meteoric rise added an extra dimension to the lure of Test cricket, which had been ambushed and held to ransom by the intimidating West Indian pacemen. For years Clive Lloyd and Viv Richards had played four specialist express bowlers at the expense of over rates, up-and-coming Caribbean spinners and the very essence of the game. There was no respite when a Malcolm Marshall or Joel Garner was spelled. In his place would step strapping young quicks like

Courtney Walsh or Colin Croft – who was so mean he even once barrelled into an umpire in an infamous temper tantrum in Christchurch.

Warne helped rekindle an art which was in retreat, and he became so influential that Test teams around the world, even the West Indies, once again started to encourage spin bowlers and play them regularly in both Test and limited-overs matches.

Thanks to Warne, the taking of the second new ball lost its significance. With his peroxide-blond hair, ready smile and M.C. Hammer dance routines, Warne was a likeable rogue with the knack of ripping big leg-breaks at will and running through bottom orders with embarrassing ease.

So excited was the game's elder statesman Richie Benaud about Warne's potential that he declared the Victorian capable of turning the ball on ice.

Benaud, the last great Australian leg-spinner, had toured England three times without taking as many Test wickets as Warne did in his very first tour.

From the time a bemused Mike Gatting lost his off bail to a warm-up Warne leg-break which jagged several feet at Old Trafford in 1993, England redeveloped its phobia against playing quality wrist spinners. Warne had torpedoed England's hoped-for Ashes revival before it had even started, and it's no coincidence that England has since slumped to the biggest losing streak in Anglo–Australian history.

Three hundred Test wickets later, Warne stands as the most successful and feted spin bowler in the game, whose achievements have surpassed even the deeds of between-the-wars spin gods Clarrie Grimmett and Bill 'Tiger' O'Reilly.

His rise was truly extraordinary considering he'd been bypassed from virtually all of the elite squad and representative carnival selections as a teenager growing up in the Melbourne bayside. Yet less than a year after starting the 1989–90 season in the anonymity of St Kilda's third XI playing at the Ross Gregory Oval, he'd been lifted into the firsts and recommended to the Commonwealth Bank Cricket Academy, Australian cricket's just-established finishing school in Adelaide.

He lacked discipline and exited the Academy in stormy fashion, but there was no doubt that he could bowl. And with Trevor Hohns's retirement, Australia badly needed a quality wrist-spinner to complement Craig McDermott and Co. Two leggies were trialled with the Australian 'B' team to Zimbabwe at the start of the 1991–92 summer: Warne (after just one Sheffield Shield appearance) and the more experienced Peter McIntyre, also from Victoria.

With 15 wickets from 153 overs on tour, including 7/49 from 36 overs in Zimbabwe's second innings in the final game at Harare, Warne telegraphed what was to come.

When Victoria showed an initial reluctance to pick him, Steve Waugh and Mark Taylor led the recruiting posse to get him over the Great Divide to New South Wales. They'd seen him in Zimbabwe. Untried as he was, he was something special.

The team manager John Benaud was also a Test selector and unfazed by normal protocols. By the New Year, Warne had been lifted into Australia's Test team.

Clearly overweight and having served the minimum of apprenticeships, Warne bowled little else than his leg-break in a nervous beginning which fast became a nightmare. He hadn't bowled his wrong'un, never a favourite delivery, for fear of it bouncing twice, and the flipper he'd been toying with was off target. The thrashing he received from the Indians Ravi Shastri and an 18-year-old Sachin Tendulkar could have reduced him to One-Test Wonder status, but for the faith of those looking at the big picture. Shastri made 206 and Tendulkar 148 not out, with Warne's first-up figures an unflattering 1/150 from 45 overs. And three weeks later, in Adelaide, he went wicketless.

Terry Jenner, who had befriended him at the Academy, reminded him of how he'd been deliberately fast-tracked through the system to be Australia's 350th Test cricketer. What sacrifices had he made to get there? Warne couldn't think of even one. His life was one big social whirl, revolving around his mates, sport, fast food, smokes and beer.

But he was smart enough to realise his position of privilege, and ingenious at implementing advice he felt particularly valuable within minutes of being told.

And for the first time over the winter months, he made some of the sacrifices Jenner was talking about. In just three months, he shed almost 15 kilograms of excess weight, thanks to a new healthier lifestyle revolving around dawn runs at Black Rock's Half Moon Bay and workouts at Trevor Barker's King Club in Sandringham. He even reassessed his diet, eating sugarless cereal and substituting water for beer.

Invited back to the Academy by new head coach Rodney Marsh, Warne's education as a cricketer went into overdrive. Working in the nets five and six hours a day with a fellow cricketing larrikin in ex-Testman Jenner, he consolidated his technique and developed fresh control and confidence. He also redefined his 'lbw' ball, the quick, skidding flipper, which inaugural Academy coach Jack Potter had first shown him years before.

From the tour of Sri Lanka in late 1992, when Warne helped win the first Test in Colombo with three late wickets, Australian captain Allan Border had an extra bow in his arsenal. So successful was the now slim-line Warne that he soon surpassed even Craig McDermott as Australia's No. 1 strike bowler.

Seventy-two wickets in 16 Tests in 1993 and 70 in 10 in 1994 saw him assume one of the highest profiles in world cricket. Admittedly, some of the rough edges remained and he didn't handle stardom as easily as others – as shown by his undignified send-off of South Africa's Andrew Hudson at Johannesburg in 1993–94 – but under Mark Taylor's firm, friendly rule, there seemed no limit to his feats.

Subcontinent batsmen are renowned for their ability to dominate slow bowlers, yet in the eventful opening Test at Karachi's National Stadium in 1994, Warne not only spun the ball sharply, he was so accurate that one in three of his overs were maidens. It allowed Taylor to set aggressive fields, with Mark Waugh within virtual touching distance of batsmen at silly point and David Boon creating a similar intimidating presence at short leg.

With his confidence ballooning, Warne was to equal Richie Benaud's 18-wicket series high dating from 1959–60 and, in time, eclipse the records of even the famed West Indian Lance Gibbs, the first Test spinner to 300 wickets.

As Saleem Malik said at the end of the 1994 tour, 'Australia is very lucky to have a bowler like Shane Warne.'

**WARNE'S RECORD (TO 20 AUGUST 1999)**

|              | Mts | Runs | HS  | Ave   | 100s | Wicks | Ave   | BB   |
| ------------ | --- | ---- | --- | ----- | ---- | ----- | ----- | ---- |
| Tests        | 71  | 1378 | 74* | 15.31 | –    | 317   | 25.65 | 8/71 |
| One-day Int. | 125 | 630  | 55  | 12.35 | –    | 202   | 24.01 | 5/33 |

'Even when we're not going too well, Mark finds positive things to say to keep us going. He's always coming up with good ideas on and off the field. Mark is always easy to talk to. He'll explain his view and then listen to you while you give yours. At times we meet halfway, other times I get my way and other times he gets his.'
– *Shane Warne, Sunday Age*

37

# FIVE

---

# CHASING
# THE TITLE

*'It was a good wicket and I was playing him
okay, only to suddenly play this horrendous slog
across the line. I don't know why.'*

---

CRICKET'S ROLLER-COASTING ITINERARY can be relentless. Just hours
after arriving home, having hardly caught even an hour's sleep on the
flight from Pakistan, Mark Taylor was again spotlighted at the official
launch of the 1994–95 international season by Prime Minister Paul
Keating at Parliament House in Canberra.

The first of the five Ashes Tests was only a fortnight away and a
platoon of journalists and media men from around the world wanted
some answers from Taylor and England's touring captain Mike Atherton:
Having squared the series with the powerful South Africans, how serious
a contender was England? Was Shane Warne's menace overrated? And
how truly potent was England's much-vaunted pace attack led by the
high-speed Devon Malcolm and perky rookie Darren Gough?

Atherton considered Malcolm, 31, a genuine threat, despite only a
semi-successful Australian tour in 1990–91. He'd taken 9/57, the sixth-
best analysis of all time, in his last start on a green-top at The Oval.
The harder wickets of Australia would suit his bowling. Others, like the

first-time tourist Gough, were less highly rated, but very promising.

Taylor was typically diplomatic in his answers. He agreed Malcolm at his best was world class, but wasn't it just a little premature to compare him with the game's master pacemen such as Curtly Ambrose and Australia's own Craig McDermott? Both had been far more consistent over a longer period. 'I've faced Devon at times when he's taken 3/30 and I've faced him when he's taken 1/100,' he said.

He expected a tougher fight from England, but reminded everyone that Australia had been beaten only once in home series in the 90s, and that was by the narrowest possible margin. And there was no reason why Warne, at the peak of his form, couldn't be just as damaging in 1994–95 as he had been in Pakistan just weeks earlier and as a rookie tourist against England in 1993.

Four days later, Taylor showed his true mettle, amassing an aggressive 150 in just four and a half hours against Malcolm and Co. at Newcastle. It was his first century of the calendar year and an innings clearly calculated to dull England's early confidence after it had gone unbeaten in four of its initial five matches.

Taylor had been an admiring, on-the-spot witness when his predecessor Allan Border unleashed a similar assault on England's bowlers on the opening day of the 1989 Ashes campaign at Headingley. He came in at 2/57 and, partnered by Taylor, added 114 in just over two hours as Australia, sent in to bat, scored at will, with Steve Waugh making 177 not out before the declaration at 7/601.

While Malcolm was fast, his four wickets were at the tail end of the New South Wales first innings. Earlier he'd been subjected to heavy punishment. With 17 4s, many from his renowned pull shot, Taylor had kept pace with Mark Waugh, 144 runs coming in the exhilarating session between lunch and tea on day two.

'We have a good cricket side and if we play to our potential, we should have no trouble in retaining the Ashes,' Taylor told pressmen.

Not only was he settling to his task, he believed the work ethic and hunger of his players was a clear indicator of their passion to become the No. 1 team in the world.

As a first-time captain in Pakistan, Taylor had felt the pressure, especially following on from a leader of Border's stature. Several times in his private one-on-ones with players, he'd wondered how they'd react to his advice. After all, only months before, he'd been one of them, without the privileges of leadership, or its associated responsibilities.

'A couple of times I've walked up to chat with an individual and had a lump in my throat because I wasn't sure how it was going to go,' he said in a interview with Kim Hagdorn at the conclusion of the Pakistan tour. 'I've got to talk to the players and tell them how I want them to play and how the team will play.'

He still shared fun times with them, his mimicking of Shane Warne's reaction after being hit for 6 – while the team waited for a transit bus at the Lahore airport – an example of his uncomplicated, down-to-earth humour. He made a habit of addressing the team before each day's play and at least once in Pakistan spoke at the luncheon break too.

One of his early initiatives in the Ashes series was to ban cards, books and Walkman machines from the dressing room. 'We're not trying to run blokes' lives for them,' Taylor said. 'It's just that we want everyone to be involved in what's going on out in the middle.'

Taylor's appointment coincided with a change in coach Bob Simpson's role. Simpson, a postwar playing legend, had been a right-hand man for Border from the time of his appointment in 1986. Never before had Australia had a national team coach so involved on a daily basis. Some, like Ian Chappell, were outspoken against the need to even have such a position. Not only did Simpson select, he often ran practice and, with Border's approval, stood in at press conferences.

But Australia's World Cup win, highlighted by new levels of expertise in the field, was immediate and compelling evidence of Simpson's effectiveness, even if some found him confrontational.

Under Taylor's command, Simpson suggested rather than directed, and surrendered his seat as a selector. However, Taylor continued to implement many of Simpson's suggestions, just as had occurred in the Border years. He wanted to create his own stamp, but not at the risk of alienating one of the game's most respected personalities.

Taylor knew that a closely followed home series, especially for the Ashes, would be crucial to his ongoing captaincy ambitions. There'd hardly been a television camera in all of Pakistan. This time, with England touring, every shot, word and expression would be subject to intense scrutiny and review.

The return of a fit-again Ian Healy and Steve Waugh had strengthened his side. Shane Warne was entering his first Ashes contest on home wickets at his absolute best, having already taken 134 Test wickets at almost five per match.

Having defeated the West Indies in a Test at Bridgetown for the first time in almost 60 years, Atherton's tourists seemed primed for battle.

However, from the opening day when Michael Slater and the Australians scored more than 300 in three sessions at almost a run a minute, England's hoped-for Ashes revival languished. The menacing Malcolm had been ordered to bed with chickenpox and Darren Gough inexplicably demoted to first change behind Phil DeFreitas and Martin McCague, the English-born paceman who'd been nurtured in Australia.

From the opening over from DeFreitas when Slater struck two 4s, including a fierce cut shot to the boundary from the very first ball of the match, the Australians were in control, Taylor and Slater being denied a century stand by only one run when Taylor, having made 59, found himself stranded at the non-striker's end. He'd driven Phil Tufnell to Gough at mid-off, called yes, only for Slater to turn his back.

Slater scored 37 in the first two hours, 68 between lunch and tea and 71 in the last session before he was dismissed for 176 in the final hour. He played with glorious certainty and free-hitting flair, striking 25 boundaries – a considerable effort, even taking into account the 'Gabba's shortened square boundaries. Mark Waugh also scored a century and, having dismissed England in four and a half hours, Taylor had the luxury of a 259-run lead.

Ever since his first match as NSW's stand-in leader in the 1990 Shield final, Taylor's preference had been to bat the opposition out of the game and bowl last with close-up fields when the wicket was at its most worn. England was so sure he'd enforce the follow-on that openers Atherton and Alec Stewart padded up ready to go out.

But by making England bat last and setting a target of 508 to win in five full sessions, Taylor had safeguarded Australia's position in true Border-like fashion. He wanted a slow death and wasn't concerned by the resultant criticism (Taylor was the first Australian captain since Bobby Simpson in 1977–78 *not* to enforce the follow-on). Only months before in Pakistan, he'd agonised over a similar decision at Rawalpindi. Eventually he asked Pakistan to bat again and Saleem Malik made 237 to force a draw.

The 15-minute periods before and after lunch on day four in which Warne struck twice with his flipper proved to be the most telling of the match. Having hit six 4s in a highly attacking 33, including a cut shot to the boundary from Warne earlier in the over, Stewart went for his favourite pull shot only to realise too late that it was Warne's flipper, delivered 20 km/h quicker than his trademark leg-break. It cannoned into his stumps with Stewart hopelessly late with his shot. After the break, Atherton played back to a flipper which swung and skidded, catching him on the creaseline clearly in front.

If Slater's cavalier attack and McDermott's revitalised outswing had stunned the English early, Warne had thrown the knockout punch. By taking 8/71 from 50.2 overs, he masterminded England's slump from an overnight 2/211 to 323 all out. None of the visitors used their feet with confidence, especially with Warne spinning the ball prodigiously. They hoped to hit the loose one, but few were forthcoming and even the shorter ball was looked upon with suspicion in case it was the flipper.

Damien Fleming, who was Australia's 12th man, said the English treated Warne as if he were bowling 'hand grenades'.

'Having seen how the Pakistanis played Shane using their feet and taking the attack to him at every opportunity only weeks before, compared with the way the English played him was chalk and cheese,' Fleming said.

Warne very nearly finished the match with a hat-trick when a wrong'un to England's No. 11 Phil Tufnell grazed his off-bail. Most satisfying of all the eight wickets was the dismissal of 41-year-old Graham Gooch, neatly caught by Healy low down trying to hit Warne into the grandstand. Only minutes before, he'd told the spin star: 'You're getting all the others, but you're not going to get me!'

Having made 56 in two and a half hours of studious concentration, Gooch's demise signalled the end of England's resistance. DeFreitas was bowled around his legs without playing a shot and by mid-afternoon on day five, the Australians, led by master of ceremonies David Boon, were into a rousing rendition of their famed victory song, 'Under the Southern Cross I Stand'.

'It was a good wicket and I was playing him okay only to suddenly play this horrendous slog across the line. I don't know why,' said Gooch. 'Heals took a great catch off the bottom edge. I was really depressed after that. It was my major disappointment of the series. When you put yourself against the best players in the world, that's where you test yourself. That's what gives you the greatest satisfaction if you're successful.'

Significantly, Atherton and Stewart, England's two team leaders, borrowed binoculars and went up high behind Warne's arm, where the TV cameramen were located, looking to determine some tactics for playing him in future matches.

It had been 40 years since England had come from behind to win a Test series in Australia (in 1954–55, Len Hutton's side lost the first Test, then won three of the next four to take the series 3–1), but the firepower of earlier teams was missing. Gough had taken six wickets on his Ashes debut, but the rest of the attack was flat and the fielding pedestrian.

Australia had played with enterprise and authority and at the beginning of the second Test in Melbourne, strangely scheduled for Christmas Eve rather than Boxing Day, England was a 6/1 outsider. Several key players including vice-captain Alec Stewart were affected by injury. Martin McCague had already returned home, having confessed to carrying stress fractures of the feet into the first Test. A second paceman, Joey Benjamin, had also succumbed to chickenpox and would hardly play again on tour.

Malcolm's much-heralded MCG return was only semi-successful. He bowled with fire but could take only one wicket for the game, at a total cost of 164 runs.

England showed marginal improvement early, only to capitulate in astonishing fashion in just three hours in its second innings. Set 388 to win late on the fourth day, the tourists were bowled out for 92, their lowest score in Ashes Tests for 36 years. They lost 6/13 in just 56 minutes on the final morning, McDermott taking 5/42 in another stunning display of high-quality pace bowling. Included was his 250th Test wicket, Graham Thorpe caught behind by Healy.

However, as in Brisbane, he had to again share the spotlight with Warne, the Victorian taking a hat-trick to the roars of 9000 home-town fans who'd come to witness the last rites.

With England 6/91 and Taylor contemplating a bowling change, after some stern resistance from wicketkeeper Steve Rhodes, Warne dismissed DeFreitas, Gough and Malcolm with the fourth, fifth and sixth deliveries of his 13th over, the final fingertip catch being brilliantly taken by Boon diving full-length to his right at short leg.

Before the burst of wickets, Tim May had been warming up at mid-off, having been told by Taylor that he was on next. He wasn't sure which end.

Hemmed in by a battery of close-in fieldsmen, Malcolm, with a batting average of 6, could hardly have been expected to survive for long. Stewart, the non-striker, turned to Warne and said, 'You'll never have a better chance of getting a hat-trick!'

Warne had considered bowling a flipper to Tufnell, or a wrong'un as in Brisbane just weeks earlier. He consulted with his team-mate Fleming, who'd taken a hat-trick on debut at Rawalpindi earlier in the year.

'What do you think, mate?' he said.

'I closed my eyes and tried to get an outswinger going,' Fleming told him.

'He got lucky so I closed my eyes and tried to bowl a leg-spinner,' Warne said later. 'I bowled it and "Babs" [Boon] took a really good catch. It had a bit more overspin and it bounced and it got the bat-pad. Luckily

Boonie took an absolute beauty. He just about threw himself off his feet when he caught it.'

Having dived prodigiously to his right and emerged with the ball in his outstretched right hand, the normally poker-faced Boon jubilantly threw it skyward before being engulfed by Warne and other equally delighted team-mates.

Umpire Steve Randell, who had been unsighted, did not raise his finger immediately, but after consulting with square leg umpire Steve Bucknor confirmed the catch. 'If I hadn't given him out, they would have killed me!' he said.

The Englishmen had been humbled for the second Test in a row. The Ashes, once a symbol of world cricket supremacy, was again a no-contest.

Inside the rooms, Warne said, 'I suppose I'll wake up soon.' It was the first Ashes hat-trick in 91 years.

In his eighth Ashes Test, Warne had snared nine wickets for the game to become the third-fastest Australian to 50 wickets. In his last two Tests alone, he'd taken 20 wickets.

Just days before, against the Indians, the world champion West Indies had extended their unbeaten series run to 15 years, thanks to a series-squaring victory at Mohali. They were still the kings, but the gap was narrowing.

# SIX

---

# A
# WINNING
# COMBINATION

*Winning a Test match after being bowled out for
only 116 in the first innings would be something
to tell their grandchildren.*

---

CRICKET'S FINEST XIs have invariably possessed world-class openers.
Hobbs & Sutcliffe, Morris & Barnes, Simpson & Lawry and Greenidge
& Haynes were four of the very best combinations, who all flourished
in world-rated teams.

Mark Taylor's combination with Geoff Marsh was stable and
forthright, with one partnership during the Ashes-winning tour of
England in 1989 worth 329 runs at Trent Bridge when they batted
through the entire first day's play. With his close-cropped haircut
straight out of the 1930s, Marsh was a reassuring, steady figure at the
head of the Australian order. He was the right man for tough times
and, for Allan Border, the consummate right-hand man.

But use-by dates are inevitable and when Marsh was controversially
replaced by little-known Victorian Wayne Phillips for the final Test
of 1991–92, he knew his time was up.

David Boon was a resolute stand-in against the West Indies in
1992–93, but more valuable at No. 3. Coming into the 1993 Ashes

tour, finding a suitable partner for Taylor was a priority. Prolific Queenslander Matthew Hayden and another first-time tourist Michael Slater, who had started the previous summer with NSW's second XI, were trialled. Hayden played the three Texaco Cup matches on the eve of the first Test, but in the last first-class game before the team was selected, at Grace Road, Leicester, Hayden made only 2 and 15 while Slater scored 91 and 50 not out.

Slater played in the opening Test and was remarkably successful. In the years to come, he and Taylor were to forge a wonderful association. In this maiden series together they averaged almost 70 runs per partnership, including 128 in the first Test at Old Trafford and 260 in the second at Lord's. Taylor's poise and patience seemed to complement Slater's flair and exuberance. Opening also for NSW, they developed a strong understanding and bond.

Slater, 23, had first been chosen for Australia after just 11 state games and a stint at the Australian Cricket Academy most notable for him being hit by a car while cycling around Adelaide. Like Taylor, he hailed from Wagga Wagga and possessed the same country-style affability and enormous pride in the baggy green cap.

In their first home Ashes Tests together in 1994–95, they'd started with 99 and 109 in Brisbane followed by 10 and 61 in Melbourne. Coming to the third Test in Sydney with Australia needing only a draw to retain the Ashes, they were again central in an epic match that didn't finish until almost 7.30 p.m. on the fifth and final day.

England had dominated much of the game, thanks to Darren Gough's inspired all-round efforts early on day two. In making a cavalier 51 in just under an hour and lifting England's score to 309, he highlighted the deficiencies in his own team's top order – then claimed 3/21 in an irresistible opening spell as Australia, in reply, limped to 6/57 at lunch.

'Darren loves the big-time,' said England's selection chairman Ray Illingworth of his fellow Yorkshireman. 'He's like a breath of fresh air. We need four more like him.'

Taylor's 49 was easily top score as Australia was bowled out for 116, only just avoiding the follow-on thanks to a Malcolm bouncer which ballooned over the head of wicketkeeper Steve Rhodes and into the pickets.

Mike Atherton's conservative captaincy had been questioned in each of the opening two Tests, and he was again under fire in mid-match. Not only did he declare England's second innings closed with Graeme Hick on 98 not out, he delayed the declaration until mid-afternoon on day four when England's lead was 450. Few teams had ever made 300 in the fourth innings of a Test in Sydney, let alone chase such a huge target.

While Hick was denied his maiden Ashes century by his own captain, reviving memories of a similar decision made by Bill Lawry which left Rod Marsh 92 not out almost 25 years earlier, he had batted for more than four hours without showing undue urgency. But at the mid-afternoon drinks break, when he was 92, he had been warned by vice-captain Alec Stewart that a declaration was imminent.

With wickets in hand, England should have been far more purposeful, especially as Taylor deliberately restricted the number of overs sent down. So long was he in resetting his field on one occasion that a spectator asked Taylor if he also wanted a cup of tea. It was one of the rare occasions in which the captain's judgement was not accepted unequivocally.

Having survived a close lbw appeal, Hick played out a maiden to Damien Fleming before Atherton called his batsmen in. It was 2.58 p.m. Explaining his controversial decision, Atherton said it was unfortunate for Hick, but he wanted to have two cracks at the Australians with his new-ball bowlers, for half an hour before tea and again immediately after.

Having already batted for five hours, most believed Atherton's best option was to allow Hick an extra 12 minutes until 3.10 p.m., when a declaration would have triggered an early tea interval and given England an uninterrupted, extended session against the Australian top order.

Atherton's tactics of using his pacemen in short bursts each side of the tea interval were roundly condemned, especially when Taylor and Slater made a flourishing start, as if they were in a one-day chase. In the eight overs available before tea, the two Australians added 41 and at stumps were still together, at 0/139, Taylor 64 and Slater 65.

Taylor's 50 from 69 balls was the second fastest of the match. He'd played adventurously and, along with Slater, run brilliantly between the wickets. Malcolm was genuinely fast and Taylor looked to play shots at every opportunity. One cover drive, off the back foot against Gough, fairly hurtled to the fence.

Coach Bob Simpson said he'd never seen him bat better.

News of their great stand spread quickly and in the hour between 5 p.m. and 6 p.m. on the penultimate night, more than 5000 reserved seats were sold for the following day's play.

Australia's fifth-day target was 310. It was achievable, but still a huge ask, especially on a wearing fifth-day wicket.

After the team's warm-up, Taylor hosted the meeting where it was decided to go all out for a win. The top-order batsmen would play their natural games and attack as often as they could. Winning a Test match after being bowled out for only 116 in the first innings would be something to tell their grandchildren.

However, Australia's hopes of a historic victory evaporated early in the opening session when Phil Tufnell, bowling at leg-stump to a 4/5 field, conceded just six runs from his opening six overs.

The Australians could score only 65 runs for the session, and while they went to lunch at 0/206, 243 runs were still required at four an over with rain interruptions forecast.

Ladbrokes the bookmakers rated a draw 4/1, an Australian win 7/2 and an English win 11/2.

Slater's dismissal, from a skied pull shot soon afterwards, effectively ended Australia's winning chance. With 103 he'd again batted superbly. He reached his ton in thrilling style during the final over before lunch, helping himself to a 4 and a 3 from Graham Gooch's friendly slow-mediums.

Batting in drizzling rain, Taylor offered no shot to Malcolm and lost his off stump at 113. Thanks to Angus Fraser, who'd reinforced the touring party, England resumed control before rain, bad light and some stalwart defence from a typically stubborn Boon and tailenders Shane Warne and Tim May halted the tourists' advance.

Remembering Australia's lamentable collapse against the South Africans at the same ground just 12 months previously, Taylor spent the final hour of the game nervously biting the ends of his finger-nails.

The biggest Test crowds in Sydney in 10 years, including 25 760 on the final day, had revelled in the riveting contest, the closest of the series so far. Because of the rain break and the need to make up for lost time, the final session extended to three hours 55 minutes, another Anglo–Australian first.

Taylor had accelerated to his maiden century as a Test captain and he'd done it with style and purpose, reminiscent of his career-best form from England in 1989. Over a beer with Boon and Mark Waugh later, he said it was his finest Test innings. 'Once Mark decided to take on Devon [Malcolm] with his cut and pull shots, the momentum really built and we started scoring quickly,' Slater said, in an interview with Mark Ray of the *Sunday Age*.

Until the early-afternoon rain, which was to cost the Australians eight overs, the emphasis had always been to win. However, Taylor was more than satisfied to draw as it ensured Australia's successful defence of the Ashes for a record-equalling third consecutive time. Only Don Bradman-led Australian teams boasted a similar record.

As soon as Taylor was dismissed, he started worrying that the game might not be safe. He was pleased to force the draw, and particularly at the spirited way in which the Australians played.

Wedged between the final Tests of the summer was the World Series finale, England faring so badly that it failed to beat either Australia or series newcomer Australia 'A' into the finals. Taylor spoke for everyone in the senior team when he said the concept should never be repeated where two Australian sides opposed each other. The International Cricket Council were also unimpressed, ratifying only the games which were truly representative as official one-day internationals.

On several occasions, most notably in Adelaide, the crowd supported Australia 'A' players and several of the senior Australians were booed. And in Sydney in the first all-Australian final, Glenn

McGrath clashed with Australia 'A' opener Matthew Hayden after he'd been hit for 4. Both were reprimanded by referee John Reid. They also were spoken to by Taylor, who said even seemingly trivial incidents were magnified when played and re-played on television.

Taylor's involvement, even with Hayden, who wasn't a direct member of his side, was a further example of how seriously he was taking his overall responsibility of lifting the image of the game, so tarnished less than nine months previously by the Warne and Merv Hughes flare-ups in South Africa.

Shane Warne was at his cheekiest and most inventive bowling to Australia 'A' captain Damien Martyn in the second World Series final in Melbourne in 1994–95. Poking his tongue out and making a face at Martyn, he captured his former Cricket Academy buddy leg before wicket after he'd made the fastest half-century of the one-day summer, from just 34 balls.

## PROFILE: MICHAEL SLATER

MICHAEL SLATER PUNCHED THE AIR and planted a joyous kiss on the Australian badge on his helmet after reaching his maiden Test 100 in only his second Test in England in 1993 – but many considered he'd taken his personal celebration a little too far. After all, this was Lord's, the traditional home of the game.

Thankfully, Slater took the ribbing and refused to compromise. All of his 12 Test centuries have featured the same bubbly show of affection for the green and gold.

For many, his overt enthusiasm and emotion is symbolic of all that is good with Australian cricket. Why not play your natural game? Why be stereotyped? One of the game's great entertainers, Slater refused to compromise, even after his barely defensible 18-month exile from the international scene in 1996 and 1997.

On return, he played with all his old flair, thumping his cover drives from the first ball of matches just like the great Charlie Macartney from a bygone age. His uninhibited strokeplay and unique on-field celebrations made him, with Mark Waugh, the most watchable of all the Australians.

There have been players with finer techniques, but none at the very head of the order who have enjoyed such a rare run of success against England, or been as essential a member of a team rapidly becoming the best since Don Bradman's Invincibles.

Seven of Slater's Test 100s to the start of the 1999–2000 summer came in Ashes contests at a rate of one century each 2.2 Tests. Only The Don himself, with a century every two Tests, has a finer record in Anglo-Australian Tests.

'I'm an adrenalin player and I'm still going to get out playing some silly shots,' Slater said. 'But my shot selection has improved. I'm trying to keep it simple and isolate each ball on its merits. The longer you play the game, the more you mature.'

When banished back to Sheffield Shield ranks, despite a Test average of 45 and an opening partnership average of almost 60 with captain Mark Taylor, Slater refused to change the habits of a lifetime. He was stunned and disappointed, but he'd always believed cricketers had a duty to entertain and play aggressively. In the first half hour of the Barbados Test in 1999, he struck spinner Neremiah Perry high onto the top deck of the Challenor Stand. Another foot or two, and it would have gone clean out of the ground. For an opening batsman, few play the finger spinners with such obvious enjoyment.

His flamboyant strokeplay prompted Bob Simpson to remind him that he could score only four and not eight for boundary hits! So hard did Slater smite the ball that his NSW captain Geoff Lawson felt sure that he had shares in picket companies.

From his first days in Australia's elite XI, everything Slater did was full-on. In his anger at being dismissed in the Adelaide Test in 1995–96, he stuffed his pads, bat, gloves and thigh pad into a toilet and repeatedly attempted to flush the lot away!

Slater's century habit had started at the age of 12 when he was so prolific in the southern Riverina juniors that his coach at the Wagga RSL club asked authorities to change the rules so some of the other kids in the team could get a chance to bat! Having to retire at 50 was an initial frustration, but even when he returned at No. 11 he still got to three figures, farming the strike cleverly with hard-run singles at the end of overs and hitting 4s at the start of the new one.

His coach from the age of seven, NSW Cricket Association development officer Warren Smith, had always advocated that the best form of defence was attack. 'You have two hands and a bat – use 'em' was his catch-cry to all of his juniors.

Smith thrilled to Slater's freewheeling flair. He threw him hundreds of balls, urging him to play full-blooded shots with the fullest possible follow-through. Sometimes he'd have him playing his shots without a ball, calling in turn for Slater to play an off-drive, cover drive or on-drive, all at match pace.

Even at 12, Slater was playing shots that few in the senior XIs could play. His idol Viv Richards used to intimidate opposing attacks. Slater wanted to do the same. His favourite shot was the straight drive, lifted up high over the new-ball bowler's head. If he could do it the first ball of a match, so much the better!

The third of his three centuries in the 1998–99 Ashes summer effectively ended England's winning chance.

In one of the finest solos in Test history, he scored 100 out of 148 runs in Sydney. So jubilant was he on reaching three figures, he waved and re-waved his bat and did a mini lap of the oval to the acclamation of his home town fans.

Life as a cricketing exile had been tough, and it made his comeback successes all the more sweet. 'Unless you go through a hardship and adverse times, I don't think you grow as a person,' Slater said. 'I can't think of too many people where it's all been high, high and higher.

'There wouldn't be too many who could go through what I did, disregard what went on and still be on top of the world.'

In retrospect, Slater's controversial Test dismissal surpasses even Dean Jones's demotion as Australian cricket's greatest selection puzzle of the 90s.

He'd erred in India in the one-off Test in 1996–97, making a second-ball duck at a critical time to the otherwise-forgettable debuting medium pacer David Johnson. But in the first innings he'd top-scored with a very responsible 44 and only three Tests earlier, had pummelled a Sri Lankan attack in Perth, making a glorious Test-best 219.

The Australian selectors were to be commended for lifting stars-to-be in Ian Healy and Shane Warne from virtual obscurity into the Test side in the late 80s and early 90s. But they'll forever be embarrassed by demoting Slater after one loose shot. He was unfairly and unjustly made the scapegoat of a defeat.

## MICHAEL SLATER'S RECORD (TO 20 AUGUST 1999)

|  | Mts | Runs | HS | Ave | 100s | Wicks | Ave | BB |
|---|---|---|---|---|---|---|---|---|
| Tests | 49 | 3792 | 219 | 44.61 | 12 | 1 | 4.00 | 1/4 |
| One-day Int. | 42 | 987 | 73 | 24.07 | – | 0 | – | – |

## AUSTRALIA'S LEADING ASHES 'CENTURIONS'

| Name | 100s | Tests v Eng | Average frequency |
|---|---|---|---|
| Don Bradman | 19 | 37 | 1.94 |
| Michael Slater | 7 | 16 | 2.28 |
| Arthur Morris | 8 | 24 | 3.00 |
| Greg Chappell | 9 | 36 | 4.00 |
| Bill Lawry | 7 | 30 | 4.28 |
| David Boon | 7 | 31 | 4.42 |
| Steve Waugh | 7 | 37 | 5.28 |
| Allan Border | 8 | 47 | 5.87 |

**EXPERT OPENERS: MARK TAYLOR & MICHAEL SLATER IN TEST CRICKET**

| Season | Opponent/Venue | Tests | Runs | Ave | 100s | 50s |
|--------|----------------|-------|------|-----|------|-----|
| 1993 | England (away) | 6 | 676 | 67.60 | 2 | 2 |
| 1993–94 | New Zealand | 3 | 380 | 95.00 | 1 | 2 |
| | South Africa | 3 | 177 | 35.40 | 0 | 2 |
| | South Africa (a) | 2 | 132 | 33.00 | 0 | 1 |
| 1994–95 | Pakistan (a) | 3 | 288 | 57.60 | 1 | 1 |
| | England | 5 | 766 | 76.60 | 3 | 3 |
| | West Indies (a) | 4 | 215 | 35.85 | 0 | 1 |
| 1995–96 | Pakistan | 3 | 271 | 54.20 | 2 | 0 |
| | Sri Lanka | 3 | 306 | 76.80 | 1 | 0 |
| | India (a) | 1 | 51 | 25.50 | 0 | 0 |
| 1997–98 | India (a) | 3 | 201 | 33.50 | 0 | 2 |
| 1998–99 | Pakistan (a) | 3 | 131 | 26.20 | 0 | 0 |
| | England | 5 | 294 | 29.40 | 0 | 2 |
| Total | | 44 | 3898 | 51.28 | 10 | 14 |

**NEXT MOST PROLIFIC AUSTRALIAN PAIRS**

| | Runs | Ave |
|--------|------|-----|
| Bill Lawry & Bob Simpson | 3596 | 59.93 |
| David Boon & Geoff Marsh | 1871 | 46.78 |
| Mark Taylor & Geoff Marsh | 1846 | 40.13 |

(Most prolific openers of all:
Gordon Greenidge & Desmond Haynes (WI) 6482 runs at 47.31)

## TEST CENTURY PARTNERSHIPS BETWEEN MARK TAYLOR & MICHAEL SLATER

| | | | |
|---|---|---|---|
| 128 | 1st inns | v England | Old Trafford, first Test, 1993 |
| 260 | 1st inns | v England | Lord's, second Test, 1993 |
| 198 | 2nd inns | v New Zealand | Perth, first Test, 1993–94 |
| 176 | 1st inns | v Pakistan | Rawalpindi, second Test, 1994–95 |
| 109 | 2nd inns | v England | Brisbane, first Test, 1994–95 |
| 208 | 2nd inns | v England | Sydney, third Test, 1994–95 |
| 128 | 1st inns | v England | Adelaide, fourth Test, 1994–95 |
| 107 | 1st inns | v Pakistan | Brisbane, first Test, 1995–96 |
| 120 | 2nd inns | v Pakistan | Hobart, second Test, 1995–96 |
| 228 | 1st inns | v Pakistan | Perth, first Test, 1995–96 |

## MARK TAYLOR'S TEST OPENING PARTNERS

| Opening Partner | Tests | Runs | Ave | Span |
|---|---|---|---|---|
| 1. Geoff Marsh | 25 | 1846 | 40.13 | 1988–89 to 1991–92 |
| 2. David Boon | 10 | 488 | 34.03 | 1989–90 to 1992–93 |
| 3. Mike Veletta | 1 | 33 | 33.00 | 1989–90 |
| 4. Wayne N. Phillips | 1 | 37 | 18.50 | 1991–92 |
| 5. Tom Moody | 3 | 117 | 19.50 | 1992–93 |
| 6. Michael Slater | 44 | 3898 | 51.28 | 1993 to 1998–99 |
| 7. Matthew Hayden | 6 | 132 | 13.20 | 1996–97 |
| 8. Matthew Elliott | 14 | 721 | 30.04 | 1996–97 to 1997 |
| 9. Mark Waugh | 1 | 14 | 14.00 | 1997–98 |

# SEVEN

## DEFENDING
## THE ASHES

*To upset the world champions, Australia needed to be
consistently tough and, whenever possible, repel the fire.
Intimidate them, before they could intimidate you.*

ONE OF CRICKET'S FASCINATIONS is its element of surprise. A game's
fortunes can inexplicably swing in just an hour or two. Having conceded
the Ashes by mid-tour, Mike Atherton's 1994–95 tourists were heading
for another defeat late on day four of the fourth Test in Adelaide.

Trailing by 66 runs on the first innings, England was 6/181 in its
second, just 125 ahead with only the tail to come. While Australia had
been vulnerable chasing substantial targets, it seemed anything below
250 would not greatly extend the Aussies, even batting last on a fifth-
day wicket.

Adelaide Oval was traditionally a batting haven. In the last Sheffield
Shield match at the ground just weeks earlier, the first four South
Australian batsmen (Greg Blewett, James Brayshaw, Paul Nobes and
Darren Lehmann) made centuries against Victoria, creating a South
Australian state record.

A late flurry from Phil DeFreitas and John Crawley, who had played
the dangerous Shane Warne as well as anybody on first sight in

Sydney, raised English hopes. DeFreitas, an all-rounder of infinite ability, had under-achieved on tour, and lost his place in Sydney. He received an unexpected recall when the team's major strike bowler Darren Gough so severely injured an ankle during the World Series one-dayers that he was immediately sent home.

Looking for the breakthrough on the last morning which would have exposed England's three non-batsmen, Angus Fraser, Devon Malcolm and Phil Tufnell, Mark Taylor opened with his two matchwinners, Craig McDermott and Warne. For once, neither could create the breakthrough which surely would have ensured Australia the match.

Instead, DeFreitas launched an astonishing counter-attack such as has rarely been seen in Tests. With Warne rested in favour of the second new ball after his workload hastened shoulder soreness, DeFreitas thumped the fast bowlers unmercifully down the ground and to the short square boundaries. Scoring at a run-a-minute, he made 88 in two thrilling hours. One of McDermott's overs with the second new ball went for 22 (44•446). It was an extraordinary rally which saw 89 runs added for the seventh wicket and 47 for the eighth. Instead of having to chase 200, Australia's task ballooned to 263 in the final two sessions, at a rate of four an over.

The momentum had swung England's way and Malcolm, who had been threatening all summer with his extreme pace, at last found the right line. In his first five overs he took 3/8, including the prize wicket of Steve Waugh, who was beaten for pace first ball and had his off stump uprooted. Fraser was also superb, one leg-cutter to Mark Waugh seaming away wickedly like a fast leg-break.

From being the hunters, Australia was suddenly fighting to save the game, and when Waugh was miraculously caught by short leg Mike Gatting (he hit the ball at pace into Gatting's boot only to see it dolly up into his hands) England seemed destined to score a shock win.

Ian Healy and Damien Fleming bravely forced the game into the final hour with a 69-run stand before Fleming was lbw to a long hop from pace reinforcement Chris Lewis, and No. 11 Peter McIntyre fell identically to Malcolm. A patched-up England had won by 106 runs

Shane Warne's extraordinary record was assisted by some marvellous close catching, including this one-hander by Mark Waugh to dismiss Pakistan's Ramiz Raja in Brisbane in 1995–96.

*Stephen Laffer*

The Taylor–Warne combination became the most lethal of any fielder-bowler. Together they shared 51 wickets including this one, Keith Arthurton caught at Antigua in 1994–95.

*Gordon Brooks*

The 1994–95 series was billed as a two-man battle between Shane Warne and Brian Lara, but neither was overly dominant, despite occasional flashes of brilliance.

*Gordon Brooks*

The proudest moment: Mark Taylor holds the Frank Worrell Trophy aloft after
Australia's victory in three and a half days at Sabina Park in 1994–95.

*Ray Titus*

The beginnings of the party of a lifetime. In the rooms in Kingston after David Boon
had just led a rousing rendition of 'Under the Southern Cross I stand'.

*Ray Titus*

Michael Slater's double century in Perth in 1995–96 was a thrilling affair, highlighted by an imperious attack on Sri Lanka's No. 1 bowler Muttiah Muralitharan.

*Sergio Dionisio*/Australian Cricket *Magazine*

Australia's Ashes comeback in 1997 including a match-winning double-century stand between first-time tourists Matthew Elliott and Ricky Ponting at Headingley.

*David Munden/Sportsline*

Matthew Elliott writhes in pain after colliding with Mark Waugh in mid-pitch, having made 78 against the West Indies in Sydney, 1996–97.

*Stephen Laffer*

Having bowled poorly in his Ashes debut in England, Glenn McGrath found top form at Lord's with 8/38. Only rain saved England.

*David Munden/Sportsline*

The Australians gather at the 'Gabba for 'Advance Australia Fair' before the first of their near clean-sweep of wins against the 1997–98 New Zealanders.

*Stephen Laffer*

Mark Taylor and South African Hansie Cronje toss in Melbourne in 1997–98. Taylor won and Australia dominated throughout – until the fifth day when a Jacques Kallis century saved the tourists.

*Ken Rainsbury*/Australian Cricket *magazine*

For the first time in his illustrious career, Mark Waugh batted through an entire day to save the Australians from defeat against South Africa in Adelaide in 1997–98. He's pictured in the first innings, batting against Shaun Pollock.

*Stephen Laffer*

Ashes 1998–99: Jason Gillespie celebrates the dismissal of Graeme Hick, second ball in Perth. The gangly South Australian speedster took seven wickets for the game, only to be made 12th man for the next Test!

*Stephen Laffer*

with 35 balls remaining. DeFreitas was man of the match. Healy's 51 not out was easily top score. No other Australian reached 25.

The success of the two West Indian-born pacemen, Malcolm and Lewis, who'd taken 13 wickets for the game, seemed ominous in light of Australia's imminent Caribbean visit. Lewis, 26, had answered a team SOS from Melbourne, where he'd been playing with northern suburban turf team Seddon. His aggressive send-off of McDermott on the final day was straight out of a Clint Eastwood movie.

In between Tests, Taylor made a lightning trip back to Sydney to witness the birth of his second son, Jack, before heading to Perth determined to restore some of Australia's lost pride. An English win at the WACA Ground would square the series 2–2.

From the time 'centurion' Michael Slater was dropped from the third ball of the match at third slip by Graham Gooch, Australia was never extended, and registered a 329-run victory by early afternoon on day five. With 0/41 and 6/38 for the match and 32 wickets in five Tests, McDermott was man of the series. On the penultimate night, England slumped to 5/27 after a nightmarish final hour. Among McDermott's victims were ex-captains Gooch (aged 41) and Gatting (37), playing their farewell Tests. On the final day, after England was bowled out for 123, Taylor led the call for three cheers for the much-capped pair, who between them had played almost 200 Tests.

Taylor felt the 3–1 result adequately reflected Australia's superiority. But Australia would have to play better again and be mentally tougher to defeat the West Indies in Australia's coming Caribbean showdown. The Poms had not always played with absolute focus. Ructions existed within their ranks. They'd even been beaten twice in two days by the kids from the Australian Cricket Academy.

As enthused as he was about the spirit in the team, Taylor warned that the frenetic schedule was taking its toll, especially among his bowlers. Burn-out was an undeniable factor. Warne had averaged 55 overs per Test since the first Test against Pakistan, and noticeably was spinning the ball less and less. He and McDermott had bowled 54 per cent of the overs against England, taking 44 per cent of the wickets. While truly world class, they needed support.

Fleming and Tim May were fighting injuries. Opening batsman Slater was nursing a broken thumb and all-rounder Steve Waugh hadn't bowled for almost four months.

It seemed bizarre that, after eight Tests and two full-scale one-day tournaments in five months, another short tour could be wedged in before the tour of the West Indies. But it was, to New Zealand, the Australians playing four games and defeating NZ in the final of the Bank of New Zealand Centenary Series. In 20 weeks, the Aussies had played internationals against Pakistan, South Africa, England, Zimbabwe, India and NZ. No wonder there'd been casualties.

And 10 days later, having hardly had time for even some beach cricket in Barbados, the Aussies were into a five-match one-day series, preceding the West Indian Tests.

Addressing the team in London, just hours before their connection to the Caribbean, Taylor said the biggest aspect of the coming series was that the West Indies had everything to lose and Australia everything to gain. He said the '91 tour had been tough, probably the toughest of his career. But this team was a harder, more professional unit, which, but for the hiccup at Karachi in October, had been winning virtually everything at both Test and one-day level.

Taylor urged his batsmen to play naturally and use all their shots, even the hook shot, as they would in any other game. The strength of West Indian cricket still revolved around fielding four express bowlers in each Test. To upset the world champions, Australia needed to be consistently tough and, whenever possible, repel the fire. Let the West Indians know that they'd come to win. Pepper their fast bowlers with short deliveries. Intimidate them, before they could intimidate you.

● The biggest crowds in 12 years saw the 1994–95 Tests, 478 000 being aggregated at the five Tests, including 144 492 for the Christmas Test in Melbourne. With results in four of the five games, plus a gripping draw in Sydney, Test cricket was clearly alive and well.

## PROFILE: GREG BLEWETT

IN THE 1950S AND 1960S, emerging cricket stars with an appetite for tall scores often had to endure Bradman-like comparisons. Ian Craig, Norman O'Neill and Doug Walters were three batting virtuosos who burst onto the Australian first-class scene to be labelled 'the next Bradman' by ambitious pressmen.

Critics are more realistic now. Don Bradman's colossal runmaking feats are an integral part of cricketing lore and likely to remain untouchable long into the new millennium. Whenever the all-time best cricket teams are named, Bradman is invariably No. 1. His talents were unique, his hunger for runs unsurpassed.

Occasionally a starlet emerges who reminds of The Don. India's Sachin Tendulkar is similar in build and performance. And not even Bradman debuted in Tests as a teenager or had scored 20 Test 100s by the age of 25.

Among Australians, the closest in style has been the right-handed Greg Blewett from one of Adelaide's foremost cricket schools, Prince Alfred College. Replacing Michael Bevan in the Australian top order in the last Ashes Tests of 1994–95, Blewett scored 102 not out and 12 on debut in Adelaide, followed with 20 and 115 a week later in Perth.

ABC Radio's Roger Wills was on the spot in the Adelaide members' grandstand with Blewett's father Bob, mother Shirley and sister Kerry, when he reached his maiden ton, with a force behind point for two. 'To think that the larrikin kid has grown up and made it to play for Australia,' Blewett snr told Wills after the rangy 23-year-old debutant had been accorded a standing ovation. You could almost hear his heart thumping with pride.

It had been a drama-packed opening hour as Craig McDermott, who was due to bat at the fall of the seventh wicket, had been taken to hospital for an examination after complaining of stomach pains during morning practice. With wickets falling around him, Blewett, who was 91 not out overnight, was joined by last man

Peter McIntyre, McDermott still being absent.

Somehow McIntyre survived long enough against the pace of Devon Malcolm and Co. for Blewett to achieve his first-up ton. He was dismissed for a duck just as McDermott had returned to the ground and was dressing to take his place at the crease.

No one had made two centuries in their debut Tests since the brilliant Walters, in 1965–66. And Blewett's mannerisms and methods, especially his pull shot, were uncannily Bradman-like.

When taking his stance, Blewett closed his bat in between his feet à la Bradman, allowing him full scope for his favourite cut and pull shots. When moving into a drive, his habit was to move his front foot past, rather than just to the ball – another Bradman habit that lessens error, especially on seaming or slower tracks.

Former Australian Test bowler Terry Alderman had initially thought Blewett too impetuous, especially early in his innings, to be a long-term Australian prospect.

But by making 125 in the first Test against England at the start of the next Anglo-Australian series, at Birmingham in 1997, Blewett became the first player to score 100s in each of his first three Ashes Tests. He also was to build an enviable record replacing David Boon at short leg.

### GREG BLEWETT'S RECORD (TO 20 AUGUST 1999)

|              | Mts | Runs | HS  | Ave   | 100s | Wicks | Ave   | BB  |
|--------------|-----|------|-----|-------|------|-------|-------|-----|
| Tests        | 34  | 2003 | 214 | 35.14 | 4    | 11    | 52.54 | 2/9 |
| One-Day Int. | 32  | 551  | 57* | 20.40 | –    | 14    | 46.14 | 2/6 |

# EIGHT

---

# THE
# PROUDEST
# MOMENT

*'That tour was the Steve Waugh show.*
*He dominated it from start to finish.'*

---

FROM THE TIME the young Barbados express Patterson Thompson whistled a welcoming bean ball, the very first of the tour, past the nose of a retreating Michael Slater, Australia knew just how tough it would be to inflict upon the West Indies the first series defeat on their home wickets in more than 20 years.

Thompson was playing only for Barbados 'B', but was as quick as anyone in the Caribbean. The only trouble, however, was that he had no idea where it was going. His nine overs cost 64 runs, and provoked five wide and seven no-ball calls.

However, he did have Slater caught off his gloves with a wicked lifter third ball, to the roars and whistles of the Bajans, who delight just as much in bumpers as they do in big hits.

Enter a helmeted Steve Waugh, Australia's toughest competitor and a man destined later in the year to become the world's new No. 1 ranked batsman. By the finish of Thompson's furious first over, he'd spanked two 4s, and in an entrancing two hours of clubbing counter-attack, raced to a match-winning century from just 89 balls.

Within days, however, the breakdowns of Damien Fleming and Craig McDermott, Mark Taylor's two foremost new-ball bowlers, had added a darker perspective. Fleming's shoulder had given way, the start of long-term problems, while McDermott had freakishly injured tendons in his ankle while jogging.

By winning four of the five one-day games, the Windies had started the tour buoyantly and, come the first Test in Bridgetown, were confidently fielding their usual flotilla of flamethrowers: the intimidating pace bully Curtly Ambrose, his thoroughbred partner Courtney Walsh, plus the two Benjamins, Kenny and Winston, well-versed in their roles in cricket's version of assault and battery.

By comparison, Australia's pace attack was inexperienced and unproven. Glenn McGrath had played nine Tests, Paul Reiffel 12 and mid-tour inclusion Brendon Julian, just two.

At the team's traditional pre-Test dinner, held two nights before the match, Taylor told of the opportunity which existed for some of the junior members in the team to step up and become regular Testmen. Emphasising the importance of enjoying the challenge, he said there was no need to treat Test cricket like war.

He spoke of 1973 and how Australia last won the Frank Worrell Trophy in the Caribbean against the odds. Dennis Lillee had broken down in the first Test, while Bob Massie, a star during his maiden tour in England just months earlier, was ill and lost form so dramatically that he failed to play a Test. Back-ups Max Walker and Jeff Hammond revelled in their new frontline roles and were instrumental in one of Australia's finest series wins overseas.

Taylor's game tactics revolved around his unsung bowlers concentrating on an off stump line and allowing little scope for the usually uninhibited strokeplay of opposing captain Richie Richardson, returning to international cricket after a break of almost 12 months. New world No. 1 Brian Lara was a danger, but early in his innings he had a habit of playing back, even to good length bowling. The plan was to bowl full and hope that he'd tickle an early catch. Carl Hooper was a strong driver of the ball, but sometimes went for his shots prematurely. Bowl short of a length around off stump and wait for him to make a mistake. Jimmy Adams, too, could stick around, but he often played with his bat at an angle and, particularly early, was always a candidate for a slips catch. The strategy against the tail was simple. Bounce 'em and enjoy their discomfort!

Kensington Oval was full by 9.35 a.m. when Taylor and Richardson went out to toss, triggering a fresh round of drum beating. There is no more passionate or informed cricket crowd in the world than in Barbados. The showdown for world cricket supremacy had brought the locals into Bridgetown by their thousands. The pitch looked flat and full of runs. And as the Australians were enthusiastically applauded by the hundreds of their own fans attending with Melbourne and Sydney tour groups, there were almost as many outside looking to get into the ground.

The start will long be remembered as one of Australia's very best:

- Julian, sharing the new ball with Reiffel, induced a wild flay from rookie Stuart Williams which was gleefully accepted at slip by Taylor – 1/1;
- Sherwin Campbell, also making his Frank Worrell Trophy debut, then nicked Reiffel through to a delighted Healy – 2/5;
- and captain Richardson, from only his third ball, fanned rashly at Julian to give Healy another present – 3/6.

It was a fairytale start for the challengers and particularly for Julian, the athletic New Zealand-born bowling all-rounder, playing only his fourth Test. The wicket was producing steepling bounce and the world champions were lurching. The tension was electric. Allan Border had long believed that the team that dominated day one of the first Test would win the series.

Hooper and Lara momentarily wrested the ascendancy with some thrilling, almost daredevil batting, which drew the Bajans away from the rum stands dotting the back of the bleachers and into every available vantage spot.

When Taylor introduced his trump card Shane Warne at first

. change, Hooper hit each of his first three balls to the boundary. It was a premeditated, daring assault designed to shake Warne's confidence.

Lara, too, was very aggressive before being controversially given out on 65, caught in the gully by Steve Waugh. Television replays showed that the ball may have hit the ground before Waugh completed the catch, but he was sure it was a clean take and Lara walked off. Even a third umpire wouldn't have been able to adjudicate, as powers weren't to be extended to allow a third umpire to use TV replays for disputed catches until 1 September 1997.

Later Waugh told reporters that the ball had bobbed out of his hand and onto his wrist before he controlled it again. He believed that at no stage did it hit the ground. 'It all came as a shock to me that people said I didn't catch it,' he said later.

Taylor, at first slip, couldn't tell conclusively that the catch had been taken, but when assured by Waugh that the catch was okay, he stood by him. 'Then, after Viv Richards came out against Stephen, I went around to the commentary box myself and got them to replay the dismissal and I still couldn't tell conclusively either way,' Taylor said. 'When Steve said yes he caught it, that was good enough for me.'

The great Viv Richards had fanned the controversy by claiming Lara had been robbed of a certain 100 by Waugh's poor sportsmanship. 'Lara was batting like a dream,' Richards was quoted as saying. 'Who knows? He might have got 200 the way he was going. The player must have known it had hit the ground. Some Aussies have been doing it for years, not all, but some since I started playing in 1975. It's a poor thing when you have to resort to that.'

Mark Waugh squarely backed his brother. In an interview with Robert Craddock, he said: 'I don't think there is any doubting the fact that Stephen is honest,' he said. 'He has been playing for a long time. He thinks he caught it and I will back him up and say he has caught it.'

Steve Waugh accused Richards of deliberately inciting trouble between the teams. In his *West Indian Tour Diary* Waugh said, 'His word is gospel with the locals, which he knows only too well ... he should be more responsible in his actions.'

The Australians had established a 151-run lead with sensible forthright batting in mid-match, and thanks to McGrath (who took 5/68) and Warne (3/64) the Australians dismissed the Windies a second time for just 189. The match finished late on day three when openers Taylor and Slater needed just half an hour to score 39. The winning run came via a Kenny Benjamin no-ball.

CALYPSO CRACK-UP was the banner headline in Melbourne's *Herald Sun* newspaper. The Windies had capitulated almost without a whimper, being bowled out twice in less than 120 overs and at their most renowned venue. Barbados was to West Indian cricket like Karachi is to Pakistan. It was a cricketing citadel where their team of so many generations had rarely been tested, let alone beaten. It was the West Indies' first three-day loss in 30 years and there was particular spring in David Boon's step when he leapt onto a table and began the first line of Australia's victory anthem, 'Under the Southern Cross I Stand'.

Inter-island jealousies invariably bubble in the Caribbean, and given the number of capped players, plus manager Andy Roberts, to hail from the Leeward Islands, there was talk of nepotism and upheaval. 'I was really frustrated because the guys weren't geed up for the Test,' Richardson told Phil Wilkins of the *Sydney Morning Herald*. 'When you are playing the first Test match, you should be very enthusiastic. For some reason we could not get it right.'

Taylor had led by example, playing his hook shot and being aggressive from the outset, much as he had against the Englishmen in Newcastle back in mid-November.

Describing it as the best Test win he'd ever been involved in, Taylor said it was especially satisfying to see some of the team's unsung players performing so ably. Julian, with five wickets for the match, had been a revelation, while McGrath's dismissal of the in-form Lara in the second innings had been a turning point, the ball of his career. A delighted Taylor gave him a stump as a souvenir.

The Australians had outplayed the Windies in '91 without being able to put them away. Now they had done so, in the very first Test, the pressure would intensify. Taylor forecast that the Windies would come at the Aussies in Antigua with a ferocity that only a truly formidable side could repel. Once stung, the world champions had a history of defying the odds. Overconfidence may have been a problem at Bridgetown – players were said to be out until the wee hours during and after the first Test – but they would not relinquish their title without a supreme fight. It was the West Indian way.

Australia expected a bumper barrage in the second Test, and particularly on the second evening, batting was perilous as Taylor and Slater fought as hard to preserve their physical safety as their own wickets. At the end of the first Test, Slater had said the West Indian attack held no fear for the Australians. What was meant to be an innocent throwaway line, highlighting the new team psyche, enraged the Windies. Ambrose advised Slater to have '19 ambulances waiting for him' at St John's.

Trailing by 44 on the first innings, Australia had just nine overs to bat to conclude day two and home town hero Ambrose and Walsh went on full attack. Bodyline revisited. Four balls an over were pitched short and at the body. Two outriders were positioned for the skied hook, a bat-pad was in for the fend, while three slips and a gully were in for the nick. Every time a ball whistled past Taylor's head, the crowd at the Recreation Ground roared like they were at a bullfight. With the hi-fis, drums and trumpet players all going full bore, it made for an extraordinary atmosphere.

Taylor felt the attacks were intimidatory and went against the spirit of the game. He said he felt quite punchy walking off the ground, on 4, with Slater 9 and Australia 0/16.

Every available ice-pack and then some were utilised by physiotherapist Errol Alcott in the cramped Australian rooms. It had been a ferocious attack; 'chin music' at its most lethal. The two Australians felt like they'd been at a coconut shy. Walsh eventually dismissed them both, but the rain, which had briefly interrupted the lunch-to-tea session on day two, was the ultimate winner, each of the last three scheduled days also being interrupted. Set 257 to win in 36 overs on the final afternoon, the Windies were 2/80 when the game was abandoned, Walsh's nine wickets the match highlight along with an extraordinary catch by Richardson at third slip and a one-hander by David Boon at short mid-on, just when Brian Lara looked set to power to the first ton of the series.

Mark Waugh, who made 61 in the second innings, said he'd never faced as many short deliveries as on day three. He'd been greeted with his normal two first-up bouncers. He was also struck flush on the back by a beamer from Walsh.

The experimental rule limiting bowlers to two bouncers an over was rarely policed.

Taylor, dismissed twice on the hook shot, said he would continue to challenge the West Indian pacemen by being aggressive. He told reporters: 'If a side bowls five half-volleys an over, you have to play the drive. If a side bowls a lot of short balls, you have to hook and pull.'

Part of Taylor's role was to change the thinking within the Australian team that the West Indians were untouchable. Previous sides had been loath to return the volleys of bouncers to Ambrose and Co. Taylor's attitude was that the Australians would be bounced and it was up to them to repel and return in kind. Every time a McGrath bouncer whistled head-high past a tailender, the Australians would laugh, genuinely enjoying a predatory role.

Coming to Trinidad for the third Test, where 12 months previously England had been humbled for 46 (Ambrose 6/24, Walsh 3/16), Australia was confronted by a soft, under-prepared green-top which unfairly loaded the importance of the toss.

The pitch had originally been soaked to cater for the month-long dry spell in Port-of-Spain, but rain pelted down on match eve and with the covers on, it was unable to dry sufficiently by the start of the game.

As resolute as the Australians were on the occasion of David Boon's 100th Test, they couldn't stop the West Indian charge, led by a pumped-up Ambrose, who was at his most venomous, taking nine wickets as the Windies squared the series decisively in just three days.

Sent in to bat, the Aussies were bowled out in 47 overs for 128 in the first innings and in just 37 overs for 105 in the second. Only one player, Steve Waugh, scored more than 50 for the game. His 63 not out stretched early into the second day and was as fine and courageous a display as any of his far larger contributions in the 1990s. As good as Brian Lara and the Indian Sachin Tendulkar undoubtedly were, both would have been proud to have lasted three hours on this deck, especially after being booed onto the ground!

Having taken 5/45 in the first innings, Ambrose claimed 4/20 in the second. Warne, batting at No. 10, was almost relieved to get a nick to be caught behind, only to hear the call of no-ball. 'Oh no!' said Warne.

If the Australians felt the heat at St John's, they were cornered at Queen's Park, where it was hard to distinguish between the outfield and the wicket area. Tempers flared, especially when Steve Waugh was confronted mid-pitch by a furious Ambrose minutes before noon.

With Australia 3/37 and Waugh and Boon trying desperately to halt the West Indian advance, Ambrose bounced Waugh, the ball flying harmlessly over his shoulder, so much so that he barely had to duck.

'He followed through to within two metres away from me and gave me the regulation Clint Eastwood stare,' said Waugh in his *West Indian Tour Diary*. 'I thought he went on with the silent assassin style interrogation for longer than was necessary, so I came back with, "What the #@&%* are you looking at?"

'It was at this moment that I had done the equivalent of smashing open a hornet's nest with a large brick. Ambrose began to move closer to me and mouthed the words, "Don't cuss me, man!" His eyeballs were spinning and as he edged to within a metre, it seemed he was ready to erupt.

'At this point I gave him a short but sweet reply that went down as well as an anti-malaria tablet. Fortunately, Richie Richardson (from slip) moved in swiftly to avert what could have been my death by strangulation, and the game continued.'

Waugh felt Ambrose had deliberately and unnecessarily invaded his space. Neither he nor Ambrose was prepared to back off and match referee Majid Khan ordered an immediate 'please explain'. While he took no official action, he told both players and teams to 'cool it'.

Waugh gave only one chance, at 35, and said later he'd never experienced more testing batting conditions. Afterwards, even Richardson claimed the pitch was sub-standard. 'I don't believe Tests should be played on wickets like that,' Richardson told reporters. 'It is unfair for the players, especially the batsmen, and quite embarrassing really.'

Australia felt they could regain their early series dominance if given a hard wicket at Sabina Park, Jamaica's famous old Test ground, in Kingston. However, another soft-top would again favour the Windies.

In his 12th Test as captain, Taylor felt nothing but an Australian victory would suffice. It was a heavyweight title bout with the winner to take all. 'We had a chance at Karachi to prove we were a great side, and this is another,' he said. 'You've got to be mentally tough and mentally aggressive to beat the West Indies.'

Any reservations Taylor had in losing his fourth toss in a row were forgotten when, with the second ball of the game, Paul Reiffel had Stuart Williams caught, after a lifting delivery brushed his glove and ballooned from his chest to Greg Blewett at short leg.

A century from Richie Richardson and 65 from Brian Lara evened the fortunes, but once Lara was caught via the inside edge to Warne's topspinning leg-break and Jimmy Adams and Carl Hooper fell meekly, the Australians assumed control, bowling the Windies out for 265 right on stumps. The Sabina Park pitch was firm and highly polished and so brown in colour that the tourists dubbed it 'Cadbury'.

It was a gutsy effort by Warne to even take his place in the XI after he'd suffered a chipped thumb, courtesy of Ambrose, at Port-of-Spain. The key wicket of Lara was his most satisfying of the series. When Warne had first come into the Australian team in 1991–92, his goal wasn't necessarily to spin opposing teams out; rather to take the wicket which changed the match.

The underrated Reiffel with three wickets and Julian, two, were also instrumental in the West Indian collapse, which saw the last eight wickets topple for 134.

Day two of the Test – 30 April 1995 – will be forever remembered as one of the greatest in Australian cricketing annals.

At 3/73, after Slater had been miraculously caught on the backward square boundary by Lara from the bowling of Walsh, Steve Waugh joined brother Mark at the crease in what was to build into the most important partnership of the tour.

Ducking the customary first-up bouncer, this time from Kenny Benjamin, Steve Waugh, who'd been outstanding throughout the tour, continued imperviously against the pace. There was an early scare, at 4, when he only narrowly avoided the short leg catching trap. At 18, he almost lifted a Winston Benjamin bouncer to Adams at short leg. Mark Waugh was also close to being caught before he'd made double figures, fending at Walsh.

Encouraged by the early life in the wicket, the Windies tried even harder to bounce the twins, but too often were off line, bowling either too short or too wide. Every time their line wavered, the West Indian pacemen were punished. The two Waughs added 101 in the middle session and a further 130 in the last before Mark fell on 126 to the occasional spin of Hooper, after four and a half hours of applied concentration and sparkling strokes. Like Steve, he'd scored mainly square of the wicket as the Windies pounded the ball in short.

The West Indian frustration was graphically illustrated by fast bowler Winston Benjamin, who sat on the ground and cried.

Ex-Test fast bowler Geoff Lawson, in Kingston with a tour group, said the twins were ruthless in their domination of the Windies. He wrote in the *Age*: 'They actually had a 45-second mid-wicket conference at one stage, which is rumoured to be the longest conversation they have had since Mrs Waugh let them have separate rooms.'

Their stand was worth 231 as Australia tightened their grip.

Dropped by first-game wicketkeeper Courtney Browne at 42, Steve Waugh was 110 at the close, having defied the bowling in a rare innings of resolution. Maintaining his focus the next day, Waugh carried on to a Test-best 200, No. 11 McGrath hanging on for seven balls to help his NSW partner through the 'nervous' 190s.

Waugh had batted for 555 of the 659-minute Australian innings.

Greg Blewett's 69 and even twin brother Mark's 126 were dwarfed by Waugh's epic. It was his eighth 100 in 76 matches and, given the importance of the match and the constant physical danger he endured, the innings of his life, even superior to Dean Jones' double century against India in the tied Test at Madras a decade earlier.

At 531 all out, Australia had doubled the West Indian score. The champions were in quicksand.

'It was a big series for me,' said Waugh, who was to receive almost 400 congratulatory faxes back at the team's Kingston hotel. 'I'd always struggled against the West Indies and had a reputation for not being able to handle the quicks. There was a lot of incentive there. The [Lara] catching incident came along [at Bridgetown] and I was castigated by a lot of people. I channelled all my energies into being positive rather than being negative.

'Concentration wise and focus wise, it was the best I'd batted. Even after 10 hours, I felt I could have batted for another 10 hours if I'd needed to. I was almost in a trance-like state throughout.'

Waugh was besieged by waves of Australian supporters, who sprinted onto the ground carrying footballs and didgeridoos and draped in Aussie flags. To Waugh's amusement, one of the fans was his bulky former Test team-mate Greg Ritchie. 'Fat Cat, what are you doing here? You should know better,' said Waugh.

Having fielded for almost two days and 266 runs behind, the Windies lost all hope of saving the game when Paul Reiffel, in the most inspired hour of his career, took 3/18 from six overs, including Lara for a duck, lbw to a grubber which may have pitched outside leg stump. It was yet another magic moment for the Australians in the Test match of their lives.

With two days to play, only prolonged rain could save the West Indies, and on the fourth afternoon, with the pitch taking spiteful side-spin, the champions were bowled out for 213, giving Australia victory by an innings and 53 runs.

Appropriately, Taylor took the winning catch at slip from the bowling of Warne, whose first-innings dismissal of Lara had been so crucial.

Fifteen years of West Indian Test domination was over. The Frank Worrell Trophy was in new hands.

Taylor presented the ball to Australia's team coach Bob Simpson, who had been so central in the planning, despite missing sections of the tour after developing thrombosis in his leg. Simpson was the only Australian captain to lose two series in the islands and a third, as coach, in 1991. 'I think it's the proudest moment I've known,' Simpson wrote in the *Sydney Morning Herald*. 'We've got close before, but to beat the West Indies in the West Indies is the pinnacle.

'A testimony to the tenacity, concentration and skill of the Australian bowlers was that the West Indies' highest score was 265 and not once did they bat for a full day. While on the surface the Australian attack may not have had the colour or charisma of some of our past heroes, none of those greats of the past could have bowled with better control, nor stuck so faithfully to our game plan. A tribute to their skill was that approximately 70 per cent of the West Indies' batsmen got out in the way we had planned.'

The Australians tossed champagne around the rooms like it was water. One Tasmanian supporter handed two bottles of Boag's beer through the dressing room window for David Boon and Ricky Ponting to consume. He'd transported them halfway around the world and had them nicely iced for this very moment. The lobby at the Australians' hotel, the Pegasus, was soon packed with hundreds of supporters who carried the celebrations into the wee hours. Several of the team, including man of the series Waugh, didn't even bother to change out of their cricket gear as they partied.

Healy says watching Waugh staggering up to his room remains an enduring memory. 'Tugga was still in his whites, spikes and baggy green cap. We found him stretched out the next morning, still in all his gear, complete with baggy green firmly on his head.'

Without Waugh's monumental contributions, Australia could never have won. 'He was the rock which held the team together,' Healy said. 'That tour was the Steve Waugh show. He dominated it from start to finish.

'While the scorebook shows that we won by an innings, it was a tighter match than the scores indicate. The Waughs' stand meant everything to us. At least 100 of the 400-odd balls Steve faced were short as the West Indies looked to test an apparent weakness. But Steve had incredible spring in his footwork and, displaying all of his renowned grit, warded everything off. It was a tremendous effort, the best innings I've witnessed in my time in Test cricket.'

With more than 400 runs at an average of 107, Waugh had reinforced his ranking as the world's No. 1 batsman. Never before had he batted so effectively, felt as strong or been so controlled.

'We were fired up and really determined [to win],' he said.

'A lot of us were in our late 20s and into the early 30s. Maybe it was our last throw of the dice to win in the West Indies. We'd gone close a few times. We'd lost in Adelaide [in 1992–93] by a run. That was in the back of our mind as well. We knew they were beatable and ready to be taken down. India should have beaten them a couple of months before, but probably lacked that killer blow.'

McGrath had also been magnificent, with 17 wickets at an imposing strike-rate of one every seven overs. In *Inside Edge* magazine, Mark Waugh likened McGrath to Merv Hughes of old. 'He took it to the Windies bowlers when their turn came to bat. He let them know in obvious terms that he meant business and we weren't scared of them. The fear factor wasn't there, and that's how they've won a lot of their games.'

Taylor, who passed 5000 runs in Test cricket during the game, said he'd never felt prouder than when he kissed the Frank Worrell Trophy and hoisted it into the air to the acclamation of hundreds of the assembled Aussies. This was the original trophy, refound after a decade in which it had gone missing, forcing authorities to make a replica.

For at least an hour after the ceremony, many were still chanting '2–1, 2–1' and 'Ooh-arr Glenn McGrath, I say ooh-arr Glenn McGrath'.

Taylor had averaged only 25, but had claimed nine catches at slip and captained brilliantly.

Inside the rooms, champagne was thrown and the standards began, the ritualistic 'Khe Sanh', sang karaoke-style by Steve Waugh, Warne and Slater, followed by yet another rousing chorus of 'Under the Southern Cross I Stand' led by the little big man David Boon.

Allan Border was among the celebrities in the thick of it all. He'd been cruelly denied his greatest cricketing moment two years previously in Adelaide. Now, as a celebrity commentator for Fox Sports, responsible for the cable television coverage coming to Australians, he felt proud and privileged to be ushered into the rooms and on the spot for the changing of the world cricket order. Lawson and David Hookes were also on hand to share in the revelry.

'Seeing the Frank Worrell Trophy held aloft at Sabina Park was a very proud moment for me, because it was the one undone thing of my own Test career,' Border said.

'We didn't just beat them in close games,' said Shane Warne in the *Sunday Age*. 'We flogged them.'

## MARK TAYLOR'S FIRST 5000 TEST RUNS

| Milestones | Tests | 100s | 50s |
|------------|-------|------|-----|
| 1000 | 10 | 3 | 5 |
| 2000 | 14 | 3 | 8 |
| 3000 | 12 | 1 | 4 |
| 4000 | 14 | 5 | 5 |
| 5000 | 16 | 1 | 8 |

## PROFILE: GLENN McGRATH

EVER SINCE HE WAS A FARM BOY bowling fourth change for the Backwater under 16s in Narromine, 450 km west of Sydney, Glenn McGrath had yearned to be Australia's No. 1 fast bowler.

An invitation to play in Sydney on the recommendation of the legendary Doug Walters saw his career prosper so rapidly that Rod Marsh included him among his Australian Cricket Academy scholars in Adelaide. In 1993–94, he became the first Academy pupil to also represent Australia in the same year.

From being a somewhat hesitant new-ball apprentice to Craig McDermott in his maiden Tests, McGrath succeeded him as Australia's premier paceman during his very first Test tour overseas, in 1995.

In the opening Test in Barbados, he took the wicket of his life – world record breaker Brian Lara caught at the wicket for nine, with a seaming off-cutter pitched so perfectly that it demanded a shot. Sensing the danger too late, Lara tried to adjust his defensive push but could only fan the ball through to Ian Healy. Of all McGrath's 200-plus Test wickets, it remains his very favourite dismissal. 'We all knew we had to lift,' he said. 'And we had nothing to lose. We just went out there and gave it everything. For me, Barbados was my first chance to play as the No. 1 bowler, which is what I'd always wanted to do rather than bowling in the shadow of someone else.'

By dismissing the world champions for 195 and 189, Australia won by 10 wickets in under three days. It was a classic start to an unforgettable series. For McGrath, his eight-wicket match haul was the defining moment in his career. He was bowling faster and more consistently. Rarely did his line stray. 'Getting that first five-for was a big step,' he said. 'It's like a batsman making his first 100. Once you have proved to yourself that you can perform at that level, your confidence grows and things fall into place.'

Benefiting from an arduous gymnasium and fitness program and ongoing advice from Dennis Lillee, whom he'd first met at the

Academy, McGrath claimed 35 wickets the following Australian summer at a strike-rate superior even to spin genius Shane Warne.

Not only did McGrath operate at near express pace, powering through the crease with gusto, he moved the ball appreciably and often disconcertingly late, like the great Pakistani duo Wasim Akram and Waqar Younis. The wicket of Aamir Sohail, bowled for 99 in Brisbane, was up there with the Lara dismissal, so late did the ball move with McGrath bowling from wide around the wicket. 'Using reverse swing is an asset I never had when I started,' McGrath said. 'Now when it starts to move around for me, my confidence goes through the roof. I feel very comfortable with it, especially at places like the 'Gabba where the ball tends to move around for you. I feel I automatically pick up a yard or two in pace.'

One of the tallest men to play cricket for Australia, the 198 cm (6 ft 6 in.) right-arm fast bowler and specialist No. 11 batsman took just 23 Tests to reach 100 Test wickets and another 24 to make 200. His ability to build pressure and success against players of the quality of Lara and England's Michael Atherton underlined his value to captain Mark Taylor.

At Lord's in 1997, his Test-best 8/38 from 20.3 overs rivalled the all-time best performances by any Australian in England, stretching over more than 100 years of Ashes contests. Only four others had also taken eight wickets in an innings:

- Frank Laver, 8/31 at Old Trafford, 1909;
- Hugh Trumble, 8/65, The Oval, 1902;
- Bob Massie, 8/84, Lord's, 1972;
- Craig McDermott, 8/141, Old Trafford, 1985.

Having won the first Test comfortably, England tumbled for just 77 in its first innings on a memorable Saturday afternoon's play. ' There was a little bit in the wicket so I thought instead of going overboard and trying to do too much, I'd just stay patient,' said McGrath. 'It's probably the most patient I've been with my bowling and that makes it so much better.'

He'd never played in England before, even at club level. It was little wonder that he took time to settle and learn the lessons of bowling a fuller, tighter length. However, he was to thrive from mid-tour, appreciating the set of greenish wickets which seemed to follow the Australians, a reaction to the astonishing success of first-time tourist Shane Warne on far drier wickets in 1993.

An amiable giant off the field, McGrath cuts an intimidating and aggressive persona on it. He believes no bowler can be successful-without a certain competitive edge. Sometimes his temper can run out of control, like at St John's in 1999 when he was accused of spitting in the direction of West Indian opener Adrian Griffith. A fine of $2000, suspended from a previous altercation months earlier in Melbourne with England's Alan Mullally, was enforced. So frustrated had McGrath become at seeing Lara put down from his bowling that he'd kicked the fence at fine-leg in his frustration and wrenched his ankle so badly that physiotherapist Errol Alcott was up most of the night treating it with ice.

It was appropriate that two days later McGrath took the final wicket, of Corey Collymore, to give Australia the victory which squared the series. With 30 wickets in four Tests, he'd bowled with passion, pace and outstanding durability.

Like Merv Hughes, he built his reputation around taking the important wickets when they most counted.

As England coach David Lloyd said during the 1998–99 Ashes campaign, 'McGrath is everything I see in a fast bowler – he's nasty, aggressive and good.'

**GLENN MCGRATH'S RECORD (TO 20 AUGUST 1999)**

|  | Mts | Runs | HS | Ave | 100s | Wicks | Ave | BB |
|---|---|---|---|---|---|---|---|---|
| Tests | 49 | 244 | 39 | 5.80 | – | 232 | 22.60 | 8/38 |
| One-day Int. | 96 | 49 | 10 | 3.76 | – | 140 | 24.65 | 5/14 |

# NINE

---

## JUSTICE
## IN THE
## GAME

*Malik even refused to allow an Australian doctor*
*to give him an injection for fear he might*
*attempt to poison him!*

---

IT'S DOUBTFUL if there had ever been a more expensive one-night stand. With the wives and partners joining the players for a 10-day holiday in Bermuda, a victory party was organised, with the blessing of the Australian Cricket Board and team manager Jack Edwards, who until then had been expertly budgeting and balancing the books, keeping a little aside for a night such as this.

Most of the girls and many of the touring party drank nothing but Moët champagne and the total bill, including VAT and the gratuity, came to $US6777, almost $A10 000!

When the tour expenses ballooned further thanks to more than $20 000 in excess baggage, several board men claimed cricket money had been flagrantly wasted. As the tour party broke up, Steve and Lynnette Waugh heading for Egypt and Shane Warne and fiancée Simone Callahan holidaying in the United States, Edwards, an innocent party, had to face a please explain!

'I said to Mark Taylor and Steve Waugh to go down to a decent restaurant and have a good night,' Edwards said. 'Many of the girls had come over for a holiday and there were 28 in total. I calculated roughly what it would cost and told the players to get a couple of bottles of champagne too. It turned out that they drank nothing but Moët and not just your two bottles. I had to pay for the lot! Even now Steve Waugh asks me if I managed to balance the books. Steve was the culprit. As far as food and drink bills go, it's still the all-time record.'

In June, a ticker-tape parade was held through the main streets of Sydney before a crowd estimated at 150 000. It had been 20 years since Australia had last been world champion, and the victory at Jamaica had captured the imagination of the entire nation.

Having challenged and beaten the mighty West Indians, Taylor believed Australia had every right to the title. 'The West Indies have been the best side in world cricket for 12–15 years,' he told Phil Wilkins of the *Sydney Morning Herald*. 'Now I think we are the better cricketers. Pakistan play us next summer in three Test matches. If they beat us on our soil, they are the world champions.'

However, his views weren't necessarily shared, even by his team-mates. Long-time deputy Ian Healy said any world champion needed to be unbeaten over several series, for a period of two or three years. 'I don't believe this talk of us being world champions – just yet,' he said. 'At the moment, I believe the title is in limbo.'

Despite Australia's domination of the series everywhere but on lush Queen's Park where it was difficult to distinguish the centre square from the outfield and the toss virtually decided the winner, Richie Richardson declared that the West Indies should continue to be considered the No. 1 ranked team in the world, until beaten again. 'I can't believe we lost [to Australia],' he said. 'In my opinion this is the weakest Australian team I have played against.'

Richardson had an ally in team manager and fast bowling legend Andy Roberts. Asked who was No. 1, he said: 'West Indies – still. The thing is, you have to go to Pakistan and beat Pakistan.'

The fact that cricketing minnows Sri Lanka accomplished an upset 2–1 series win in Pakistan, on the eve of the 1995–96 Australian season, fuelled speculation that Pakistan might not be quite as powerful as some thought. Zimbabwe had also recorded its first-ever Test win against the Pakistanis in Harare earlier in the year, prompting the sacking of captain Saleem Malik and manager Intikhab Alam in one of the country's darkest cricketing hours.

Key players remained embroiled in the bribery scandal. News months later that Malik had been acquitted of any wrongdoing was virtually dismissed down under, as the Pakistani inquiry had glossed over (and, in fact, largely ignored) the statements of the Australians who claimed they'd been offered bribes by Malik in 1994.

Malik's reinstatement enabled him to tour Australia for an eighth time, under the captaincy of premier all-rounder Wasim Akram. Intikhab was back as manager.

Warne had been particularly keen to oppose Malik after the Pakistani had downgraded his bowling at the conclusion of the '94 tour. 'Warne is a great bowler, but to pick him is not difficult,' Malik said. 'He can bowl only three different deliveries and has a completely different action for each one. The angle of his hand is different for each ball. I pick each one as it leaves the hand. I was confident and he knew that.'

Malik's tactics included taking block wide of leg stump when Warne started operating around the wicket and playing only straight-bat shots, to negate the chance of Warne's deadly flipper skidding through undetected. The slow and low wickets found on the subcontinent had helped him master all of the Australians in a display of rare domination. However, like many of his highly rated countrymen away from their own wickets, he'd regularly been discomfited by the extra bounce.

In between his international travels and his springtime marriage, Warne's winter off included time back in Adelaide with his mentor Terry Jenner. There he reassessed his technique and made some slight action adjustments, convinced that his signature ball, the big-spinning leg-break, had lost a little of its bite. Jenner had been a soulmate of Warne's ever since they'd first met in 1990, at the Australian Cricket Academy. His own Test career in the early 1970s had been racked by self-doubt and lack of opportunity at the highest level. But as a coach of leg-spin, he was regarded as the very best in the world. Warne was not only a keen and willing student, he possessed the rare gift of being able to carry out instructions within minutes of being shown.

Jenner's reinforcing talks also centred on Warne's psyche and tactics against certain batsmen. While subscribing to the theory that slow bowlers should mix up their deliveries, he believed Warne should never sacrifice his biggest trump, the leg-spinner, which even in unfavourable conditions could spin the width of a set of stumps and more.

In interviews leading into the first new-season Test in Brisbane, Warne echoed much of what the pair had discussed. 'I think you can get a bit carried away bowling a lot of different stuff,' Warne said. 'The biggest weapon for me when I bowl leg-breaks is the amount of spin [I get]. I can't lose that.'

Warne had had a cortisone injection in his battle-scarred finger at the start of the summer, the first major warning that his work-rate was leading to a breakdown. Previously, when working on improving his googly with Jenner, his finger had blistered so badly that he'd virtually discarded the delivery altogether, resolving instead to rely on his leg-break, back-spinner and flipper.

In Victoria's opening Sheffield Shield match of the season, in Brisbane, he'd bowled 61 overs, followed by almost 50 a fortnight later in Melbourne. As the State's new vice-captain, he'd been keen to make the most of his only appearances for the summer.

Malik's confrontation with Warne cornered almost all of the pre-match publicity, dwarfing Craig McDermott's return. The Australians had for a long time referred to Malik as 'The Rat', not through any slur on his integrity, but because of his long, rodent-like face. After the affair spilt into the public arena and the Pakistani bribery judgement branded the Australians as concocters, it became team policy to refuse to acknowledge Malik in any fashion.

Malik became so paranoid about his critics that he even refused to allow an Australian doctor to give him an injection, for fear he might attempt to poison him!

Having arrived a week after his team-mates because of visa problems, Malik had played only one lead-up game before the opening Test, against South Australia in Adelaide when he was dismissed cheaply in both innings.

The absence of classy opener Saeed Anwar, who was unable to join the team because of typhoid fever, had severely weakened Pakistan's batting. The bowling was also suspect and in the opening two first-class fixtures, five players (Mike Hussey and Brad Hogg from Western Australia and Darren Lehmann, Greg Blewett and Jamie Siddons from South Australia) made centuries against Wasim Akram, Waqar Younis and Co.

Even the most pessimistic Pakistani supporter, however, could not have predicted how badly their team was to fare in the first match of the three-Test series. After all, it was barely a year since Pakistan had defeated a full-strength Australian team 1–0.

Australia batted the best part of two days for 463 before Pakistan capitulated meekly for 97 and 240, to lose by an innings and 126 runs with a day and two full sessions to play. Malik had six stitches inserted in a gashed thumb after diving to dismiss Taylor on the first day, and failed to bat in the first innings. Sent in at No. 8 in the second, he lasted only four balls before meekly surrendering his wicket to Warne. 'It shows there is justice in the game,' said the Australian, who pumped the air with both fists as a scrambling McDermott cupped the ball safely in both hands at mid-off.

'I really enjoyed that [Malik's dismissal], for obvious reasons,' Warne said. 'He has obviously got a bit of a sore hand, but I thought he could have batted in the first innings. I know if that was one of the Australians, he would have batted and would have just about gone out with a broken leg. I don't know if he will play in the next Test, but hopefully I'll get him out for a duck in every innings he plays.'

With 11 wickets for the game, including a flattering 7/23 in the Pakistan first innings, Warne produced the best figures by an Australian against Pakistan.

He spun the ball sharply in a flashback to his best spells against England at the same ground 12 months previously. But his performance was abetted by some stunningly poor Pakistani batting. Other than

Aamir Sohail's 32, no one else made even 20. Several self-destructed in a manner demeaning to Test-standard cricket.

In three Tests in Brisbane, Warne had taken 30 wickets at the extraordinary average of 10.4: 4/66 & 4/59 against New Zealand in 1993–94; 3/39 & 8/71 against England in 1994–95; and 7/23 & 4/54 against Pakistan.

Intikhab Alam rated Pakistan's batting in Brisbane as the worst he'd ever seen. 'We got ourselves out,' he said. 'If someone is bowling well, you have to be sensible and patient.'

Imran Khan said Pakistan cricket had lost its way since its World Cup triumph in Melbourne in 1992. He blamed greed, lack of leadership and internal wrangles for Pakistan's woes.

The tourists dropped eight catches on the opening two days, including Michael Slater three times in the opening hour. While Slater did not take full advantage of his good fortune and was out for 42, Steve Waugh, who was also dropped three times, motored to his ninth Test century, and batted for six hours in all. Since the 1993 Ashes tour, he'd averaged 80-plus to warrant his elite ranking as the world's top-ranking batsman, ahead of even the record-breaking Brian Lara.

So telling had Warne's wrist spin been in Brisbane that the Pakistanis were virtually forced to re-include Mushtaq Ahmed, their own world-class leg-spinner, for the second Test at Bellerive Oval. Mushtaq had been omitted from the starting XI at the 'Gabba in favour of a late arrival, 21-year-old reinforcement Mohammad Akram, making his Australian debut.

In the true spirit of spin fraternity, Warne had discussed technique with Mushtaq during net practice at the 'Gabba.

Mushtaq's googly, while internationally acclaimed, had essentially become a stock ball and for years the senior Australians had played him as a virtual off-spinner, a little like Anil Kumble, the world-ranked Indian.

In Hobart and Sydney, Mushtaq revived Pakistan's fortunes, taking 18 wickets in two Tests. Instead of concentrating on his googly, he used it only sparingly and showed he could consistently rip his leg-break. At Bellerive he bowled 27 overs unchanged in a rare spell of slow bowling, to take 5/115 as Pakistan immediately became more competitive.

While beaten by 155 runs late on the fourth day, six of the Pakistanis falling to lbw decisions, several of which were dubious, it had been a far more positive showing. In Sydney, given the opportunity to bat first, Pakistan forced a 74-run victory, its first in Australia since 1981–82.

With 5/95 and 4/91, Mushtaq was man of the match, ahead of a back-in-form McDermott and Warne, who each took eight wickets. Warne had been unable to bowl in Hobart after having a toe broken by Waqar Younis' famed in-swinging yorker. He seemed to benefit from the enforced break, six of his wickets being in Pakistan's top order. The most extraordinary dismissal was Basit Ali, who was bowled through his legs with Warne operating around the wicket during his last over of the third evening. Before bowling the ball, Warne called wicketkeeper Ian Healy into a mid-pitch conference in a delaying tactic aimed at unsettling the young Pakistani. Later it was revealed that rather than discussing immediate tactics, they'd been talking about that night's dinner arrangements!

The Sydney reversal extended Australia's winless record at the ground into a seventh year. Needing 247 runs to win, Australia collapsed from its overnight 3/121 to 172 all out, continuing their habit of faltering on last-day run-chases. The last four wickets fell for just two runs, three to the high-speed Waqar, including an out-of-form Greg Blewett to a swinging full toss. 'It's always tough chasing here,' said Taylor. 'They outplayed us from the start.'

After the second Test in Hobart, Wasim Akram conceded that Australia deserved to be Test cricket's new No. 1. While pleasantly pleased by Pakistan's comeback win at the SCG, Akram said the rubber was dead and his team's central focus was on successfully defending their World Cup title early in 1996. He would, however, have enjoyed the opportunity of playing a five-Test series with the Australians.

Taylor had again excelled, as opening batsman and slipsman and as a leader, where his bowling and fielding changes were innovative and often inspired. In Hobart, Taylor's explanation after little-used seamer Blewett had taken two important wickets in Pakistan's second innings was that he was 'just trying something different'.

In just 12 months at the helm, many thought Taylor had taken Australian cricket to a new level. Taylor's confidence in each player automatically led to a positive attitude in the field and at the crease. 'I take my hat off to Mark,' Ian Chappell said in an interview with Malcolm Conn of the *Australian*. 'He has the ability to immediately assess what he's got and fully utilise it and encourage the guys to play that way ... the last thing this side needs with its ability it has got is a conservative approach.'

Another ex-skipper in Kim Hughes was also congratulatory. 'The captaincy sits well with him,' he told Mark Ray of the *Sunday Age*. 'He keeps the game simple. I believe he'll be one of the great captains.'

A three-Test series against Sri Lanka preceded the World Cup and was most notable for the controversy and ill-feeling it generated.

The Sri Lankans were consigned to a bush circuit and didn't play at a major capital city in their first three weeks on tour. Not only did they have to combat poor practice facilities, the match wickets were slow and second-rate compared with city wickets. Asanka Gurusinha broke a thumb in Cairns while Aravinda de Silva suffered a split finger in Launceston.

Once the internationals started, the tourists plunged into a series of sensations:

• At the WACA Ground in Perth where the tourists lost the first Test by an innings, ball tampering allegations were made by the International Cricket Council referee Graham Dowling. He claimed the ball had been deliberately tampered with in the 17th over of the Australian first innings;

• On day one of the Boxing Day Test in Melbourne, Sri Lanka's No. 1 bowler Muttiah Muralitharan was no-balled seven times for throwing by umpire Darrell Hair, standing at the bowler's end;

• Asanka Gurusinha accused Steve Waugh of cheating during a one-day game in Perth. In the same game Aravinda de Silva caused $200 damage to the visiting players' viewing room after a disputed dismissal;

• Glenn McGrath and Sanath Jayasuriya jostled in mid-pitch and Ian Healy and Arjuna Ranatunga's feud continued to bubble after Healy questioned the out-of-condition Ranatunga's use of a runner in the second one-day final in Sydney;

• And in the season low point, Sri Lankan players refused to shake hands with Taylor after Australia clinched the World Series Cup in a clean sweep at the SCG.

Michael Slater's cavalier 219, the 500th century to be scored for Australia in Test cricket, highlighted the opening Test where Ricky Ponting, aged 20, and Stuart Law, 27, made their debuts, both sporting goatee beards.

Slater and Taylor (96) added 228 for the first wicket and almost passed Sri Lanka's first innings of 251 themselves. Slater's audacious straight driving of Muralitharan was a highlight.

The controversial Sri Lankan conceded 35 runs from his first five overs, with Slater clubbing three 6s down the ground. In all, he hit five 6s before finally falling caught and bowled to Muralitharan after being dropped by the same bowler at 136 and 159. Leading into the tour Murali had been touted as the finest finger spinner in the world, capable of imparting incredible side-spin with his unique action. First-up figures of 2/224 highlighted the gulf between bowling on the slow turners of the subcontinent compared with the harder, pacier Australian wickets.

Mark Waugh's 111 was full of polish but he was dropped before scoring, thereby avoiding a fifth duck against Sri Lanka in a row. Veteran David Boon, with 13, missed out again, raising speculation that his place might be in jeopardy. Ponting seemed certain to become a third Australian centurion in a huge score of 5/617 declared when inexplicably being given out lbw, by international umpire Khizer Hayat, at 96 to a Chaminda Vaas delivery which may have pitched in line but struck him high. Side-on replays confirmed the ball was clearly bouncing over the stumps.

More than 55 000, the biggest crowd to attend a day's Test cricket in 10 years, witnessed the Muralitharan no-balling in Melbourne on Boxing Day. Standing several metres back from the stumps, Hair called the off-spinner twice in his fourth over, three times in his fifth and twice in his sixth before captain Ranatunga rested him and later, having consulted with ICC referee Dowling, switched him to the northern end without further incident.

Hair said later he could have called Muralitharan 27 times, rather than just seven. He considered his action diabolical.

Taylor's 100th catch in Test cricket, centuries by veteran Boon and Steve Waugh, Australia's fourth Test win of the summer and even the growing doubts about Warne's fitness were virtually overlooked in the ruckus.

Having had their integrity doubted over the ball-tempering affair in Perth, the Sri Lankans were again bristling. If Muralitharan's action was so suspect, why had it taken 23 Tests for him to be called? And was this just a one-off action by an umpire wanting to make a name for himself?

Australia's clean sweep was completed in Adelaide where Waugh, who had recovered from a hamstring injury, clinched the man of the series award after making 170 and 61 not out and passing 5000 runs in Tests. His series average was 362. For the first time his Test career average reached 50. He even helped finish the Sri Lankans off with 4/34 from 19 overs.

In an emotional farewell, Boon, in his 107th Test, was fortunate to escape a first ball duck in Australia's second innings after a lifting delivery tipped the little finger of his glove on its way through to the 'keeper. Umpire Lloyd Barker disallowed the unanimous appeal and when Boon got up his end asked if he had, in fact, hit it!

Sanath Jayasuriya's 112 in the Sri Lankan second innings following his whirlwind 48 in the first provided a preview of what was to come during the World Cup.

The tourists may have been beaten 3–0 in the Tests, but they had qualified for the World Series finals ahead of the more highly rated

West Indians, and with their efficient spin-based attack were dangers, with or without Muralitharan, who'd been no-balled again, even when bowling leg-spinners in Brisbane.

New coach, the Australian Dav Whatmore, had instilled a high degree of fielding expertise and with the dash and daring of the top five batsmen – Jayasuriya, the pocket rocket Romesh Kaluwitharana, Asanka Gurusinha, Aravinda and provocative captain Ranatunga – the Sri Lankans were not to be underrated leading into cricket's version of the Olympic Games – the World Cup – on the sub-continent.

Taylor also had reason to be confident. Underrated Victorian Paul Reiffel had carried some of his West Indian form into the Sri Lankan Tests, finishing with 5/39 and 1/60 in Adelaide. McGrath was a class act already threatening to assume centre stage from McDermott as Australia's premier pace bowler, Mark Waugh had taken to opening at one-day level with alacrity and poised Tasmanian Ponting was fast becoming regarded as the next Big Thing.

However, on a more sombre note, his champion spinner Warne was showing signs of strain, having had three cortisone injections into his over-used third finger without the soreness clearing. Clearly his leg-break was not spinning as consistently or anywhere near as prodigiously as in 1993 and 1994. Doctors had asked him to consider operations on both his ring finger and his shoulder. For the first time since his career took off, Warne was feeling vulnerable.

## PROFILE: DAVID BOON

WHEN ALLAN BORDER released his autobiography, *Beyond Ten Thousand*, in 1993, he reserved one of the leather-bound limited editions for his long-time friend and team-mate David Boon. Inside is the inscription: 'To Babs, My Rock of Gibraltar, Best wishes, Allan Border.'

Border knew just how integral Boon was in the rebirth of Australian cricket and the team's transformation from easy-beats to world champions. Not only was 'The Keg on Legs' the consummate team player, loyal to the extreme and as tough and determined as anyone in the game, he was also among the premier batsmen in the world.

From day one in Brisbane when he almost ran himself out from the first ball he faced in Test cricket, opposing bowlers celebrated his wicket as if he were Viv Richards. No matter the match fortunes, they knew they'd have to be at their absolute best to budge him. A scrapper with style, Boon never shirked issues or bypassed challenges.

As coach Bobby Simpson said, Boon was strong, uncomplaining and brave, with a work ethic matched by few. He was also highly durable and only the second Australian, after Border, to play 100 Tests.

So pivotal was he to the Australian team for a decade that when he was omitted from the one-day squad at the start of the 1995–96 summer, he felt almost lost. He didn't want to play only one brand of the game at the highest level. Soon afterwards, he resolved to end his Test career, on his terms. Parting with a century in Melbourne and 43 and 35 in Adelaide, he received a rare set of accolades befitting a champion. It had been a momentous journey in which he'd always felt nothing but extreme privilege in wearing the baggy green Australian cap.

As cricket great Greg Chappell said when launching Boon's Australia-wide testimonial later in the year, 'Boonie is one of Australia's favourite sporting sons, a role model and a good bloke to boot.'

Being man of the match and winning the World Cup final in 1987 remained his all-time favourite moment, ahead even of the world championship in the Caribbean in 1995 and hitting the winning runs which reclaimed the Ashes at Old Trafford in 1989.

'Even though it was one-day cricket, winning the World Cup was the catalyst for Australian cricket to improve,' Boon said.

'The young guys now talk about the West Indies in 1995. It was great, as we'd never beaten them for a long, long time, but they hadn't experienced all the down times.

'They are walking into a team which is very confident and successful. In the mid-80s, we had a team which was struggling and not succeeding. It took longer for me to get into Test cricket than maybe someone today starting off.

'That's what made it just a bit sweeter in England in '89. Up until that stage, more often than not, we'd basically been getting our backsides kicked. To go to England and win 4–0 and, but for the weather, to have been a big chance of 6–nil, was fantastic.'

In his earliest days in Australia's team, Boon admits he wasn't as tunnel-visioned as he was in the early 90s. It took him years to become comfortable with his responsibilities as a batting specialist. Youngsters today tend to adapt more quickly, especially as they're entering a winning team.

He thanks Simpson for badgering him about being complacent and encouraging him to be more single-minded and make the most of good form, hold his wicket and string more big scores together.

Eight of his 21 Test centuries came in his first six years of Test cricket and 13 in his second six. The most cherished were his 164 at Lord's in 1993 (his first century in three tours of England) and his unbeaten 109 against the West Indies in the opening Test at Sabina Park in 1991. During the innings, he was hit flush on the jaw by a bouncer from the West Indian express Patrick Patterson, but refused to go off and only later had some stitches inserted, without anaesthetic.

Technically, his best century was his 143 against New Zealand in Brisbane in 1987–88, a year after a poor Ashes summer against England when he averaged 18 and was dropped in late summer.

'I can't remember playing and missing,' he said of the innings. ' I made Richard Hadlee bowl to me, rather than him dictating the terms. Everything hit the middle of the bat.'

Boon said his send-off in Adelaide after his final Test innings was 'truly memorable' and 'an absolute highlight'.

'I never expected the people of Adelaide and others from all over Australia to be so public in their appreciation. It was very gratifying and a great honour.'

Thankfully he was not lost to cricket and played three more seasons with Tasmania – for 21 in all – and three in county ranks with Durham. He was 38 in his last match. Typically, even then it was a wrench to end it all. He decided before Christmas 1998 that he wouldn't play again. But it wasn't until the following March, on the eve of his last Shield game, that he confirmed the speculation. As always, he wanted to avoid the fuss.

**DAVID BOON'S RECORD**

|  | Mts | Runs | HS | Ave | 100s | Wicks | Ave | BB |
|---|---|---|---|---|---|---|---|---|
| Tests | 107 | 7422 | 200 | 43.65 | 21 | 0 | – | – |
| One-day Int. | 181 | 5964 | 122 | 37.04 | 5 | 0 | – | – |

'David Boon was the gutsiest cricketer with whom I played. He wasn't the most gifted, but he was definitely the toughest, both physically and mentally. There is no doubt that for about five years there he had as good a claim as anybody to being the best batsman in the world.'
– *Geoff Marsh, Boon's long-time opening partner.*

After being given out in Brisbane one day, David Boon was so upset by the decision he stormed from the ground, muttering oaths and repeatedly looking back over his shoulder at the umpire.

He was still red hot when he got into the rooms and was told there was a phone call for him.

It was his mother, Lesley, calling from Launceston. Never has a player's mood swing been quite as emphatic. He ended up apologising to his mum and rarely again allowed himself to be quite as openly emotional walking off a ground again!

# TEN

---

# THE ULTIMATE
# BOILOVER

---

*The ever-provocative Arjuna Ranatunga hit a full toss*
*from Shane Warne over the midwicket boundary and*
*promptly poked his tongue out at the Australian!*

---

BRIDGE-BUILDING AND DIPLOMACY were an additional part of Mark
Taylor's portfolio approaching the most glamorous one-day tournament
of all, the 1996 World Cup. Relations between the touring Sri Lankans
and in particular their captain Arjuna Ranatunga and the Australians
had so soured that the Sri Lankans refused to shake hands with
Taylor, or even acknowledge the Australians, during the World Series
Cup victory presentations in Sydney.

After the storms of Perth and Melbourne, the Sri Lankans felt
persecuted and it wasn't until the Australians brought beers into
the Sri Lankan rooms a week and a half later at the end of the
Adelaide Test that the normal friendliness which exists between
teams, at least outside of cricket hours, returned to anything like
normal.

Taylor believed at least some of the discontent could have been
avoided had the Australians relaxed socially with the Sri Lankans
earlier in the tour.

The World Cup in Sri Lanka, India and Pakistan was notable for Sri Lanka's giant-killing victory against the Australians, one made even sweeter for the international cricketing minnows by Australia's boycott of their scheduled opening fixture in Colombo. A bomb had exploded killing dozens and injuring more than 1000 in downtown Colombo, just a block or two away from the Taj Sumadra Hotel where the Australians were due to stay.

For weeks, the Australians had been agonising over whether to play the game at all after threats to some key players. Fast bowler Craig McDermott had been told a bomb would be planted at his house on the Gold Coast. Shane Warne had also had death threats.

Already the players had vetoed the initial plan to spend an acclimatising week practising in Colombo. It was to their unanimous relief when the Australian Cricket Board executive opted not to venture into what was effectively a war zone, thus forfeiting the match.

After a week's training in Brisbane, Australia's campaign started in Visakhapatnam against the Kenyans. The West Indies also boycotted their Colombo commitment, sparking a broadside of criticism, the most stinging from Indian cricket great Kapil Dev, who said that both the Australian and the West Indian teams were wimps and should be banned from all international cricket for 12 months.

After three wins out of four, to ensure a place in the quarter-finals, the Australians were thrilled to squeeze through to the final, after two incredible victories against New Zealand and the West Indies.

Chasing the Kiwis' record 286 in the quarter-final at Madras, Australia responded with 4/289, winning in the 48th over thanks to Mark Waugh's third century of the tournament. Three days later in Mohali, the West Indies were cruising to semi-final victory at 2/165 chasing Australia's 207, only to see their last eight wickets fall for 37. It was one of the most embarrassing reverses in West Indian cricket history and a humiliating end to Richie Richardson's international career. 'It was the most unbelievable win I've ever played in,' said

Taylor. 'We were almost unable to comprehend what had happened to us,' said Steve Waugh.

Australia's good fortune couldn't hold, and with Aravinda de Silva making a century in the final, Sri Lanka cantered to a boilover seven-wicket win with 22 balls to spare. The ever-provocative Arjuna Ranatunga hit a full toss from Shane Warne – an attempted flipper – over the midwicket boundary and promptly poked his tongue out at the Australian! Muttiah Muralitharan, controversially no-balled in Australia, had reappeared as Sri Lanka's major bowler and in the final took 1/31 from 10 overs in another frontline contribution.

With almost 500 runs for the tournament, Mark Waugh emphasised his class. India's Sachin Tendulkar headed the aggregates with 523 runs, yet he, too, was overlooked when the player of the series was decided – that honour went to Sri Lankan opener Sanath Jayasuriya.

The bravest player of the tournament was Sultan Zarawani, captain of the United Arab Emirates, who opted to face South African express Allan Donald without a helmet!

Australia may have faltered at the line, but there was now no doubt that the team was the best all-round XI in world cricket, the depth and competition for places a major factor in their consistency.

McDermott's breakdown at Visakhapatnam with a calf strain was an early downer for the team and a forerunner of his retirement later in the year. His replacement, Jason Gillespie, fresh out of the Australian Cricket Academy, wasn't to play a game, but the selectors were taking a long-term view and believed the experience would be invaluable.

The tournament was to be Bob Simpson's last as coach. He'd initiated much of the success of the team with an insistence on superior fitness, swifter running between wickets and a greater emphasis on fielding skills. But the parting was messy, Simpson critical that he couldn't have spent his 11th year working in tandem with his successor, West Australian cricket great Geoff Marsh.

Marsh was considering an offer to coach the Victorian state squad when told the national job was also available. He'd been a Simpson disciple in his playing days, but this was a once-in-a-lifetime opportunity, a full-time, high-profile job suited to a younger and fitter man. The

ACB wanted to gradually phase in its personnel changes, from players to coaching staff. Taylor, the Waugh twins, Ian Healy, Tim May and McDermott were all in their thirties. With Simpson's contract expiring, this was seen as the first step in the ushering-in of a new era.

From August, the team was embarking on a two-year period of virtually non-stop cricket which would take it up to autumn 1998. In what was virtually one extended and continuous summer, in 20 months the team was scheduled to play 24 Tests and up to 50 one-day internationals, taking in four different countries and playing seven different nations. It was a hectic period in which not all were to survive.

Marsh, 37, a veteran of 50 Tests and 117 one-day internationals, had retired on the eve of the 1994–95 Sheffield Shield season and in the 12 months preceding his appointment served an initial term as an Australian selector. 'Anyone who has played Test cricket and retired and tells you they do not miss it is telling a lie,' he said.

Marsh saw himself working alongside Taylor, but without the power or authority of the Australian captain. He'd been his opening partner for 25 Tests, but now there were definite lines of demarcation. 'I'll have to sit down and talk to Mark before I say what I want to happen,' Marsh said on his appointment. 'He is the captain of Australia and I've got to make sure he's happy with my ideas. At the end of the day he has to walk on the paddock with the boys and he's got to be happy doing that.'

Marsh knew an important part of his coaching role would be to keep training fresh and players interested. 'The amount the boys play now, it would be very easy to just arrive in town and sleep for a couple of days. You've got to keep your work ethic up,' he said.

Simpson, 60 and one of the game's greatest survivors, had worked hard since the New Year to rally support. He believed he'd been let down by Board members. He was the head of a reliable management team underrated for its role in lifting the Australian performances.

'If you're doing well, then surely you don't change,' he told the *Herald Sun*'s Bruce Wilson in an interview from his holiday getaway in Amalfi, Italy. 'If you take this [change] theory, then you should change all the members of the Board every 10 years, you should change the selectors, my goodness, change the players suddenly after they've done 10 years and be told, "ah you've passed your usefulness".'

Marsh's initial appointment was for two years and had the firm approval of Taylor, who said the team personnel was likely to radically change by the year 2000, adding to the importance of having one coach overseeing continuously.

'I wouldn't want anyone to think I'd want Bob Simpson to go, but players are getting younger and the Australian board obviously thought it was time for a younger man at the helm,' he said.

He believed Australian cricket owed Simpson a debt, especially with the improvement of fielding standards encouraged by daily skill sessions. 'Simmo's ideas were very good,' said Marsh. 'You can't beat Simmo's fielding routines. I learned a lot from him.'

The story of Simpson once batting Tim Zoehrer back into a barbed wire fence during catching practice on the subcontinent is part of Australian cricket lore.

Marsh promised to be just as tough. Some of his charges had been old team-mates. But he considered that to be a plus rather than a negative. His own playing career had been built around hard work. Now he was ready for fresh challenges and any player not prepared to go with him and make the sacrifices faced immediate exile.

## PROFILE: CRAIG McDERMOTT

FEW FAST BOWLERS OF REPUTE have been anything but feisty. Dennis Lillee was famous for his volatility and Fred Trueman had a maverick streak, while Merv Hughes constantly flouted the game's code of conduct. As Richie Benaud once said: 'Show me a fast bowler who isn't moody and I'll show you a medium pacer.'

Craig McDermott was a fiery redhead renowned for his temper, but before injuries reduced his effectiveness and finally forced him into premature retirement, he was as quick, nasty and successful as anyone in international ranks. Bowling his outswing at speeds approaching 90 mph, McDermott's ability to take wickets was unquestionable. Among Australia's premier pacemen, only Dennis Lillee, Jeff Thomson and Glenn McGrath have a superior strike rate.

McDermott's importance to the Australian team was highlighted in the '91 series in the Caribbean when the West Indian speedsters Patrick Patterson, Courtney Walsh and Curtly Ambrose targeted him for a campaign of intimidation, believing him to be crucial to Australia's victory hopes. He was struck and stitched up in Jamaica as part of the softening-up process designed to break his spirit. But with 24 wickets in five Tests, he out-bowled everyone, being particularly lethal in Antigua where he took five wickets, including the great Viv Richards lbw for the only duck of his career in the Caribbean.

Injuries, which so often plagued him in his final years, ended his '95 Caribbean campaign almost as soon as it had started, and after breaking down in the World Cup in 1996 and again in the 1996–97 Australian summer, he retired to club ranks, aged 31.

If a player ever deserved to be part of a world championship side, it was McDermott, despite the warts. Few were as successfully fast-tracked or performed with the same spectacular result early in their careers. But his inconsistencies were a constant frustration and he was sent back into Sheffield Shield ranks to grow up, as much as to improve his own performance.

His second coming, triggered by the example of world champion ironman Trevor Hendy, ushered in new levels of fitness, mental toughness and success. In his first six years of Test cricket, he took 80 wickets; in his next six, 211.

Greg Chappell regarded McDermott's re-emergence as one of the great comeback stories in Australian sport. 'I admired him much more for regaining his place in the Australian side at the age of 25 than I did when he first won a place in the team at the age of 19,' he wrote in McDermott's book *Strike Bowler*.

'The other remarkable thing about his comeback is that he returned a far better bowler than he had been during his first flash of success.'

Chappell said McDermott deservedly should be rated with

Australia's finest postwar pacemen, including Lillee and Thomson.

Opponents agreed. Malcolm Marshall, the great West Indian, said Australians should be proud of McDermott. 'To play over such a long period as a quality fast bowler is a big achievement,' he told *Inside Edge* magazine.

Throughout his career, as illustrious as it was, McDermott oscillated between glorious highs and despairing, even life-threatening lows. In 1993, doctors told him he was only 24 hours away from death because of a twisted bowel. Through injury or illness, he completed none of his last five tours, a damning record which he felt keenly, yet with 291 Test wickets, he remains among Australia's finest three Test bowlers of them all. He was also the first Australian to 200 one-day wickets.

Few were as focused on the field and this occasionally led to unrest, even on one notable occasion from his captain Allan Border in an early tour game in England in 1989.

While at his best with the new ball, he could also bowl effectively with the old ball, as in Durban in 1993–94, when he had the highly rated Springboks struggling to put bat on ball in an inspired effort, despite problems with his knee.

Australia was fortunate that McGrath was able to step up so quickly and assume central responsibility, otherwise the new world champions would not have been anywhere near as formidable given their day-to-day reliance on the classy Queenslander with the God-given ability to dismiss anyone in the game.

Known for the white zinc which he plastered over his face before matches, McDermott refused all advice to slow down and extend his career by bowling at a slower pace. He took an all-or-nothing mentality into his cricket. Ultimately, it was his body which couldn't keep up. Four knee operations, two groin operations, three hernias, a twisted bowel and cyst and melanoma removals were undeniable evidence of his body's failure to adapt to cricket's ballooning schedule.

## CRAIG McDERMOTT'S RECORD

|              | Mts | Runs | HS  | Ave   | 100s | Wicks | Ave   | BB   |
|--------------|-----|------|-----|-------|------|-------|-------|------|
| Tests        | 71  | 940  | 42* | 12.20 | -    | 291   | 28.83 | 8/97 |
| One-day Int. | 138 | 432  | 37  | 7.08  | -    | 203   | 24.71 | 5/44 |

# ELEVEN

---

# A
# WAKE-UP CALL

*Ricky Ponting and Steve Waugh were asked*
*to share a double bed. When they refused*
*it caused offence.*

---

JUST HOURS after being announced as Victoria's new cricket captain in 1996, Shane Warne booked himself into hospital, unsure if he'd ever play again.

Many had warned the champion against such a delicate operation, but he felt cornered. His ring finger – the one which imparted his incredible flick – had all but seized up during the World Cup tournament, and while one specialist in the United States prescribed nothing but rest, Warne knew he had no other option. Numerous painkilling injections into the knuckle had provided only temporary relief, and he feared long-term ramifications from their continued use. His overworked shoulder was also a concern, but he ruled out any surgery. One operation was bad enough, let alone two.

Specialist Greg Hoy cleaned the joint and tightened the ligaments and declared the surgery an unqualified success. But neither he nor Warne truly knew if the finger would ever allow the champion to impart the same work on the ball.

Daily physiotherapy sessions were part of the rehabilitation, not just to his spinning finger, but to his wrist, arm and overworked right shoulder. Hoy warned that there would be stiffness from the scar tissue but that this was normal. He placed the arm in a sling and advised Warne to use his left hand rather than his right for virtually everything. Shaking hands was out, as was any sort of bowling, even without a ball.

Meanwhile in two other capital cities, two other elite Australians were struggling with their wintertime fitness. Mark Taylor had a serious disc problem while Craig McDermott's battle-scarred knee had collapsed, raising concerns that he might not play again.

After holidaying with his family at the tiny New South Wales coastal hamlet of Halfway Creek, Taylor was back into full training under the direction of Sydney-based physical fitness expert Kevin Chevell. He shed 9 kilograms in 10 weeks, before so badly injuring his back lifting weights that he was unable to lead the Australian team on its one-day matches tour of Sri Lanka in August. A piece from the bottom disc in his back had broken away and was interfering with the nerve that ran down his left leg. An immediate rest was ordered, ensuring Ian Healy the captaincy for the one-day tournament in Sri Lanka. He was also on standby to lead the tour of India, which included a one-off Test and Titan Cup one-day tournament soon afterwards.

McDermott, having missed selection for his first major tours in six years, had been preparing for a Christmas-time comeback, looking to join Dennis Lillee as the only Australian to take 300 Test wickets. However, an October operation, his fourth to his knees and 12th overall, proved unsuccessful. 'I realised it wasn't going to get better. Basically I'm out of comebacks,' he said at his farewell press conference. 'I've had four and come back from four very strong. But there's another part of my life that I want to get on with. I've lost the will to train as hard as I used to.'

It wasn't until days before the team's departure for India that Taylor, badly short of fitness, finally declared himself a starter. His left leg was still worrying him and he rated himself no more than 65 per cent fit. But the hectic program demanded that he be involved from the start. The absences of McDermott and Warne and the retirements of Tim May and David Boon had tested Australia's depth. Only Steve Waugh had had previous Test experience in India, in 1986. With the upcoming challenges against the West Indies, South Africa and England, which inevitably would lead to new faces being involved, Taylor felt a duty to be there from the start. 'To think that the same 11 blokes can get through a schedule of the next year-and-a-half is crazy,' said Australian coach Geoff Marsh in *Inside Edge*.

Life was tough from the team's arrival in Bombay, when the new world champions first learnt one of the two lead-up games before the Test had been cancelled. The team's normal accommodation was changed and at Patiala, venue for the opening game against the Board President's XI, Ricky Ponting and Steve Waugh were asked to share a double bed. When they refused it caused offence.

Not only were the Australians to be beaten in three and a half days in the Test in New Delhi, they lost all five completed one-day matches against India and South Africa.

The upcoming tour by the West Indies rather than the six-week campaign in India seemed to be the team's primary focus and Marsh, on his first tour as coach, was ropeable. 'It comes down to hunger, doesn't it?' he said. 'You can look for all the excuses in the world why these blokes didn't play well, but they are professional sportsmen. It's an excuse to say it was our first hit-out. We played poorly.'

Marsh accused the team of training like millionaires. Too many were too casual in their work in the nets and the fielding had lacked its customary sharp edge. There had been an unhealthy reliance on Warne and when confronted by a powder-dry spinner's wicket, the Australians, bar Steve Waugh in the second innings, had not been prepared to be sufficiently patient. The rookie spinners, Brad Hogg in his first Test and Peter McIntyre in his second, had taken only four wickets compared to 14 by the Indian trio of Anil Kumble, Sunil Joshi and Aashish Kapoor. Neither had bowled with the bounce or bite of Warne. Nor could they have reasonably been expected to do so. Warne had been a security blanket to Australian cricket for years. Without him, Taylor's options were severely reduced.

Kumble snared nine wickets with his combinations of fizzing in-swing and straightening breaks. Wicketkeeping batsman Nayan Mongia batted for more than eight hours to score 152 and was man of the match ahead of Kumble, who was instrumental in Australia being bowled out so cheaply twice in 72 hours. Later, both Taylor and India's Sachin Tendulkar deemed the Feroz Shah Kotia Stadium's wicket was totally unsuitable for Test cricket. Taylor said he'd never before seen balls run along the ground as they did frequently from the opening day. Having a single Test match decide the Border–Gavaskar Trophy was a further frustration.

Taylor saw the loss to India as a wake-up call, one which he hoped would galvanise the Australians into action in their three upcoming series against world-rated opposition. The West Indian summer was to be followed by tours to South Africa and England. Taylor's aim to win all three would silence all those who believed Australia vulnerable, especially any time its spin bowling champion Warne was absent.

On return from the subcontinent, the programming of the two short tours with the barest of preparations was an agenda item at Australian Cricket Board level. Steve Waugh said the players needed to have more of a direct input into future programming. 'Ultimately it is our careers on the line, not the administrators',' he said in *Australian Cricket* magazine.

Ten years between Indian Test tours, however, was considered an anomaly given the Board's ambassadorial approach to the worldwide promotion of the game. With the need for two international teams to tour down under each summer for the lucrative World Series Cup tournament, reciprocal visits, even for three and six-week periods, were not only a sign of the times, they were an absolute necessity.

And increased player payments automatically led to more matchplay. With the top six Australians each receiving upwards of $300 000 a year purely in contracts and match fees, the team's commitments were spiralling to eight and nine months each year.

It took Don Bradman 20 years to play 50 Tests. Warne played his 50th in just five.

# TWELVE

## SUMMER
## OF SPEED
## AND SPITE

*'You don't have to use the press as a tool to say*
*everyone is ganging up on you, as Lara did.*
*That was disgraceful.'*

THE WEST INDIES boasted a new captain, coach and manager on
arrival in Australia for their seventh Test tour in two decades. Courtney
Walsh, Malcolm Marshall and Clive Lloyd represented a redoubtable,
unifying leadership team for a side which had suffered the ultimate
embarrassment during the World Cup when beaten by cricketing
minnows Kenya at Pune.

With a fast bowling six-pack, led by the still-hostile Curtly Ambrose
and Walsh and with no specialist spinner, the Windies were staking
their comeback purely around speed and an improving top six. In their
only series of the calendar year, a two-Test affair against New Zealand
in the Caribbean, pocket-sized Sherwin Campbell and Jimmy Adams
each made double-centuries. Opener Robert Samuels, in only his
second Test, was another centurion. Despite his walkout midway
through the English tour 12 months previously, Brian Lara remained
a world-class batsman and the player the Australians most feared.
Fellow left-hander 22-year-old Shivnarine Chanderpaul shared Adams's

liking for crease occupation. And unlike Adams, whose technique could be exposed by the short ball, he seemed impervious to pace. Four of the tourists' top six were left-handers, a fact not lost on Shane Warne, whose most lethal deliveries had invariably been delivered to right-handers.

Warne's battle to regain his fitness was a daily talking point leading into the Australian season, which began without the touring internationals. After the first uncertain wintertime weeks when his spin finger ached and he wondered if he could possibly play for Australia again, his enthusiasm and confidence slowly returned. A springtime Victorian team training camp at HMAS Cerberus on Melbourne's Mornington Peninsula saw him swimming in mud pools and clambering through concrete pipes as part of an exhausting fitness examination. Ever since schoolboy days with his mates at Mentone Grammar, he'd always revelled in the team involvement and leadership roles, and his desire to set an example as Victoria's new skipper helped him overcome many of his own self doubts. By October, he was making his first tentative steps back into domestic cricket and setting his sights on the first Test in Brisbane, one of his all-time favourite venues where he'd been so central in recent Australian victories. A limited-over haul of 5/35 against Tasmania at Carlton's Optus Oval, his best-ever one-day figures for Victoria, was a green light to Trevor Hohns, the national chairman of selectors, that he was once again ready for higher honours.

The publicists had labelled the Frank Worrell Trophy series as *The Decider*. The Australians had always measured Test runs and wickets against the West Indies as the most important. They believed many had written the Windies off prematurely with the retirement of captain Richie Richardson and the apparent decline of ageing pace pair Ambrose and Walsh. The world championship title was squarely on the line.

Before the opening Test, Taylor presented newcomers Matthew Elliott from Victoria and Michael Kasprowicz, Queensland, with baggy green Australian caps, to the applause of team-mates, who had formed a guard-of-honour. It was an innovation other Test teams were soon to replicate.

Speculation that Ian Healy would be replaced as Taylor's deputy for the series proved unfounded, and as had so often happened when he felt his position under challenge, Healy bounced back with a premier, man of the match performance, his 161 not out in the first innings in Brisbane the highest by an Australian wicketkeeper in Tests. With more than 200 runs and four catches for the match, Healy made the most decisive contribution in Australia's 123-run victory. Team-mates had never seen him bat better. Hohns said Healy's career-best first innings knock was one of the great Test innings.

More than 17 000 attended the opening day's play, the biggest single Test crowd at the 'Gabba for more than 50 years.

Warne's comeback produced a modest 2/88 and 2/92. The psychological scars from his May operation clearly remained, and he was spinning the ball noticeably less than in his prime. He was also relying almost exclusively on variations of his leg-break, plus his quicker, sliding delivery which saw him claim three of his four wickets lbw. The fourth, Samuels, was caught by Taylor, via Healy, at slip.

With 68 overs for the game, including 31 on the final day, Warne had again shouldered an enormous workload. As satisfied as he was to be back in the Test team, he was far from happy with the lack of bite of his signature delivery, the leg-break.

Impatient to regain his best form, he enlisted the help of coach and confidant Terry Jenner in between Tests. 'He wanted to get the old feeling back in his finger,' said Jenner. 'He'd been bowling tightly without spinning it much and it wasn't until Ian Healy joined us in a side net and Shane bowled a few leg-breaks with his old spin that he began to consistently rip the ball like old times.

'I was next to him and seeing one spin almost at right angles, said to Shane all excited, "That's it mate. That's perfect!"

'Shane looked at me with a querying look, "Was that good? It didn't feel like it."

'It was a matter of him getting to know in his own mind all over again what felt good and what didn't.'

Elliott, having controversially displaced Michael Slater at the head of the order, made 0 and 21 on his maiden appearance. The second debutant, Kasprowicz, went wicketless.

Australia's joy at winning inside the final hour on the fifth day was tempered by confirmation of the seriousness of Steve Waugh's groin injury. He'd overstretched while bowling in the West Indian first innings and been unable to bat when Australia chased quick second-innings runs to set up a declaration target.

As to Slater's non-selection, an overreaction by the selectors to a poor shot at New Delhi a month earlier, captain Taylor said: 'We have opened for 30-odd Tests together so I feel for him. I've known him for a number of years and it is a sad day for him. I know he's feeling it.'

With an overall Test average of 47, Slater was mystified by his omission. He knew he'd played a loose shot in India, but couldn't understand why his previous in-Australia Test performances could possibly have been ignored. It had only been less than 12 months since he'd made his Test-best 219 against the visiting Sri Lankans in Perth.

'Everywhere I went people were bewildered as to why I was out of the side,' Slater said. 'I was doing my best to come to terms with it all and that brought out all the emotions and issues again. I never thought I'd lost my bubble. I'm certainly playing in the same fashion as I pretty well always have.'

Elliott, 25, had started the summer with 25 and 187 for Victoria against New South Wales in Sydney and 158 and 12 not out for an Australian XI against the West Indies in Hobart. At Bellerive he and Queensland's Matthew Hayden batted through the entire opening day's play, scoring 316 in an extraordinary start. Raised on the concrete wickets of Lancaster in Victoria's Goulburn Valley, Elliott's pull shot was lethal, and when the West Indies pitched up he drove through mid-off and cover with the assurance of a player at the top of his form.

In Sydney, where the Australians clinched back-to-back Tests for the first time against the Windies in more than 20 years, the tall Victorian left-hander seemed set for his first Test century, having made a match-high 78, before colliding in mid-pitch with Mark Waugh and so severely injuring his knee that he left the field in the drinks cart and played only once more all summer.

The Sydney Cricket Ground was in sub-standard condition for the match. Not only was the wicket dry and uneven, the outfield had been scarred after two Michael Jackson concerts several nights before.

Having seen the Australians establish a narrow lead on the first innings, Taylor's aggressive instincts saw the Australians decline the offer of a light appeal late on the third day. While Taylor was out cheaply for the second time soon afterwards, the Australians finished at 2/77 – an overall lead of 104. And from the fourth morning they so dominated that by mid-afternoon on day five victory had been attained by 124 runs.

The West Indian fielding fell apart late on the fourth day. Noted commentator Tony Cozier declared 'any self-respecting school team would have done better'.

Set 340 to win, a challenging target, given the history of low scores by teams batting fourth on the final days at the SCG, the Windies made an exhilarating start, accelerating from 0/27 at stumps on the penultimate night to 4/152 at lunch on the fifth day. In a dynamic counter-attack, the little Guyanese master Chanderpaul, known as 'Tiger' to the Australians for his ability to fight like one, raced to 50 from just 38 balls. Four Warne overs cost 37.

Reintroduced for several overs just before lunch, Warne, bowling around the wicket, produced a gigantic leg-break which pitched in footmarks wide outside Chanderpaul's off-stump, gripped and spun back wickedly to hit middle and leg. The delivery was estimated to have spun almost a metre and was compared to Warne's much-vaunted 'Ball of the Century' which castled Mike Gatting at Old Trafford in 1993. Warne raised two clenched fists in his jubilation, as did coach Terry Jenner back home in Adelaide. With 4/95 in the West Indian second innings, Warne was again the linchpin for Australia's success. Several of the deliveries he bowled in the second innings were as good as he'd ever bowled.

Carl Hooper, who'd made his first century against Australia in Brisbane, was again in form, reaching 57 before falling to the catch of the summer, a remarkable juggled effort from Taylor at slip from the bowling of Michael Bevan, who had stepped up to share the specialist spin duties with Warne.

Lara made only 1 before being caught low down by Healy in a controversial, disputed catch. It so enraged the West Indian that he stormed into the Australian dressing room, still in his pads, and confronting coach Geoff Marsh, claimed the Australians had cheated and Healy, in particular, wasn't again welcome in the West Indian dressing rooms. Team manager Clive Lloyd issued an immediate apology, but notably, Lara didn't. As Healy was to say later, 'a leopard doesn't change its spots'.

Taylor said that the replay showed Lara was quite correctly given out caught behind, and if the catch *hadn't* carried he believed Healy wouldn't have claimed it.

Taylor accused Lara of being immature and predicted that in years to come he would look back upon the incident with embarrassment and regret.

Healy said Lara hadn't made an issue of his dismissal on the ground. 'Frankly, I couldn't understand all the fuss,' he said. 'It was all unnecessary from my point of view, though I can understand the pressure Brian obviously felt under. He and all his supporters wanted it to be his day. When it wasn't, you can't help but feel disappointed.'

The Australians only had to force a draw in Melbourne to retain the Frank Worrell Trophy, but in an extraordinary form reversal, the West Indies bounced back into series contention, winning in three days on a grassy Melbourne Cricket Ground wicket with the pace and bounce reminiscent of the lightning decks of the 50s.

Ambrose had been a sleeping giant in the opening two Tests, taking just three wickets at an average of 93 and earning censure from ex-Australian skipper Allan Border, who wrote in his syndicated column that Ambrose seemed to lack fire in his belly and was merely aiding and abetting Australia.

'Unless Ambrose is carrying an injury that is being shielded from public knowledge, he needs a rocket,' said Border.

The West Indies believed even a 60 per cent Ambrose was as good as any bowler in the world. 'When he's on song, I don't think anyone in the world can beat us,' said coach Malcolm Marshall.

Marshall felt Ambrose erred by bowling too short in Brisbane and Sydney, and from his first overs in Melbourne, Ambrose produced a far fuller line which saw both openers Taylor and Hayden fall early. When Mark Waugh was trapped lbw first ball, Ambrose's figures were 3/3 from seven inspired overs.

The Boxing Day crowd of 72 891, the biggest for a Test match day in Australia for more than 20 years, witnessed the Australians under siege at 4/55 by lunch. Though Steve Waugh and Greg Blewett each reached half-centuries, the all-out score of 219 showed a top-order vulnerability which had not been seen for years. With 5/55 from 24.5 overs, the old warhorse had been superb, bounding to the crease and bowling with much of his old purpose in what effectively was his Melbourne farewell. He even granted the media a rare interview, afterwards saying how keyed up he was and knew if he could take 10 wickets for the game, the Windies would win easily.

As to his mediocre form early in the series he said: 'From the time I made my debut for the West Indies, people were always saying things about me. If I had a bad game or two, I'm all washed up. So things like that don't really bother me. As a matter of fact, I thrive on things like that.'

The Australians failed again in the second innings. Only Steve Waugh with 37 and brother Mark, 19, lasted for more than an hour. Newcomers Hayden and Justin Langer were out for ducks, Hayden not offering a shot in Ambrose's first over and losing his off stump, and Langer being caught at slip from an ill-advised hook shot. With 4/17 from 12 overs, Ambrose passed 100 wickets against Australia and by 6 p.m. on the third night, the Windies were locked away under the MCG member's stand, celebrating a victory which had not seemed possible in the early injury-plagued weeks of their campaign.

It was Australia's first loss at the MCG in almost a decade. The team had batted for just 75 overs in the first innings and 46 in the second. Not for the first time in his career, Taylor found himself under increasing fire for his own batting performances. It was the first hint of any discontent, however, since he'd become captain. His Midas touch may have placed him among Australia's elite postwar leaders, but he was also in the team to open the batting. Runs were just as important as his win–loss ratio, however impressive it was (including this Test, Taylor's win rate was 55 per cent [12 wins, 6 losses and 4 draws], which compared favourably with the two finest long-time leaders Don Bradman [63 per cent] and Lindsay Hassett [58 per cent]).

Taylor agreed with Phil Wilkins of the *Sydney Morning Herald* that he was not batting like a genius, but he believed it was just a trough. 'The thing I have to do, as a few other guys also have to do, is to come out of it, keep working and try different things,' he said.

It had been 12 innings since Taylor had made a Test half-century. His batting average as captain of 38 was well behind his overall average of 44.

'I have to find a way of turning an hour into three or four or five hours of batting, turning 10 or 20 into 50 or 100,' he said. 'I'm not getting myself knocked over first ball every game. I'm generally batting for an hour or so, but not getting on top.'

His form bypass had seen him fail to make 30 in any of the one-day internationals and speculation was increasing that his mandate to lead at all levels was being reappraised. Talk that the selectors were pushing for separate Test and one-day teams was gathering momentum.

Thanks to six losses in a row, the Australians had failed to make the World Series finals for the first time since 1979–80. Even the normally upbeat and cheerful Taylor was struggling to smile, though the extra days off with his family leading into the Adelaide Test were welcome.

HAVING SEEN THEIR much-vaunted top order so exposed in Melbourne, the Australian selectors flouted convention and went with an extraordinary balance for the fourth Test in Adelaide. Not only did they name seven batsmen and just three frontline bowlers, one of the three bowling specialists in Queensland's Andy Bichel was yet to play a Test.

The responsibility on Glenn McGrath (who'd dismissed Lara in five of his six innings) and Warne was enormous, although NSW's Bevan had also been chosen as a spinning sidekick, despite having only part-time bowling status, even at Sheffield Shield level.

Any misgivings Taylor had at losing the toss on a flat and dry Adelaide Oval wicket were forgotten when McGrath struck almost immediately, and Warne, used at second change behind Bevan, disposed of the star left-handers Chanderpaul and Lara. Lara was dismissed for his fifth consecutive single-figure Test score.

Five wickets went down before lunch and another five in the first 75 minutes of the next session, leaving the Windies bowled out for just 130 in under 50 overs. Warne, having benefited from more tuition from Jenner, took three important wickets, and Bevan snared four.

Years before in Adelaide when he was first attending the Australian Cricket Academy, Bevan had so impressed coach Jack Potter with his left-arm spinners that he advised him to forget about the medium pace he preferred to bowl in matches and slow down.

Bevan's first four overs went for 19 before he returned to capture top-scorer Junior Murray and clean up the tail, bowling briskish topspin and bosies.

Taylor fell cheaply again but at a stumps score of 2/139, Australia's position was formidable, with the absence of the injured Ambrose robbing the tourists of their most lethal strike bowler.

By making 577 and dismissing the West Indies a second time for just 204, the Australians clinched an overwhelming victory in a little over three days. They'd played with great purpose and focus throughout. The cluster of keen, close-in fieldsmen who surrounded the Windies for both Warne and Bevan from early in the match made it almost impossible to survive for any period of time. By contrast, the Windies had been strangely uninterested; the dismissal of Lara, who holed out to mid-on from the first ball Warne bowled him, a prime example of their lethargy.

Bevan, with 6/82 and 10 wickets for the match, enjoyed a Boys' Own return. He'd also made 85 not out, having led a charmed life, especially early when he was bowled by an Ian Bishop no-ball and dropped by wicketkeeper Murray before having reached 20.

Hayden's 125 and Blewett's 99 were also contributing factors, which helped both into the touring team to South Africa, named at the conclusion of the Test. Blewett could well have made 100, but for being sent back by Bevan when calling for a run wide of slip. It was one of the few negatives for the Australians, whose status as the world's No. 1 Test team was no longer in dispute. Those who had been in the one-run loss to the Windies at the same ground four years previously particularly savoured the moment. Taylor said there was a deep, almost numbing feeling of satisfaction.

The newspaper headlines summed up Australia's dominance: BEVAN HEAVEN, TOURISTS FLOORED BY A TWIRLING TORNADO, TAYLOR'S MEN RESTORE ORDER and WINDIES GO TO PIECES.

West Indian manager Clive Lloyd accused the selectors of picking a poorly-balanced side, which was ravaged by injury even before their arrival down under. An all-rounder with experience like Phil Simmons and a specialist spinner were lacking, while the top-order batting all too often lacked discipline. Of Bevan's match-winning spells in Adelaide, he said the reluctant spinner tended to bowl two bad balls an over, but the Windies batsmen had been too impatient and their shot selection wayward. 'Cricket is played from the neck up,' he said.

While the Windies were to hit back with a 10-wicket win at the WACA Ground – their fifth win in five Tests in Perth, in heatwave weather on a wicket noticeable for its gaping cracks – the series was effectively over, a point not lost on the Australians who reminded centurion Lara that he'd saved his best for a match of little or no consequence.

Tempers flared late in the game when Lara, acting as a runner for Walsh, was accidentally knocked down by close-in Australian fieldsman Hayden. Mark Taylor accused Lara of being a stirrer and it wasn't until both Taylor and Walsh were called in for an extraordinary mid-pitch conference by umpires Peter Willey and Darrell Hair that on-field order was restored.

Lara had been angered by the verbal grilling the Australians reserved for rookie opener Samuels, who battled five and a half hours for 76 and at one stage responded to the chat by poking his tongue out at

Steve Waugh. 'When there is all-day sledging and stuff like that of one particular player it is unnecessary,' Lara said. 'They admonished a youngster who is trying his best. We're going to bounce back and we've got them in two years time [in the Caribbean]. I promise you we will not be losing.'

Warne, who took two wickets in the game, said gamesmanship was part of international cricket. 'If you think the odd jibe can get you a wicket, fine,' he told reporters. 'Everybody who plays sport knows it happens. You don't have to use the press as a tool to say everyone is ganging up on you, as Lara did. That was disgraceful.'

The Perth Test provided yet another milestone in the outstanding careers of Steve and Mark Waugh. It was their 44th Test together, equalling the mark of Ian and Greg Chappell, who had so dominated Australia's world championship teams of the 70s.

'Personally I feel I'm still reaching my peak,' Steve told reporters. 'I've got a lot of cricket to play and don't want to retire while I know I've got my best cricket ahead of me. I don't see age as a factor. It's how you feel and how you're playing and whether you're still keen to do all the travelling and spend time away from the family.'

Mark said playing cricket for a living was 'better than working. Hopefully I've got a few years left in the tank yet. I'd like to average 50 in Tests and think I'm good enough to do that. It's a matter of turning 100s into big 100s. I'm happy with the way I'm batting. I don't think I can improve too much more.'

Not one minute of play was lost due to bad light or rain during the five Frank Worrell Trophy Tests between Australia and the West Indies in 1996–97.

# THIRTEEN

## SPEAKING OF SUCCESSORS

*In Afrikaans, captain Hansie Cronje said as
much to Adams. Waugh grinned and said,
'You're dead right. I can't pick him.'*

JASON GILLESPIE was still attending the Australian Cricket Academy,
the game's noted finishing school, when he first played Sheffield
Shield cricket and soon afterwards was catapulted into the 1996 World
Cup as a replacement for the injured Craig McDermott. Not only
was a teenage Gillespie a fast bowler of uncommon pace, it was all
still a novelty to him, as he'd been bowling off a long run for only
three years.

His remarkably rapid rise that saw him lifted from the third XI
competition in Adelaide pennant ranks into the firsts stemmed back
to one practice night. His thirds captain believed the spindly youngster
showed more potential with his batting than his bowling and told him
so. 'I wasn't happy with that,' Gillespie said, 'so I measured out a long
run one day and starting bowling quick. The "A" grade captain noticed
and I went straight from the thirds to the firsts.'

Known initially at representative level for his 30-metre run-up and
his flowing ponytail, Gillespie played a debut Test against the West

Indies in Sydney before breaking down with a muscle strain after having bowled just three overs in the next Test in Melbourne.

While injuries restricted his progress, there was no denying that his fast-tracking was a selection masterstroke. It reminded observers of the gilt-edged treatment Shane Warne received earlier in the 90s after quitting the Cricket Academy and being immediately lifted into Victoria's Sheffield Shield team because of the dearth of quality wrist-spinners.

As fine a prospect as Gillespie appeared to be, like Warne, he was fortunate to be in the right place at the right time, with Merv Hughes having lost favour, Craig McDermott prematurely retired and the experienced Paul Reiffel struggling for full fitness. Despite only one appearance with South Australia all summer, Gillespie was one of four pacemen chosen for the 1997 tour of South Africa. He was given immediate new-ball status alongside Glenn McGrath after Reiffel suffered a recurrence of a back-related hamstring injury at Durban and subsequently missed selection in the remaining two Tests.

With 13 wickets in four lead-up games, Gillespie was named in Australia's first Test XI at Johannesburg ahead of Queensland's Andy Bichel, who'd taken 10 wickets in three. From his opening overs, Gillespie produced consistent, searing pace which had the South African batsmen ducking and wicketkeeper Ian Healy retreating.

After taking two wickets in the first Test, he took eight in the second on a green-top at Port Elizabeth and four in the third at Centurion Park, to be Australia's most improved player.

Despite a 2–1 loss in India just months before, the South Africans had billed the series as a world championship.

However, after faltering badly at The Wanderers, where they were thumped by an innings and 196 runs, they also lost, albeit narrowly, at St George's Park before hitting back in the dead rubber at Centurion Park.

The world's foremost-ranked batsman Steve Waugh was once again the man of the series with his now familiar percentage game and admirable focus. His tour highlight came at Johannesburg in the opening Test when he and Greg Blewett became only the 10th pair to bat through the entire third day's play, adding 288 as Australia declared at 8/628. Waugh made 160 and Blewett, 214, the highest score by an Australian in a Test in South Africa. Their stand of 385 was the 11th highest in Test history.

When he first came in, Waugh played and missed twice at South Africa's unorthodox left-arm slow bowler, Paul Adams, both times being beaten pointlessly by balls spinning sharply away. He'd never sighted Adams before and was clearly struggling to pick his spin. In Afrikaans, captain Hansie Cronje said as much to Adams. Waugh grinned and said, 'You're dead right. I can't pick him.'

Midway through a slower patch in their epic stand, Cronje approached Waugh and said, '$50 you don't win this game,' a subtle way of adding an extra edge to the contest, in the hope that Waugh might self-destruct in a bid to lift the run-rate.

But he was far too focused. Earlier in the match, while waiting his turn to bat, he'd looked at the scoreboard and imagined 156 against his name.

As he and Blewett assumed total control, the much-repeated theme between overs was, 'Grind 'em down. Be patient. This is a Test match.'

Australia's landslide win was completed early on the fifth morning, with Michael Bevan taking the final four wickets in just 14 minutes as the South Africans plunged to their worst Test defeat since 1949–50. Glamour spinner Adams, a national hero among South Africa's black population, went for 163 from 52 overs, his only wicket coming at the conclusion of Australia's record innings.

Taylor admitted afterwards he'd never played in a superior all-round team. Even the decision to bat Matthew Elliott, a renowned opener, at No. 3 had paid off, the Victorian stamping his return to Test cricket with a highly-accomplished 85 from just 115 balls.

Both Warne (in his 50th Test) and Bevan took six wickets, Warne continuing his mastery over star South African Daryll Cullinan by dismissing him for a duck in the second innings – the seventh time he'd taken his wicket in seven internationals. He also bowled Jacques Kallis around his legs with a leg-break delivered from wide on the outside popping crease. With 4/43 from 28 overs, Warne seemed back to his best, having made an astonishingly rapid recovery after finger surgery. 'In the first innings he probably didn't get it through as nicely as he probably would have wanted but it was different in the second,' Cronje said. 'The pace of his flipper was back again.'

Taylor had asked Warne to address the team leading into the match. Stressing the importance of focus, he recalled how he had lost control four years previously in the infamous incident with Andrew Hudson and warned that for Australia to win, everyone had to ignore the taunts, sheep calls and barracking, and rally around each other.

Australia's new selection policy of pairing two pacemen with Warne and the growing-in-confidence Bevan was paying a continuing dividend. While Bevan still rated his bowling as an incidental, his blend of topspinners and the left-armer's bosie were proving irresistible, especially against the tail.

The only chink in the team's aura of invincibility, especially on hard, flat wickets, was the continuing fragile batting form of captain Taylor. His run of low scores in Australia had been an almost daily talking point and by making just 16 at Johannesburg before inside-edging a ball back onto his stumps, he was again fair game. Many were conveniently forgetting that he was playing as an all-rounder, that his sure hands at slip and captaincy were just as important assets as his batting.

A back injury, sustained in running-between-wickets exercises before the fixture against Border, was a further complicating factor. Vice-captain Healy filled in for him in East London and Steve Waugh for a one-day match in Zwide, a black township on the outskirts of Port Elizabeth, venue for the second Test.

Quizzed about his feelings on the captaincy, should Taylor's injury be serious enough to force him out of the remaining Tests, Healy said it was a tough enough task keeping wickets to contemplate the captaincy on anything but a part-time basis. He favoured Steve Waugh as Taylor's long-term successor and, if necessary, as early as the coming English tour. In an interview with Malcolm Conn of the *Australian*,

Healy said: 'If it's a fill-in thing, then I have no reservation. But long-term either the team is going to suffer or my keeping will suffer and it's just not worth it if you've got a candidate just as good [Steve Waugh] standing at gully.'

If he'd had anything but a week to recuperate in, Taylor would surely have been stood down, on fitness if not form grounds.

Once his back had settled, however, the decision was made to continue with an unaltered XI, despite the promise of the greenest wicket of the tour, at St George's Park.

Taylor had gone 17 innings without a half-century. So hesitant was his footwork that he seemed either to be out deflecting the ball back onto his stumps, or giving 'keeper Dave Richardson and the South African slips cordon catching practice. For the first time, coach Geoff Marsh, always so upbeat when discussing Taylor's performances, went public about his concerns. 'It's got to be getting to him,' he told reporters. '[But] he's a stronger man than you or I are. He's tough. It's a credit to him the spirit he's shown in the dressing room, for a guy who deep down is obviously very disappointed with his form. The longer you go without scoring runs the harder it gets. He's not batting as well as in 1989. He just needs some time at the crease.'

Taylor was to miss out again, twice, at Port Elizabeth, prolonging the worst run of low scores by any Australian captain in history. But his team's extraordinary fightback averted the spotlight, albeit momentarily.

Outplayed on the opening two days after Taylor had won the toss and sent the opposition in for the first time in his 26 Tests as captain, the Australians had conceded a 184-run break and, given the unpredictability of the wicket and the side's poor record in chasing fourth innings targets, were massive outsiders beginning day three.

But Gillespie, who'd taken a Test-best 5/54 bowling with a gale on the opening day, again broke through early, castling the hard-to-dismiss Gary Kirsten. Soon afterwards Greg Blewett ran out Jacques Kallis with a direct hit from midwicket and it was South Africa's turn to stumble. They slumped from an overnight 0/83 to 168 all out. With eight wickets for the match, Gillespie had silenced those who felt him undeserving of a Test place after only one full season of Shield cricket. Warne with 2/20 and Bevan 3/18 maintained their psychological hold on the hesitant Proteas middle and late order.

The target of 270 was still an enormous challenge, especially after both openers fell for a total of 30. Matthew Hayden's dismissal was particularly embarrassing: run out after both he and Elliott finished at the same end.

Elliott's free-scoring 44, including 32 runs in boundaries, lifted Australian hopes, but almost everything depended on the Waugh twins, who were not out overnight with Australia 3/145, still 125 runs from victory.

The gripping final day's play saw first Australia and then South Africa assume control. At 5/258 the Australians were cruising before losing three wickets for just seven runs.

Five were still needed with just two wickets in hand. So nervous had Warne been, coming in at No. 9, that he couldn't feel his feet.

Gillespie, the unheralded new star of Australian cricket, grittily played out a maiden over of Kallis in-swing to roars of appreciation from the small Australian contingent in the public reserve. Healy was hoping for a shorter one around off stump so he could play his trademark square cut. Instead Cronje overpitched on leg stump and Healy lifted it high and mightily into the bleachers backward of square leg before saluting his excited team-mates in a rare and uninhibited show of emotion.

Only once had Australia ever achieved a narrower victory batting last: in 1951–52 by one wicket against the West Indies in Melbourne.

'It was a lottery,' Healy said. 'I just watched the ball and played the moment, which is what we are all taught.

'The big thing was that Hansie Cronje took second slip out and put him at midwicket. If he pitched outside off stump I was going to try and run him through gully. But the ball drifted onto my pads and I thought I'd go for it.'

It was the first time an Australian had hit a 6 to win a Test match. The sweetest of all wins gave the Australians an unassailable 2–0 lead and their first series win in South Africa since 1957–58.

The instigator in the extraordinary escape was Mark Waugh, who played the innings of his life in scoring 116 in the true blue-collar manner of brother Steve. For years he'd been overshadowed by his twin, but this time with Steve failing – to the catch of the match by a somersaulting Cronje – it was Mark who assumed central responsibility. He'd made 105 before he gave his first semblance of a chance, to slipsman Cullinan, and it was a genuine surprise when he lost his bearings to a Kallis off-cutter and was bowled at 116.

It was a new, grittier Mark Waugh who'd lasted for five and a half hours on a green seamer against a world-class attack. He played handsomely on occasions, especially when whipping the ball off his pads. But the rest of the time he concentrated fiercely, waiting for the right ball and playing scrupulously straight. 'It was the best of my 11 Test 100s and also my best innings in first-class cricket,' he said.

With Australia still 100 runs short, he'd touched a delivery from Adams through to wicketkeeper Richardson, but no one appealed! It was a rare stroke of luck which ultimately was to cost the South Africans the game in one of the most climactic finishes of them all.

'To win a Test match like that was just an incredible buzz, maybe the best I've had in Test cricket,' said man of the match Waugh in his book, *A Year To Remember*.

Within days he had been named No. 2 batsman in the world behind brother Steve, an unheard of honour for two people from the same family.

'It's undoubtedly the biggest Test win I've played in by an absolute mile,' said Taylor. 'I just can't think of a win which rates with it. To climb off the canvas like we did was very special. There is no better Australian side I have played in than this one. I think we are a better side than we were in 1995. I can't think of a win which tops this. And no side in the world could have chased like we did and won.'

The last Test, a week later at Centurion Park, was an anticlimax. Several of the Australians had been told they were to go home at the conclusion of the match, rather than be a part of the one-day team.

It was unsettling and affected morale, normally an Australian strongpoint.

Having conceded a large first-innings lead, this time the Australians couldn't recover. South Africa won by eight wickets, thanks mainly to Allan Donald (who took eight wickets) and a fit-again left-arm paceman Brett Schultz with six.

Steve Waugh, with 67 and 60 not out, was again the outstanding batsman of the match. Replays showed that Waugh (in the first innings) and Healy (in the second) had been wrongly given out caught at the wicket. Healy's much-publicised response was to gesture at the umpire as he walked off the ground and to angrily throw his bat up the steps towards the dressing room door. It was a rare show of petulance which saw him suspended from the first two matches of the one-day series. It was a sombre end to a milestone match in which he'd become only the second Australian wicketkeeper to achieve 300 dismissals.

His removal, soon afterwards, as Australia's vice-captain for the soon-to-start tour of England was a further blow. He'd telegraphed Steve Waugh's appointment months earlier by saying Waugh should be Taylor's long-term successor, given the focus wicketkeepers had to have on their own performances in the field. His frankness probably cost him any chance he had of captaining Australia beyond one-day level. But had Taylor been in any sort of form, the selectors might not have been as alert to the need to groom a replacement. Despite his durability, Healy, 32, wasn't considered a long-term leadership prospect. And the selectors were insistent that the vice-captaincy should also go to the next captain. If Taylor's poor form continued in the UK, Steve Waugh would be his immediate successor.

The headline in the *Australian* at the conclusion of the Test, TAYLOR CRISIS HITS TEAM COHESION smacked of a 'Let's-Get-Tubby' campaign. Australia had won an important series, but Taylor's woes were still being highlighted. Something had to give, soon.

## PROFILE: **MARK WAUGH**

CRICKETING ARISTOCRAT Mark Waugh's elevation to the ranking of No. 2 batsman in the world, behind twin brother Steve, at the conclusion of the South African series in 1997 was confirmation of the unqualified success of the new, hard-nosed approach he'd adopted. He wanted to not only cement his place, but to become one of Australia's all-time best Test batsmen.

Years before, after four ducks in a row in Sri Lanka, he'd given away all his equipment to the team's room attendant in Colombo. Dropped from the Test team just 12 months after his fairytale first century in Test cricket when he was dubbed an 'instant super Test hero' by his captain Allan Border, Waugh not only revived, he played with such charm and artistry that he was easily the most-watchable of all the elite Australian batsmen.

As one of Mark Taylor's indispensables, not only did he score runs consistently, he did it with a joyous, effortless grace which thrilled old masters like Greg Chappell, who, four centuries into Waugh's Test career, had predicted he'd go on to make 20.

From the mid-90s, Waugh joined brother Steve as Australia's premier batsmen, his centuries in Jamaica in 1995 and at Port Elizabeth in 1997 confirmation of his ability to perform, even under the most enormous pressure.

The following Australian season, against the South Africans in Adelaide, he was to bat through an entire day's play and for the first time in his Test career – to his supreme satisfaction – was instrumental in Australia *saving*, rather than winning, a match. Almost as fulfilling among four centuries for the 1998 calendar year was his Test-best 153 not out in oppressive conditions against India at Bangalore. It enabled Australia to win its only match of its autumn tour. His ranking as Australia's leading one-day batsman continued.

Waugh believed his career-best form was more to do with extra experience, but he'd also developed a harder edge to his batting. No longer was he flustered by the inevitable initial volley of bouncers which, at one stage in the 1992–93 campaign against the touring West Indies, prompted Brian Lara to accuse him of being frightened. 'No heart man,' he called from slip. 'Get behind it.'

Waugh's whole game continued to be built around being positive and refusing to allow even the sharpest bowlers to dictate. He improvised, reviving the deliberate steer over the top of the slips made famous years before by the South African Eddie Barlow. He was also concentrating better and seemed to have a little of brother Steve's focus, without losing his flamboyance. Sometimes he was victim of a so-called 'soft' dismissal, like Englishman David Gower, but it didn't mean he didn't care. Poor shots pained him just as much as they did Steve. He just didn't tend to show his disappointment quite as openly. In Perth, in 1995–96, however, having broken a run of ducks against Sri Lanka with 111 in the first of three Tests, he responded to some heckling from one section of the crowd when he was slowly progressing through his 90s by angrily waving his bat having finally reached his 10th Test 100.

Invariably of happy disposition, he started signing his name 'M. Wog' in India, to tie in with the way Indians pronounced his and Steve's surname.

In the new era of professionalism, he regarded cricket as better than having to work for a living and believed himself capable of remaining a frontline choice for the Australian Test and one-day team well into his 30s.

'There have been a lot of players who have made a lot of runs in their 30s,' he said. 'Graham Gooch got better with age. David Boon and Allan Border were very competitive. From 30 onwards there's no reason why you shouldn't be batting well. You know your strengths and weaknesses. You've played a lot of games and have the confidence to play well at the level. You know the conditions around the world and the grounds and the wickets.'

Asked his runmaking goals, he said: 'It's *when* you score your runs which is important. Hopefully I'm contributing to Australia winning and maybe saving a few Tests, rather than the pure statistic of runs. When you get them in the tough times it counts more.'

Rather than there being any brotherly rivalry with Steve, Mark said the pair were proud of each other's performances. 'Maybe [there was] when we were younger, but there's no point now,' he said. ' We're both playing for Australia and both doing well. I hope he does well and I'm sure he thinks the same.'

The highest of the Waughs' six century stands leading into the spring Tests against Sri Lanka in 1999 was 231 against the West Indies at Kingston in 1995. They also added 190 against England in the Sydney Test in 1998–99, a daring, dominant display which thrilled the holiday crowd after Australia had lost 3/52.

Waugh had once rated a key career goal to average 50 in Test cricket, but has since modified it. 'It takes a lot of big 100s and not outs to get your average up around there. It's beyond me now. Anywhere around 45, give or take a couple, is a pretty good average.'

Standing tall at the crease, with a bat two inches longer than most, he says he just goes out and hits it. But his artistry is reminiscent, according to the old timers lucky enough to have been witness, of Alan Kippax and Stan McCabe, two of Australia's most-revered between-the-wars batsmen.

More flamboyant at the crease than Steve, he is also more athletic in the field, having taken a series of memorable catches, at second slip, silly point and in short, run-saving positions. In the 90s, he took more 'blinders' than anyone, Mark Taylor rating him the finest all-round fieldsman in his time.

**MARK WAUGH'S RECORD (TO 20 AUGUST 1999)**

|  | Mts | Runs | HS | Ave | 100s | Wicks | Ave | BB |
|---|---|---|---|---|---|---|---|---|
| Tests | 90 | 6042 | 153* | 42.85 | 16 | 48 | 40.66 | 5/40 |
| One-day Int. | 191 | 6636 | 130 | 38.58 | 12 | 81 | 32.81 | 5/24 |

While Steve Waugh was lifted into Sheffield Shield and Test ranks before his twin brother, Mark Waugh was first to be named by Bankstown-Canterbury for his 'A' grade debut.

Mark, 17, made 97 in his maiden game and for the 1982–83 Sydney grade season, scored 427 runs at an average of 30.5. He played 13 matches and Steve just four. Both were regulars as 18-year-olds in 1983–84, Mark scoring 350 runs at 19.4 and Steve, 445 at 40.8.

'From their earliest days with us, they made a remarkable contribution,' said Bankstown president Brian Freedman. 'Bankstown is a rough-and-tumble place and the feats of sporting people such as Steve and Mark lift the profile of the whole area.'

In late 1999, a new 800-seat grandstand, named in their honour, was due to be opened at the ground.

# FOURTEEN

---

# HITTING
# THE
# WALL

*'Well, that's about it. I'm just about
ready to give up.'*

---

MARK TAYLOR'S BATTING SLUMP dominated the headlines on Australia's arrival and the traditional press grilling at Heathrow. He'd even failed in a 40-over friendly against a Rest of the World XI in Hong Kong during a team stopover, making just 4 before being caught behind from the bowling of the otherwise nondescript Pakistani Mohsin Kamal.

Taylor had to field just as many questions about his own form and future as his team's make-up and ability to win the Ashes for a record fifth consecutive time. Some of the talk was demeaning and deliberately provocative, yet he refused to crack, parrying the media questioning with poise and diplomacy, even if he was burning inside. The back surgery which had forced his 11th-hour withdrawal from the Sri Lankan tour nine months earlier had forced him to rest at just the wrong time. He was beefier than normal and hadn't regained all his flexibility down his left side, which disadvantaged his runmaking.

Legendary Australian ex-captain Greg Chappell suggested Taylor was not mentally fit to lead, aligning some of his problems to his own.

He'd been the last Australian captain to make a run of low scores, in 1981–82 when he was out for five ducks in seven innings. Even in those days, the itinerary was exhausting and allowed little respite to a player struggling to see the ball.

Others said his eyes were gone, his feet immobile and no longer should he be entitled to an automatic place. As hard as he tried to rectify his embarrassing run of outs, it was a theory Taylor had been unable to bury even a month into the tour after nine innings without a 100. He was forever trying to play the perfect innings, looking to start with a Mark Waugh-like cover drive, instead of waiting and watching and making the bowlers come to him.

It has always been the Australian way to pick their best XI before naming a captain. Taylor had been bumbling along as out-of-form as he'd ever been in his career. The statistics were damning. Clearly he wasn't worth his place in the side. He knew his form slump was upsetting team focus and having dropped out of Australia's XI for the last of the three Texaco Cup internationals – after a similar demotion in mid-tournament in South Africa only weeks previously – he privately conceded his role as Test captain might be over before the Ashes campaign had even begun.

Potential replacement Michael Slater, recalled to the team as a reserve opener, hadn't played a first-class match prior to the first Test. Neither had another of the batting specialists, Ricky Ponting. Both were victims of a batting-rich squad and Taylor's desperate desire to play himself back into form via fixtures he normally would have missed.

Having failed once in an otherwise inconsequential county game at the Racecourse Ground, Derby, Taylor finally hit the wall. In the split second after nibbling at a wide half-volley from Phil DeFreitas early in the second innings and nicking the ball to slip and Derbyshire's Australian import captain, Dean Jones, Taylor decided to end it all. He was preparing to walk off before realising Jones had muffed it.

While reprieved, he felt nothing but anger at yet another indecisive shot, and at the change of ends told his batting partner Justin Langer, 'Well, that's about it. I'm just about ready to give up.'

The nightmares of the extended Australian summer, coupled with

One of Mark Taylor's central missions on succeeding Allan Border as captain in 1994 was to retain the Ashes, cricket's most famous urn.

*David Munden/Sportsline*

Mark Taylor and Michael Slater's opening responsibilities initially also included one-day cricket.
*Ken Rainsbury/Australian Cricket magazine*

Together Mark Taylor and Michael Slater averaged 51 and amassed 10 century opening stands, including two doubles.
*Ken Rainsbury/Australian Cricket magazine*

Thanks to a memorable Shane Warne hat-trick, it took the 1994–95 Australians only an hour on the fifth day to clinch a 295-run victory and go to a 2–nil lead with three Ashes Tests to play.
*Ken Rainsbury/Australian Cricket magazine*

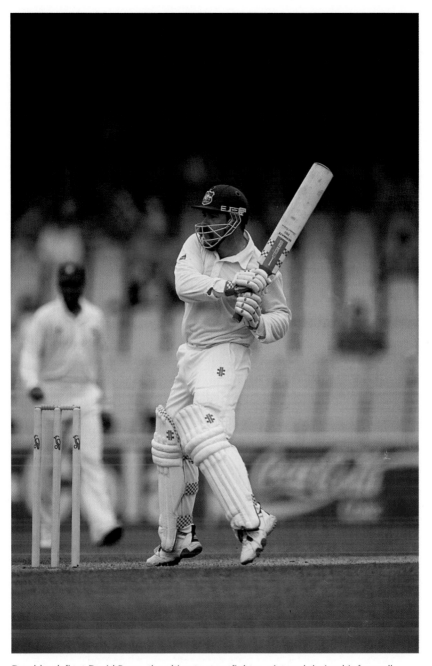

Durable, defiant David Boon, the ultimate streetfighter, pictured during his farewell
Test summer, against Pakistan in Sydney in 1995–96.

*Stephen Laffer*

Every time Ian Healy's right to a Test place was questioned, he'd respond emphatically. His 161 not out against the West Indies at the 'Gabba in 1996–97 was a career-best performance.

*Stephen Laffer*

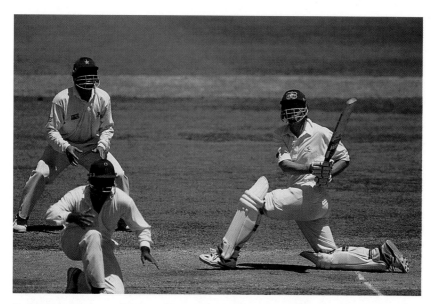

Despite missing the Perth Test with injury, Stephen Waugh's 1995–96 contributions were consistently outstanding and included three centuries and an average of 100-plus.

*Stephen Laffer*

No one span the ball further or attacked as purposefully as Shane Warne, voted the No. 1 cricketer of the 90s by his peers.

*Ken Rainsbury/*Australian Cricket *magazine*

Craig McDermott's grand career ended prematurely at the age of 30, but not before
he'd taken 291 Test wickets for Australia, second only to Dennis Lillee.

*Stephen Laffer*

Mark Waugh and Ricky Ponting enjoy the races in Bridgetown, Barbados, 1995 tour.

*Ray Titus*

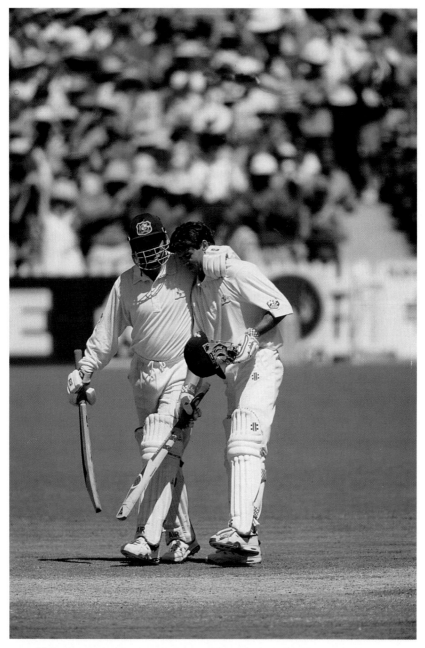

Greg Blewett's maiden century in his debut Ashes Test in Adelaide in 1994–95 wouldn't have been possible without some late-order resistance from fellow first-gamer Peter McIntyre.

*Ken Rainsbury/*Australian Cricket *magazine*

Without Steve Waugh, the Australians could not possibly have won the Frank Worrell Trophy in 1994–95. Not only did he average 107, he took this crucial catch to dismiss Junior Murray at Bridgetown when the Windies were threatening.

*Ray Titus*

The 1994–95 Australians, Test cricket's new world champions.
Back row, left to right: Errol Alcott (physiotherapist), Shane Warne, Justin Langer, Ricky Ponting, Glenn McGrath, Brendon Julian (mid-tour replacement), Carl Rackemann (mid-tour replacement), Paul Reiffel, Michael Slater, Greg Blewett, Mike Walsh (scorer). Front row: Bob Simpson (coach), Tim May, Steve Waugh, Ian Healy (vice-captain), Mark Taylor (captain), David Boon, Mark Waugh, Jack Edwards (manager).

*Ray Titus*

an even poorer run in the opening weeks in England and the constant media quizzing as to his future, had so sapped Taylor's morale that he was ready to stand down, then and there.

Langer, a junior member of the team, blinked and said: 'That's rubbish about giving up. Absolute rubbish. Just watch the ball. You'll be right.'

From a shaky 9 not out at tea, Taylor finished 59 not out at stumps, only his second half-century in eight months since returning from back surgery.

After the one-on-one with the highly-positive Langer, he'd reassessed his standing, suppressed his negative thoughts and hung in. Late in the day he even played a couple of meaty drives and leg-side flicks, once his bread-and-butter shots. By stumps, he was actually *enjoying* himself again, playing the way he always had, loving the game.

A week later, having deflected more broadsides and condemnation after his and Australia's first-up failure on the eventful first morning of the Ashes series in Birmingham, he made a memorable, back-to-the-wall century in the second innings, and by the fifth Test in Nottingham, Australia had re-claimed the Ashes and Taylor resurrected his career.

Taylor admits that his whole career was in the balance as the edge flew to Jones. Had 'Deano' not dropped him, his international career was as good as finished.

Taylor's ambassadorial abilities and his right to be regarded with Don Bradman, Richie Benaud and Ian Chappell as Australia's finest postwar captains were not in question. But when you can hardly put bat on ball, even those with the steeliest resolve have nowhere to hide. In Australia, the captain is not only a leader of men, traditionally he's the team's best player.

Having failed to make 50 in his previous 20 Test innings, Taylor was the subject of ever-increasing ridicule. The Melbourne *Age* published an office sweep forecasting how many runs Taylor would make in the first Test, with the majority of categories from 0 to 10.

Even ex-Australian coach Bobby Simpson joined the critics, declaring in the *Daily Mail* that the Australian captaincy issue was fostering resentment among the players. He believed Taylor's record as captain shouldn't allow other key issues to be clouded. 'I know Taylor is admired for his leadership, but that can't compensate for what is not just a bad run of form but a basic flaw in his technique,' he said.

At dinner the night before the first Test at Edgbaston Taylor's parents, Tony and Judy, said they'd never seen their son more morose. 'It was his absolute low point,' Tony said.

Bowled out in just two and a half hours in a sensational opening day's play of the new series, the Australians were comfortably beaten, but Taylor reclaimed at least some of the lost ground in the second innings with a triumphant 129 in six and a half hours. As comebacks go, it was the full monty and prompted a wave of congratulation, including a note from Australia's cricket-loving Prime Minister John Howard, who talked about 'true Aussie grit' and how 'all Australians are proud of you'.

Taylor's parents were staying at a local bed & breakfast close to Edgbaston and were applauded coming down for breakfast. 'That was very, very moving,' said Tony Taylor. 'We'll never forget that or the reception when he made his 100 having struggled for so long. He's so popular and respected in England.'

Before the game the Australian team watched film of Kieren Perkins' extraordinary 1500 m freestyle gold medal swim in Atlanta. Soon afterwards a fax arrived from Perkins, willing Taylor to re-focus on his immediate tasks, ignore the distractions and succeed.

As a youngster, Perkins had constantly referred to a motivational message stuck on his bedroom wall, highlighting the importance of persistence and determination. He told Taylor that he shouldn't underrate his own ability and that he could again make big scores. He wished Taylor and the whole Australian team every good fortune in the forthcoming series.

WITH AUSTRALIA HOPELESSLY POSITIONED, 360 runs behind and Mark Waugh in hospital with suspected appendicitis, it seemed the game would finish in three days, maybe four. A fifth day seemed out of the question.

Taylor had survived less than half an hour in the first innings and the Englishmen anticipated another easy wicket. The slipsmen crouched expectantly, waiting for the edge which would end it all. But it never came. Taylor batted out the day and maintaining his focus, continued into the next. At one stage Australia was 1/327, an epic fightback, with Taylor and Greg Blewett both making 100s; Taylor his first in 19 months and Blewett his third in three consecutive Ashes contests.

Taylor's ton was hardly classical. It was more like the way he *used* to bat, all application with a couple of drives and a few pull shots intermingled with his trademark steely defence. He was exhausted afterwards, so unaccustomed had he become to the rigours of a long innings.

Others were to make higher and faster centuries this eventful summer, but none were greeted as emotionally as Taylor's. Among the headlines were: TON OF INSPIRATION, SALUTE TO A SUPER SCRAPPER and COMEBACK OF THE CENTURY.

Australia's team manager Alan Crompton broke team rules and allowed the television cameras into the dressing room to record the jubilation of the Australians for the news bulletins back home. 'It was a very courageous effort and I can assure you that there was not a single dry eye in the Australian dressing room when he achieved his century,' said Crompton.

'He'd been under such a lot of pressure. The media from both countries was very critical of his poor batting form. He handled it superbly in the face of persistent and repetitive questioning. At times I asked him if he wanted me to relieve the pressure on him by intervening or handling some of the numerous press conferences myself. He would always say, "No, Crommo, I can handle it."

'He certainly could handle it and he did so consistently superbly. He always remained calm and not once did he lose his cool.'

From being under siege, the most embattled cricketer in the game had emerged a hero. 'I didn't hit the ball like Don Bradman or Viv Richards,' Taylor told reporters. 'But I hit it like Mark Taylor and I got a 100. This is my 82nd Test and I've enjoyed the vast majority. I went out there to enjoy myself again.'

Taylor said he would have preferred to have made 0, if it meant Australia winning the game.

Bad weather interfered with Australia's winning bid at Lord's after Glenn McGrath had taken a career-best 8/38 on the third scheduled day, rain having washed out all of the first day and most of the second.

For only the second time in his 29 matches as captain, Taylor sent the opposition in and was immediately rewarded with the first three wickets going down for 47 and last seven for just 30. In returning the best Test figures by an Australian in more than 75 years, McGrath bowled at pace and jagged the ball back like he was bowling fast off-breaks.

Australia established a 136-run first innings lead thanks to opener Matthew Elliott's maiden century, before England enjoyed the best batting conditions of the match on day five and happily settled for a draw – the first involving the Taylor-led Australians in 19 matches.

The momentum had swung and by winning at Old Trafford, Headingley and Trent Bridge, the Ashes were retained in convincing fashion, Steve Waugh's twin centuries in the third Test the cornerstone of the comeback. In batting more than 10 hours on a green, moist wicket, Waugh became only the third Australian to notch twin centuries in 120 years of Ashes battles. GUNSLINGER WAUGH LEADS THE FIGHTBACK headlined the *Guardian*.

Regarding the centuries as being equal to any he'd scored in Test cricket, especially given the challenge of batting first on a green seamer, Waugh was gritty and game, refusing to come off mid-way through the second innings despite a badly bruised thumb.

He'd rescued the Australians twice, from 3/42 in the first innings and 3/39 in the second. Their 268-run victory wouldn't have been possible without Waugh's courageous double. 'It was a really tough wicket,' he said. 'I was pretty scratchy for the first half an hour [on the first morning]. I had a bit of luck, which you need on that wicket, but after that I played as well as I ever have in a Test match. It's up there with the 200 at Jamaica, but the wicket was a lot tougher so it made it even more pleasing to get runs in that situation.'

Brother Mark was equally impressed. 'I've been witness to many of my brother's best innings,' he wrote in *Inside Edge*. 'Without a doubt I have to rate his first-up 108 at Old Trafford as a great one. It was outstanding in the difficult conditions with the odds stacked in favour of the fast bowlers. He needed some luck but he also had to back himself with some positive strokes.'

Only weeks before, captaining Australia for the first time in a first-class match against Nottinghamshire, Steve had been so unhappy with his form that he had a double net session in Trent Bridge and finally started to play with the authority his game had lacked earlier in the tour. Facing three spinners, Shane Warne, Stuart MacGill (who was in England playing League cricket) and Ricky Ponting, his timing returned and he seemed sharper than he had been for weeks.

Waugh's dominance ensured an Australian win and, maintaining their ascendancy in the fourth Test at Leeds, the world champions inflicted a similarly heavy defeat on the Englishmen. Jason Gillespie bowled as fast as anyone in the world, sending wicketkeeper Healy back almost 30 metres. 'Even then I was taking "Dizzy" [Gillespie] head-high,' he said. 'It was the consistently fastest spell I've ever kept to and that includes Merv [Hughes], "Billy" [Craig McDermott], everyone.'

Leading 2–1 with two Tests to play, the Australians won in just four days at Trent Bridge, with McGrath and Warne sharing 14 wickets between them. The pitches hadn't favoured Warne as much as in 1993, but with 24 wickets in six Tests he maintained his rating as one of the world's outstanding bowlers. After the series-equalling win at Old Trafford, much was made of his skylarking which included the swigging of champagne and a couple of his favourite old M.C. Hammer dance steps. Soon afterwards he was celebrating again, this time the birth of his first daughter Brooke back in Australia.

With 36 wickets in six Tests, including 7/76 and 0/33 in the final Test at The Oval, which England won narrowly in just three days, McGrath had been the true powerhouse, confirming his strike ability with a series of high-quality performances on a set of highly conducive wickets.

Taylor had won five of the six tosses, retained the Ashes 3–2 and resurrected his own career.

Elliott's 556 runs heralded a newcomer of infinite potential, Steve Waugh continued his Bradman-like record in England, while Paul Reiffel resurrected a career he thought might have been over.

'We're as good as any side who have pulled the baggy green cap on,' said Taylor. 'We've got the players to do the business when the pressure is on. It's particularly special this time around because we were 1–0 down in the series.'

Steve Waugh and Healy became the first to figure in five consecutive Ashes-winning teams and at Trent Bridge were proudly photographed together, two old campaigners at the very core of Australia's efforts.

Another of the most important was Victorian all-rounder Reiffel, one of four reinforcements called into the side from June to replace the injured Andy Bichel. He'd made several notable contributions, particularly at Old Trafford and Headingley when Australia reasserted its authority. His 5/49 in the fourth Test at Leeds included four of the six wickets to fall on the final day as Australia clinched an innings win, a reflex catch by gifted Mark Waugh at second slip to dismiss Mark Ealham from Reiffel's bowling another of the summer's spectacular highlights.

One of the tour's most-memorable moments came during a county game at Taunton when the team met British comedian and cricket buff John Cleese. 'The hotel we were staying at was very Fawlty Towers,' said Reiffel. 'As we came in for breakfast, guess who was in the corner? Old Basil Fawlty himself, John Cleese! It was a classic.'

- Before making his resurrecting century in the second innings of the first Test in 1997, Mark Taylor went 18 months and 21 consecutive innings without a Test 50. His scores: 7, 25 not out, 21, 10 (v Sri Lanka), 27, 37 (India), 43, 36, 27, 16, 7, 10, 11, 2, 1 (West Indies), 16, 8, 13, 38, 5 (South Africa) and 5 (England).

- Leading into the English tour, Mark Waugh was outspoken about the apparent 'softness' of English cricket. 'They aren't tough enough or hungry enough on the field,' he told Jim Maxwell in the *ABC Cricket Book*. 'They don't worry as a team, they worry about themselves.'

  They were words he was to regret as in six Tests, he averaged just 20 and, for the first time since the early 90s, was under pressure for his place.

# FIFTEEN

## CRUSADING FOR THEIR MATES

*'We had no choice but to act strongly.*
*This dispute has been talked about*
*for 100 years.'*

THE EUPHORIA AT AUSTRALIA'S come-from-behind defence of the Ashes and Mark Taylor's resolution to play on was short-lived. Ahead was an old-fashioned barney which was to plunge the Australian Cricket Board into its stormiest crisis since 1977.

A breakdown in negotiations between the Board and the players threatened the whole summer season.

Believing the Board was not rewarding the players sufficiently, despite payments to the elite having doubled in a five-year period, the ACB's senior 24 contracted players crusaded for better pay and conditions on behalf of their less-influential Sheffield Shield team-mates. They also wanted more say in the running of the game – a non-negotiable point with Board men, many of whom feared the presence of a rival promoter or entrepreneur, as had occurred with Kerry Packer's World Series Cricket two decades earlier.

The confrontation became acrimonious and totally overshadowed the three-Test series against the touring New Zealanders.

Strike action was even threatened as the players, frustrated at the breakdown in negotiations, carried the fight on, looking to gain access to the balance sheets the Board had always guarded so confidentially.

The very public and divisive dispute engulfed all the leading players and administrators and gave instant notoriety to the fledgling Australian Cricketers' Association and its executive president, ex-player Tim May. It was months before any settlement was achieved, and not before tempers had reached boiling point. CRICKET IN CRISIS and ALL OUT headlined the *Herald Sun*. STRIKE ... WILL THE PLAYERS GO OUT? said *Australian Cricket*.

'We had no choice but to act strongly,' said wicketkeeper Ian Healy. 'This dispute has been talked about for 100 years. Ever since Don Bradman was in short pants, the players have been ignorant of the income the game generates and how their own payments match up.

'The players have been kept in the dark for all that time and it creates dissension. By making a stand on behalf of 120 current first-class players, we hope to improve not only their employment conditions and wages, but those of all future first-class and Test players. If we, the senior group of five or six players, didn't put our hands up now, maybe the true finances of the Board will never be divulged.'

It was a brawl which had to happen, especially with the players looking to become full-time professionals without the administrators prepared to pay full-time wages for any but its top two dozen.

Steve Waugh said he was satisfied with what he was earning from the game but believed he needed to be involved to assist his underprivileged Shield mates. The players wanted to be consulted, too, on future itineraries, so the logjam of tours in 1997 could never again be repeated.

Until their threatened boycott of the opening matches of the 1997–98 World Series Cup, the players had the public's approval.

At the height of the argument, the Board disclosed the yearly salaries of the top six players, all of whom were grossing in excess of $400 000, substantially more than Prime Minister John Howard – exclusive of their endorsements. As captain, Taylor's earnings approached $500 000 from the Board alone.

Believing their privacy had been infringed, the players resolved to intensify their battle. And when Taylor agreed to support a strike if necessary and become a central figure in negotiations, it underlined the mood and determination of the players to remain united and not to back down, even if it alienated many in the public domain who had initially been sympathetic.

The furore raged at times almost out of control and as the brawl festered, Taylor found himself locked in intensive negotiations, even in mid-match during the second trans-Tasman Test in Perth.

None of the Australian players had realised just how traumatic the dispute would be. By mid-November, the state players had voted to go on strike if one was called. It was the Test players' call. The *Australian Cricket* magazine wrote that the players deservedly should have access to more of the kitty if extra distributions could be made without affecting the flow of life-preserving dividends to the states. Improving guarantees at Sheffield Shield level would assist cricket to retain many of the multi-gifted teenagers who were preferring to concentrate on more lucrative competitions such as the AFL, where even teenagers were commanding guaranteed starting salaries of $20 000-plus, compared to as little as $2000 for a Shield squad member.

Resolutions were finally agreed upon and all threatened strike action dropped after the Board commissioned an independent report into its finances and offered a series of peace proposals, including a belated look at their accounts. The cricketers ultimately won important concessions and the Board maintained its power as the game's custodian. But cricket's good name had been tarnished. And for many, irreparably.

THE POLITICKING CUT SHORT the party for the returning Ashes heroes. Soon after his arrival home, Taylor was told that he would no longer captain both the Test and one-day teams. It was felt more specialists needed to be played at limited-overs level, as had occurred in South Africa the previous autumn with Adam Gilchrist and Adam Dale among the most impressive reinforcements. Australia's failure to make the finals of the World Series Cup the previous summer had cost the states a split of almost $2 million in anticipated revenue, with only small crowds attending the two finals between the West Indies and Pakistan. The overriding plan was to build a team capable of winning the next World Cup, in England in 1999 – even if it meant the demise ahead of their time of one or two veterans.

'His batting wasn't quite right for one-day cricket,' said selector Allan Border on Foxtel. 'We had to split the captaincy up. It was a little bit divisive at first.'

Taylor was to be replaced as captain by Steve Waugh, nine months his junior. On the eve of his appointment, Waugh said he'd be happy to captain Australia at anything, even tiddlywinks. As one of the foremost and most experienced all-rounders in world cricket, his credentials were outstanding, even though he wasn't bowling as much due to recurring groin strains.

While his likely appointment had been broadcast for some time, especially after Taylor's omission from the Australian one-day team that played the Cricket Academy in a one-off exhibition game as part of the Academy's 10th birthday celebrations in Adelaide in October, few had expected the sweeping changes to also include Healy, Australia's frontline wicketkeeper at all levels since 1 April 1988.

His replacement, Western Australia's Gilchrist, was a hard-hitting batsman with developing wicketkeeping skills. Others, like Victoria's Darren Berry, co-opted into the '97 touring team in England when Gilchrist injured a knee, were superior technicians without possessing Gilchrist's strokemaking flair and adventure, or his ability to bat anywhere in the order from No. 1 to No. 6.

Only seven months previously, however, Healy, deputising for an out-of-favour Taylor, had led Australia to victory in the seven-match one-day series in South Africa. What's more, he boasted a strike-rate of 83, unsurpassed even by the team's one-day batting specialists.

'I'm entitled to feel disappointed,' he said. 'I've been happy with my past and current form and the efforts I've put into the one-day team. I can hold my head high. I put in.'

Healy's three-year-old daughter Laura reminded him of the bigger picture on her father's return from the Hobart Test. 'Daddy, why are you disappointed? You're here with us,' she said.

The Australians had spent 312 of 365 days in 1997 on the road, either in Australia or overseas. The gruelling schedule had already claimed several victims, with Jason Gillespie once again nursing stress fractures and not expected to play before Christmas at least. Matthew Elliott was recuperating from operations to both knees. And Andy Bichel, who'd started the Ashes campaign, was only just starting to bowl again after a winter of rehabilitation.

If Taylor and the other leading Australians were distracted, the early on-field results were no indication.

New Zealand may only have been team building, but its Australian-born coach Steve Rixon was adamant the Kiwis could pinch a Test, especially after back-to-back Test wins against visiting World Cup champions Sri Lanka the previous March. But even the optimistic Rixon had to reappraise his team's goals after their thumping defeats in Brisbane and Perth.

A century from Taylor in Brisbane, Shane Warne's re-emergence as Australia's No. 1 bowler in place of the injured Glenn McGrath and a selection masterstroke which saw first-gamer Simon Cook claim seven wickets on a memorable WACA debut were features of an Australian start few had thought possible given the off-field ructions. Mark Waugh's huge six onto the roof of the Lillee–Marsh stand from the bowling of Daniel Vettori was another highlight. It soared on and on and finished so high that the ball could not be retrieved. The carry alone was more than 120 metres.

Sent in to bat in Brisbane, the Australians went to lunch at a precarious 4/62, with Taylor at one stage going 44 minutes without scoring. An in-form, combative Chris Cairns had taken all four wickets in a hostile 10-over spell, but when he was rested immediately after the break, Australia regained the initiative and never lost it again all summer.

Taylor led by example, enjoying his best year since the 1989 England tour. He was the cornerstone of Australia's top order, regaining confidence in his all-round game and once again taking some superlative catches at slip.

While slow early against the New Zealanders, making just 27 runs to lunch, he accelerated afterwards, being 72 not out at tea and scoring another 40 in quick time before falling to Simon Doull and the second new ball. The thunderous reception for his century was recognition not only for his performance that day, but also for his courage in beating the odds in England. Until well set, he'd left most deliveries outside his off stump alone, relying on his pull shot and the occasional cover drive for boundaries.

While the Kiwis remained competitive until late in the match, conceding only a 24-run first-innings advantage, the Australians dominated the closing stages, clinching victory by 186 runs after the tourists collapsed in their second innings for 132.

Taylor held back strike bowler McGrath in the first hour on day five, and when he was introduced, he responded with four wickets in four overs to decimate the Kiwi top order. He seemed even more determined than usual, and by taking 5/32 maintained his giant-killing form so important in Australia's Ashes defence. However, he inflamed an old groin injury, missed the next two Tests and struggled on his recall against the South Africans.

His replacement in Perth, rangy 25-year-old Cook, had been selected largely on the back of his bouncy spells against the tourists in Newcastle when he claimed 3/38 and 4/61. Originally from Crib Point on sleepy Western Port Bay on Melbourne's Mornington Peninsula, Cook had played only three major games in two years and in the lead-up to the Test, wasn't even in NSW's XI for the game against his old state, Victoria.

Having taken 2/36 on the opening day, he finished the Test match in a hurry, taking the last five wickets and bowling at high pace on a wicket notable for its widening cracks.

Needing to make 245 to avert an innings defeat, the Kiwis were bowled out for 174, wicketkeeper Adam Parore with 63 his team's top scorer in yet another Test which had failed to go five days.

Australia would have clinched a 3–0 series win in Hobart but for a dropped catch by Cook in the last half hour, which saw the tourists force a draw. Set 288 to win, New Zealand were 9/223 at the close, the two unbeaten batsmen Doull lasting 35 balls for 1 and Shayne

O'Connor 31 balls for 0. Openers Matthew Horne and Nathan Astle had started with 54 runs from the first seven overs in a belligerent start, Michael Kasprowicz's first three overs costing 33 runs and Cook's first four, 17.

With 99 and 56, Greg Blewett was man of the match, ahead of Elliott who made 114 and Warne who finished with six wickets for the game, including 5/88 on the last day. He would have had six but for Cook's failure to catch Doull on the sweep shot midway through the final hour.

TAYLOR HAD BEEN UNEASY about the new dual captains policy, believing the scheduling of the preliminary matches in the one-day series, wedged as they were in between the finish of the New Zealand and start of the South African Tests, was divisive and devalued his authority.

The three-week break between Test series clearly freshened him up, however, and as well as Mark Waugh played, with centuries in Sydney and Adelaide, Taylor was the outstanding batsman of the summer, finishing with an unbeaten 169 not out and 6 in heatwave conditions in Adelaide, the first time an opener had batted through the innings in Adelaide since Bill Woodfull and Bodyline. Almost as valuable a knock was his four-hour epic for 59 in the second innings on a difficult wicket in Melbourne.

Having drawn the first Test, Australia won the second in Sydney by an innings – highlighted by Warne's 300th Test wicket – before drawing the last in Adelaide, thanks to Mark Waugh's unbeaten 115 in which he batted through the entire final day's play for the first time in his illustrious career.

During the tense final half hour, Waugh, near exhaustion, embroiled himself in controversy after breaking his wicket having been struck on the shoulder by Proteas paceman Shaun Pollock.

'I'd never batted for a whole day, or on a fifth-day wicket,' said Waugh. 'I had a little luck but if you are going to bat for that long you need a bit of luck. At the end of the day you're fairly tired from batting that long. It is a matter of breaking it down into simple terms and taking each ball as it comes.'

In an extraordinary finish which saw Waugh given the benefit of the doubt despite the protestations of an incensed South African captain Hansie Cronje, who believed Waugh had broken his wicket in a reflex action immediately after being struck by Shaun Pollock, Australia limped to stumps at 7/227 to ensure the series 1–0. Cronje was so upset with third umpire Steve Davis's rejection of the South African appeal that he rammed a stump into the umpires' door adjoining the player dressing rooms at the back of the Adelaide members' stand. 'If somebody gets hit on the head and he's wobbling and walks on his stumps, he's out,' Cronje said.

Waugh believed contact had been inadvertent. He'd been fully balanced when he'd accidentally clipped the bails. He claimed his arm 'had just gone floppy' as he was walking away off the wicket to recompose himself. Had he been given out, seven full overs still remained, with the lengthy Australian tail truly exposed. In reality the South Africans cost themselves the game, having dropped five catches in each Australian innings, including Waugh four times, the first at 1 from the very first ball he faced from spinner Pat Symcox late on the fourth night.

Australia had extended its enviable record under Taylor to nine series without series defeat, an unprecedented record ahead even of Clive Lloyd's star-spangled West Indians and, a generation back, Don Bradman's Invincibles.

With 20 wickets in three South African Tests and 39 for the six-Test summer, Warne had again been dynamic, despite a noticeable weight increase which worried the Australian inner sanctum and inspired the ABC's Tim Lane to make reference to Warne's 'Billy Bunter-type figure'.

Coach Geoff Marsh conceded Warne's habit for fast food and strawberry thickshakes was a concern and said the spin champion needed to show more self-discipline if he was to avoid continuing weight increases which had prematurely ended the career of others, including one of Warne's all-time favourites, paceman Merv Hughes.

'Merv could probably still be playing [for Australia] now if he kept himself fit,' Marsh told Malcolm Conn of the *Australian*. 'We talked and talked to Merv, but you can't be with a player 24 hours a day. The biggest problem we have is that these guys live in top-class hotels, they eat out at restaurants every night and they certainly don't go without food during the day. At the end of the day Shane's the one who has to watch what he eats.'

His coach Terry Jenner said Warne's *figures* rather than his *figure* was what was important. While agreeing that Warne wasn't quite as potent or as big a spinner as he was from the ages of 24 to 26, that had nothing to do with any additional poundage. His ability to adapt and corner batsmen with his pace variations made him just as dangerous as in his prime.

'He's had to adapt his thinking to a new set of standards, not spinning it quite as far but being just as consistent,' Jenner said. 'He has to work harder for his wickets now. If he was the same bowler from the point of view of whip and grip, you just can't consistently play that sort of bowling. His great attribute has been line and length and even that has suffered a little of late. Batsmen get more free hits than they have before, but in between, the quality is still right up there.'

With 5/75 and 6/34 in front of an appreciative Sydney crowd which had taken him to their hearts ever since his very first Test against the Indians in 1991–92, Warne not only reached his 300 Test wickets milestone, he lifted Australia to a resounding victory by an innings and 21 runs.

Jacques Kallis, South Africa's leading batsman on tour, was his 300th victim after a rain delay which threatened to force the match into a fifth day. Operating around the wicket, Warne bowled three consecutive leg-breaks before unleashing a faster topspinner. Kallis misread it and padded up to it, watching in horror as it drifted and zeroed straight into his off stump.

'I set a target this summer to get 300 Test wickets and I thought if I could do that, we could win both series,' said Warne on the ABC.

Taylor took his 50th catch from Warne's bowling when Pollock fell late on the fourth day. No bowler and fieldsman had ever enjoyed such a productive partnership.

West Indian Lance Gibbs was the only other slow bowler to have also taken 300 Test wickets. He was aged 41, compared with Warne's, 28 years and four months. Only two players, India's Kapil Dev and England's Ian Botham, were younger when they achieved their triple-century milestones.

'Shane's performance in Sydney was clearly the outstanding individual effort in a summer full of highs,' said Greg Chappell in *Australian Cricket* magazine. 'But the South Africans played into his hands, being far too negative and on the opening day, squandering an opportunity to really take the game to the Australians.'

If Warne remained fit and focused, Chappell predicted he could go past Kapil Dev, the all-time Test wicket record holder, with 434. He warned, however, that Warne could be finished by the year 2000, without an extra motivation such as the Test captaincy. 'It would be a shame if he didn't go as long as he possibly could,' said Chappell. 'He deserves to be at the top of the tree. I hope he can double his present mark and get 600 wickets, but I think it's going to be closer to 500.'

## PROFILE: IAN HEALY

WHEN IAN HEALY was dropped from Australia's one-day team in late 1997, the public backlash was so marked that cricket-loving Prime Minister John Howard could easily have demanded a Royal Commission. It seemed the whole eastern seaboard of Australia was up in arms. The letters to the editor, radio talkback and television news grabs were dominated by people's indignation at Healy's axing.

Trevor Hohns, one of Australia's '89 Ashes heroes and now the national selection chairman, had never felt so unloved. Not since the dismissal of another deputy-captain, Geoff Marsh, against India in 1991–92 had there been as controversial an axing.

Healy was not unaffected, but his team ethics were so strong, he phoned his replacement, West Australian Adam Gilchrist, long-distance to offer his congratulations.

Privately he was as puzzled as anyone, but nothing was to be gained going public. He may have emerged out of left field ahead of a more-seasoned field years earlier when initially chosen as Australia's 'keeper, but he was determined not to disappear in a blaze of emotion.

He wanted to top Rod Marsh's record for the most dismissals at Test level and if possible be the first to 400 victims. Another goal was to remain his country's 'keeper, at least at Test level, into the year 2000 when he was due to turn 36.

There was a hiccup late in the West Indies tour in 1999 when he tweaked both calves so badly on day four of the thrilling Barbados Test that he worried that his tour could be over then and there. But through-the-night ice treatments from Australian team physiotherapist Errol Alcott allowed him to take the field the next morning and, while obviously restricted, he was playing his part in what should have been an Australian victory, until he dropped centurion Brian Lara in the crucial, final overs.

As in Karachi five years earlier, when the Australians lost by a wicket after Healy missed a difficult stumping chance which went for four byes, he blamed himself squarely for the defeat.

With Gilchrist having been flown into St John's early as a back-up, Healy could well have played his last Test. But the tightness in his legs lessened and with four catches and a slick stumping a week later in Australia's series-squaring victory at Antigua, he'd justified his place emphatically – and again repelled the Gilchrist challenge.

Having surpassed Marsh's 355 dismissals, in late 1998 during Australia's tour of Pakistan, Healy's Test-only commitments have proved to be a blessing.

Several of his old team-mates had literally buckled at the enormous work-load imposed by a Test and one-day program which saw players training and playing eight and nine months of the year.

Craig McDermott and Dean Jones had played their last Tests at 31 and Merv Hughes and Tim May at 32.

Wicketkeepers, however, are renowned for their longevity, and to miss only one match in more than 100 has been an extraordinarily fine effort.

Pakistan 1998 was Healy's 20th overseas tour and only a prelude, he hoped, to an English farewell in 2001.

Team-mates marvelled at his focus and involvement. Paceman Paul Reiffel said with Healy behind the stumps, he always felt it was two against the batsman and not just one. 'It sometimes is a bit lonely when you get to the top of your bowling mark, particularly if the game is running against you, but Heals gives you the feeling that he is right there with you every step of the way,' he said in *Reiffel Inside Out*.

Healy's playing intentions centred squarely around form, fitness and enthusiasm. 'While all those three things are there I'll be playing very good cricket and should never even consider retiring,' he said. 'Guys like David Boon and Dean Jones, who retired in their early 30s, did it at a time when playing only one form of the game was an entirely new thing. "Boony" had the exact same experience that I've been given: to play just Test cricket. He didn't only want to play one, but I do. If that's all I can play, I'm pretty happy to still be playing it. If there is a use-by date, it comes down to the individual involved.'

Passing Marsh's world record mark of 355 at Rawalpindi had been an ambition ever since he reached 300 dismissals. 'I'd always thought it was too way-off, but as it has got closer, I thought about it more,' he said. 'I'd like to go on and not only just pass the record but maybe get to 400 [dismissals] and maybe get 4500 runs, too.

'I wanted to pass Alan Knott's batting record of the most number of runs [4389] by a Test 'keeper and to see Australia to some more successes. There's still plenty for me to achieve.'

Another of his goals was to play in a winning Sheffield Shield team with Queensland. While the Bulls have won two of the last five titles and finished second in 1992–93 and 1998–99, Healy has been absent each time because of international duties.

Asked his secret of longevity – he has represented Australia almost 300 times at the two international levels – Healy said, 'If you're going to play for any length of time, you have to be reasonably skilful and be able to bounce back from mistakes and failures. You have to persist and make sure you're very hard to get over the top of.'

The toughest period of his career, after a nervous start on the sub-continent in 1988, was in the West Indies in 1991 when he played with four fractures of his left index finger. He'd broken it on the last day of the Ashes tour in Australia in 1990–91 in Perth. It took six weeks to heal and not only did he have to change his batting grip, he also had to learn to catch differently. 'I made the decision that I could do it, so from that time on, you're not allowed to whinge! It didn't heal straight and now grows wherever it wants.'

In 1999, on the eve of the deciding Test in Antigua, he admitted he was just one match from being axed for Gilchrist. His batting touch had temporarily deserted him, but he kept admirably, his slick last-day stumping of Jimmy Adams down the leg side standing up to Colin Miller shades of his best mid-90s form.

By match end he had his old zest back, even stuffing some rolled-up paper down his jacket and thrusting out his chest to mimic one of the local cross-dressers who'd so proudly parade through the stands at St John's at lunchtime!

He'd once again responded superbly to a challenge. As his under-study Gilchrist had said months earlier in Australia, 'Heals would have to have a broken leg not to play and even then he'd probably get through.'

**IAN HEALY'S RECORD (TO 20 AUGUST 1999)**

|              | Mts | Runs | HS   | Ave   | 100s | Catch | Stmp | Dism. |
|--------------|-----|------|------|-------|------|-------|------|-------|
| Tests        | 115 | 4326 | 161* | 28.09 | 4    | 360   | 29   | 389   |
| One-day Int. | 168 | 1764 | 56   | 21.00 | –    | 195   | 39   | 234   |

In all of Ian Healy's Test dismissals, none was quite as remarkable as the time in the fifth Test in Perth in 1996–97 when he ran out West Indian Curtly Ambrose with a direct hit. Running forward of the wicket to collect the ball, he sensed Ambrose was out of his crease and, without looking back, quickly back-handed the ball from 10 metres in the general direction of the stumps.

Ambrose, unsuspecting at first, realised his danger too late and, making a wild lunge for his crease, got his bat stuck in one of the 3 centimetre wide cracks which had opened. He could only watch helplessly as the ball hit the stumps, ending his and the West Indian innings.

# SIXTEEN

## AMBUSHED, TORTURED AND TRAMPLED

*'Cricket doesn't come any better than this.*
*Sometimes it is best simply to sit back and enjoy.'*

UNTIL BRIAN LARA'S MISADVENTURES against Glenn McGrath in Australia a summer previously, few believed he had a batting equal in the world. His sheer flair saw him rated, amongst his peers anyway, ahead of the relentless Steve Waugh and even the hero-worshipped Asian champion Sachin Tendulkar, whose stellar performances had been somewhat tainted by India's mediocre record of 13 Tests without a win.

Australians had admired Tendulkar, mainly from afar, ever since his solitary Test tour when he made two peerless centuries as a teenage prodigy in 1991–92. Other than the World Cup at the end of the same summer and several one-day tournaments on the subcontinent and in New Zealand, Australians had rarely opposed Tendulkar, whose precocious talents had seen him first playing Test cricket from the age of 16.

Just as the Shane Warne–Lara confrontation had been billed as crucial to the series outcome during Australia's world championship tour of the Caribbean in 1995, so was the anticipated battle royale between Warne and Tendulkar – the Sultan of Spin versus the Spin Master.

Tendulkar had prepared for the challenge by practising harder and longer than since his teen years. Specifically he wanted extra practice against wrist-spin. For a fortnight in Bombay, he enlisted a flotilla of leg-spinners, all of whom were asked to bowl for long periods from around the wicket to a deliberately roughed-up patch outside Tendulkar's leg stump. The pocket-sized champion wanted to simulate as closely as possible his upcoming one-on-ones against Warne. And instead of the normal 15-minute sessions, he batted for an hour and then two, and in the middle of the day when the sun was at its fiercest.

On arrival in Mumbai, Tendulkar's home town, for the start of the six-week tour, Australian vice-captain Steve Waugh conceded that Tendulkar could easily be the star of the series, such was his natural class and his ability to see the ball a little earlier than most. But he also said he might be vulnerable to overexpectation, given the incredible pressure to perform in front of the most passionate cricket crowds of them all.

It was a theory which the little Indian master was to disprove within days, when he teed off with a welcoming double century for Bombay before carrying his brilliant form into the Tests and one-day series. No Australian team had ever been ambushed, tortured and trampled quite as comprehensively by one man.

Brandishing his heavyweight 3 lb bat, sponsored by the Indian tyre makers MRF, Tendulkar simply smashed the touring Australians, Warne included.

In a scintillating set of displays which reinstated his No. 1 ranking in world cricket, Tendulkar amassed 1130 runs at an average of 100-plus.

Within days of the start of the three-Test series, Mark Taylor's plan for his bowlers to frustrate Tendulkar by bowling 'dot' balls soon disintegrated. Like Don Bradman years before, Tendulkar assessed line and length in an instant and hit it where he pleased in the ruthless, almost arrogant manner of Viv Richards. He also ran swiftly between wickets and cornered the strike, continuing his carnage at an astonishing rate which left the Australians shaking their heads in admiration.

The Australians capitulated by 179 runs at Chennai and in the mother of all thrashings, by an innings and 219 runs at Calcutta, the country's worst loss in 60 years. Though they hit back at Bangalore to win the dead rubber, it was little consolation. Taylor's unbeaten run was over, with the absence of the injured chief strike bowler McGrath and the inability of a worn-out Warne to contain Tendulkar the damning factors. Taylor repeatedly counselled a frustrated Warne, telling him that he didn't have to win the series by himself and that the Indians were renowned as being the best players of slow bowling in the world, especially at home. 'Warnie expected to knock everyone over on his own,' said Taylor in an interview later with Peter Roebuck. 'But we were very flat; we'd been playing non-stop for 20 months.'

Among the few players to emerge with enhanced reputations were surprise selection Gavin Robertson, who had played only one match for New South Wales in the three previous Sheffield Shield seasons, paceman Michael Kasprowicz who adapted quickly to the requirements of reverse swing and Mark Waugh, whose 153 not out in the third and final Test in extreme temperatures in Bangalore was a matchwinner.

Michael Slater's return for his first internationals in 18 months was important and heralded the beginning of another season as Taylor's regular opening partner. Four players, Robertson (at Chennai), Paul Wilson (Calcutta) and Adam Dale and Darren Lehmann (Bangalore), made their Test debuts. Lehmann's selection was particularly deserved. He was 19 when first chosen in an Australian XII in 1989–90, and despite enormous performances at Sheffield Shield level, had only ever previously been rewarded with one-day selection.

With 98 and 4 in a beaten side at Mumbai and 207 against a Board President's XI in Visakhapatnam, Slater was in peak form for his Test return. But it wasn't until the third Test at Bangalore that he finally came off, with 91 and 42, ensuring his ongoing selection.

Australia's demise in the Tests was surprisingly swift considering the early dogfight at Chennai which saw it lead by 71 runs on a deteriorating wicket. The final hour of the third day, featuring the blazing strokeplay of veteran opener Navjot Sidhu, dramatically changed the match and series fortunes. Consistently crashing Warne down the ground with such raw aggression that the Australian could well have been advised to bowl with a stackhat, the Sikh, underrated pre-tour by the tourists, was a blistering 55 not out at the close, with India 1/100.

While he fell at midwicket early on day four, his dismissal only hastened Australia's demise as the next man in was Tendulkar, who'd fallen for just 4 in uncharacteristic near silence in the first innings.

Beginning in far more circumspect fashion than he had on the opening afternoon, Tendulkar was soon into his stride and played with such majesty that even the Australians applauded. He took over the game as only great players can, in five hours making 155 not out, from just 191 balls. His first 50 took only 64 balls and his second, 61. Eighty of his runs came in boundary shots.

Debutant Robertson, at 31, had conceded •4141• from his first nervous over in Test cricket on day one, and was struck for 4, 6 and 4 in consecutive balls at the height of Tendulkar's hijack. When the Indian master lofted a flagging Warne for 6 over midwicket, the celebrating in the stands was something to behold. The passion was truly amazing, more than 40 000 all dancing in unison.

The Australians couldn't get any air, either to breathe or to cool them down. Ian Healy said even his socks were soaked with sweat. 'It was like standing in a wet oven,' he said.

The pace bowlers were bowling no more than three- and four-over spells as on Tendulkar sailed, seemingly oblivious to the heat or the humidity.

One forward defence against Kasprowicz was timed so sweetly it careered straight past mid-off to the fence. Other times he'd delight in steering the ball to where a fieldsman had just been.

'Cricket doesn't come any better than this,' said Roebuck in the *Age*. 'Sometimes it is best simply to sit back and enjoy.'

Set 348 runs to win, the Australians lost ground late on day four, going to stumps at 3/31 with Taylor, Slater and Greg Blewett all succumbing in the final hour.

By 1.55 p.m. on the last day, India had won, the Australian slump continuing from a lunchtime 7/96 to all out 168, the dual spin of Anil Kumble and Venkatapathy Raju almost as significant as Tendulkar's counter-attacking.

Some questionable umpiring decisions on the fifth morning denied Australia any chance it had of launching a fight, though Ian Healy added 32 not out to his first innings 90. However, the Indians had clearly deserved their victory, their first in 15 months since December, 1996.

Huge crowds, the biggest and most vocal in Taylor's time as captain, witnessed the remarkable second Test at Eden Gardens where the Australians boasted an unbeaten record in five previous Tests.

From the opening over by Javagal Srinath which produced two wickets for only the second time in the 1409-match history of Test cricket, the Australians staggered.

To roars of approval, Slater fell for a sixth-ball duck before Blewett was bowled first ball. The one run on the board was from Srinath's no-ball.

Taylor had stressed the fighting qualities of his team in even the most dire situations. At 4/29 they don't come much blacker.

Steve Waugh scored a game 80, despite acquiring a groin strain which saw him bat with a runner (in the second innings two days later he batted at No. 7 and declined a runner, preferring to hobble his way to 33 in three hours). Ricky Ponting's 60 in the first dig added respectability, but remained the only substantial contributions in an all-out score of 233, boosted late in the day by Robertson, who survived more than two hours for 29, and Kasprowicz, an hour and a half for 25.

Within minutes of the start on day two, with Sidhu once again unleashing some thunderous drives, the Australians knew they were in for the toughest of days. Taylor and Healy, deputising as vice-captain with the injured Waugh off the field, maintained the spirits, but the bowlers, one by one, lost the fight. First-gamer Wilson limped off having bowled only 12 overs, leaving Kasprowicz and Warne to bowl the bulk of the overs. Between them, they sent down 76 overs for 1/269. Robertson was also dealt with harshly, as Tendulkar (79) and Mohammad Azharuddin (163 not out) helped the Indians to 5/633 declared, their highest score against Australia and second highest in all Tests.

The Australians were so stricken that the injured Reiffel, who couldn't throw, was forced to field in the inner ring for much of the innings. It was a nightmare, the low point of Taylor's captaincy reign. By the fourth afternoon it was over, the Australians having been bowled out a second time for 181. Taylor's 45 was top score before he was slickly run out by V.V.S. Laxman at short leg.

It was a humbling defeat and as Malcolm Conn of the *Australian* said, rarely had there been a softer result from a tougher side. The heat had been physically draining and the Australians had failed to adapt to the turning wickets. The batting had been ordinary. After 18 months of continuous touring, the team was screaming for a rest.

Reiffel with shoulder stress and Wilson a groin complaint, returned home early, adding to the widening list of bowlers to succumb, both at home and overseas. Warne's overworked right shoulder was also a problem, but courageously he refused to rest, relishing his team involvement, if not the punishment. In four Tests against the Indians, he'd taken just six wickets at an average of 96. He'd continually had to bowl against the openers, in a stock rather than a shock role, and on the slow wickets was struggling to produce his old zip. Like Reiffel, his shoulder was rebelling against the repetitive nature of bowling and rapidly degenerating. In the third Test he was also to strain a groin, but not before passing Lance Gibbs's record for the most wickets by a slow bowler in Test cricket.

Indian great Bishen Bedi, in an interview with Robert Craddock of the *Herald Sun*, said even great bowlers had to have a bad series sometime. 'Shane is a very good player, but he tried too much variety in Calcutta,' said Bedi. 'There was no pressure build-up. He has got 85 per cent of his wickets through his great leg-break. He should have just concentrated on bowling it over after over.'

The nimble-footed Indians, raised on slow bowling, had carried the attack to Warne from the opening first-class fixture at Mumbai. Not only had Tendulkar shown scant respect, Sidhu and Azharuddin had also handed out some hidings.

The extroverted Warne had continued to be the most in-demand of the Australians, posing for pictures and signing countless autographs. At Visakhapatnam where a promising 13-year-old joined the Australians for a net session, Warne gave him the 700 rupees ($A28) so he could buy himself a bat.

The third Test, on a baked clay, grassless wicket in Bangalore, was again notable for some Tendulkar heroics. He made a whirlwind 177 (with 29 4s and three 6s) and with 31 in the second innings lifted his series aggregate to 441 at an average of 111.

For once, Australia had an answer with Mark Waugh scoring 153 not out, the highest of his 14 Test centuries, despite overnight illness which left him pale and listless in mid-match. In all he batted for five and a half hours and piloted Australia to its first 400 score of the tour, which was crucial in the match fortunes after India collapsed cheaply in the second innings to set Australia 194 for victory.

'I was crook all night,' said Waugh, who was 58 not out coming into day three. 'I had diarrhoea, vomiting and fever and had to call in the team doctor at about 12 o'clock. I didn't think I'd be able to turn up the next morning, but I went down the ground and thought I may as well give it a go and see how I feel. As it turned out I scored nearly 100 runs that day. The conditions were so hot and I was weak and feeling fairly ill. I lost a lot of weight. Taking all that into consideration, it was one of my best innings – not that I can remember a lot about it! I was more or less on automatic pilot. I was trying to conserve my energy and pick the right ball to hit. I didn't want to run too hard between wickets. I knew I wouldn't be able to do that and concentrate on the next ball. It was a matter of working out the best way to cope with being ill.'

Slater's 91 was also timely and in the Indian second innings, Kasprowicz started to wobble the old ball around, having Tendulkar caught and bowled on his way to 5/28, the best return of the tour.

Earlier in the match, Kasprowicz had approached Dennis Lillee and asked if he'd seen a weakness in Tendulkar's make-up. 'No, Michael, as long as you walk off with your pride that's all you can do.'

The Indian spinners sent down 55 of the 58 overs in Australia's second innings but Taylor, determined to finish the series on a high, played with freedom and refused to be intimidated by the cluster of close-in fieldsmen waiting for a bat-pad catch. His 102 not out was chanceless and ensured Australia an eight-wicket victory late on the fourth day. Some wondered if it would be his farewell, but before handing over the captaincy to Steve Waugh for the Pepsi Cup and Coca-Cola Cup triangulars, Taylor said he was keen to tour Pakistan later in the year and, if selected, would like to captain the side. He would not commit himself further than the three-Test series, however, despite the lure of his 100th Test match to begin the Ashes summer of 1998–99.

On his arrival back in Australia, he reinforced his call for more stability within the Australian side, saying the dual captaincy, especially during the 1997–98 home season, had not served Australian cricket's best interests.

'I still maintain that your best cricketers will still play both forms of the game,' Taylor told reporters. 'Stephen is not getting a fair share of the job and I don't think I'm getting a fair share either at the moment.

'The hierarchy of Australian cricket, selectors, Board members and players, need to have a direction. I don't think we really know where each other is going.'

Having called in their one-day reinforcements, including Michael Bevan, the team's most successful specialist batsman, the Australians finished their commitments in India and Sharjah strongly, defeating the Indians in the final of the Pepsi Triangular before losing to them in the final of the Coca Cola Cup in Sharjah.

Surprisingly, Warne played all 10 games, having been given the option by the selectors to continue with the tour or rest his shoulder.

All seemed well until the last matches in Sharjah when he had difficulty throwing the ball after taking a tumble. In the final, his 10 overs cost 61 and India successfully chased 272 to win by six wickets.

Why the selectors hadn't insisted that Warne stop bowling is a mystery. On an examination on his return to Australia, the Victorian was told he'd so stressed his shoulder and surrounding ligaments that without an operation he might only have 50 per cent use of his shoulder for the rest of his life.

Within a month he'd undergone an operation involving the repair of a torn rotator cuff and shoulder cartilage, an operation normally associated with javelin throwers and baseballers. The damage to Warne's shoulder was worse than expected and doctors told Warne that had he played even a few more games on the subcontinent his shoulder would have most likely fallen apart completely, ending his outstanding career.

Belatedly, the ACB said it would substantially upgrade its injury protection policy and implement a strict rotation system for its bowlers at one-day level. Unfortunately for Warne, who didn't know if he'd ever be able to bowl again, it was a decision which should have been taken years previously. As good as he was at both levels of the game, why risk the long-term fitness of the best-performed slow bowler in Test history by playing him in an insignificant series of one-day matches? Why not save him purely for Test match play and if necessary, one-day finals?

The ACB's indecision was to whiplash them into fresh controversy within a year when Warne, anxious to protect his Test place with the snowballing success of Stuart MacGill, came back prematurely and performed so poorly that he became the highest-profiled player ever to be dropped from the Australian Test team.

Australia's other injured strike bowler, McGrath, had also had off-season surgery to deaden the nerve responsible for his run of groin-related complaints. Having played only three of the six 1997–98 Tests, McGrath had also missed the tours of India and Sharjah, but hoped his rehabilitation would be speedy enough to allow him to tour Pakistan, from September.

# SEVENTEEN

---

# CHASING
# THE
# DON

---

*'They needed Steve Waugh on the* Titanic.
*They'd probably have all survived if he'd
been there.'*

---

IN LESS THAN TWO calendar years, Australia had played in 24 Tests, 52 one-day internationals and opposed every major team in the world from Karachi to Kowloon. Little wonder there'd been casualties, form swings and retirements. The opportunity for a four-month break approaching the Commonwealth Games, or almost five for the Test specialists named purely for the spring tour of Pakistan, was long overdue.

For those all-rounders who had figured in most of the extended campaign, like the Waugh twins and Shane Warne, there was no place like home. While most put their feet up, Warne busied himself overseeing the final renovations to his $1 million extended double-decker at Brighton Beach, Paul Reiffel shifted house and Stuart MacGill took an extended European holiday.

The county circuit was again popular, with seven fulfilling English contracts, including Test batting trio Michael Slater, Justin Langer and Darren Lehmann. The only bowler who had seriously contemplated continued first-class cricket – before succumbing to shoulder stress problems – was Reiffel, unsure of his long-term position in Australia's best XI.

Mark Taylor's normal preparation for a season still four months away was to take his family up the New South Wales coast on holiday, have a few beers with his golfing mates and put on weight.

However, his highs and lows of 1997 and 1998 had hit a raw nerve. He'd already forfeited the captaincy of the one-day team and after 96 Tests, despite a century at his last start in Bangalore, was feeling vulnerable. While he had committed himself to the three-Test tour of Pakistan, where he'd first captained at Test level four years previously, there was no guarantee his batting problems would not suddenly reappear – especially against the world-renowned and still-lethal Pakistani pace pair of Wasim Akram and Waqar Younis, backed by the young colt Shoaib Akhtar, who Pakistanis claimed was faster again.

Taylor didn't want a repeat of the trial-by-media he had had to endure in the first six months of '97. He'd been carried once and had too much pride in his achievements to play his forthcoming 100th Test match by default. He'd *earn* his place for the Ashes summer, just like the other five batting specialists.

For years, he'd spent at least part of his winter with Kevin Chevell, a Penrith-based personal trainer, renowned for his work throughout the 90s with leading Sydney-based cricketers and sporting teams. Since becoming Australia's captain, time restraints demanded that these were only short stints. This time, however, he committed his entire four-month break to improving his fitness to a level he had once enjoyed when exploding onto the international scene with more than 800 runs on his initial tour of England in 1989. He wanted to give himself every possible chance, not only of surviving, but of scoring runs regularly once again.

'We'd train most mornings for at least two or two and a half hours each time,' said Chevell. 'He got flogged . . . [but] he wanted it. There was unfinished business in his life.'

With an equally focused Glenn McGrath for company, Taylor spent the next 16 weeks whipping his body into shape, lifting weights, cycling, rowing and running. Everything was done at pace and at an exhausting intensity.

'Their pride and fighting spirit didn't allow them to give in,' said Chevell. 'Whatever it took, no matter how tough the routine, they went for it.'

Taylor and McGrath would be up at dawn and into their routines before most Sydneysiders were even contemplating breakfast.

Central in the Chevell workout philosophy is the need to have the heart pumping at 90–95 per cent of its absolute maximum for up to two hours each session. The work, especially early, was hellish, but the players refused to buckle. 'We always worked flat out in the zone, looking to challenge every single fibre and not just physically, but mentally as well,' Chevell said. 'Having got through something like that, the player automatically has fresh belief in himself. And that's the difference between the players who succeed and the ones who just exist.

'There were many motivations for Mark to do the work: captaincy issues, indifferent form and the exaggerated criticism of his place in the Australian team. He's tough and he may look and sound pretty good on the outside, but he's a man just like you and me. He's got feelings.'

Chevell had to remind Taylor and McGrath that they were, in fact, team-mates and instead of fighting one another, should be encouraging each other to keep going. 'They were so intense and so fiercely competitive,' he said. 'I'd have to say to them: "Let each other know that you're behind them." It didn't matter if one won one day and the other the next. They were showing each other loyalty and support.

'Mark has never been one to say he's any sort of athlete, but when he left me and he was ready for that '98 season, he was a world-class level athlete. He was sharp.'

Dubbed 'The King of Pain' by one ex-pupil, former Australian international Wayne Holdsworth, Chevell was proud of the achievements. Within 10 weeks, Taylor shed 6 kg of body fat. After 16, he'd lost 10 kg and gained 2–3 kg of muscle tissue. He remained 'Tubby' to his team-mates, but in name alone. His chest was flat and firm and his suits no longer fitted. He was wearing clothes he hadn't worn in years, triggering, incidentally, more criticism over his dress sense even his closest mates claimed had gone wrong at birth!

On return to the nets with the NSW state squad, Taylor was sharper and more in control. He was seeing the ball earlier and finishing each session fresher. By pushing himself to new limits, he was invigorated and looking with fresh enthusiasm at Australia's upcoming challenges. He had a ring of confidence which was to enable him to reach new peaks and within months allow him to share one of the most famous batting records of them all.

McGrath, too, was ready to relaunch his career after a lost 10 months in 1997–98. Having Chevell as a personal fitness coach helped redefine his goals and in time even Dennis Lillee's great mark of 355 wickets, the most wickets ever taken by an Australian fast bowler, may be his.

AFTER LENGTHY CONSULTATIONS, including several meetings with Taylor, who reaffirmed his opposition to the dual captaincy principle, the Australian Cricket Board revamped its 1998–99 season's Test and one-day programs and separated the Tests from the limited-overs component of the draw.

The five Ashes Tests were scheduled to finish early in the New Year before the start of an expanded one-day triangular series, involving England and Sri Lanka.

A successful tour of Pakistan was the immediate priority, however, especially with Australia's failure to win a series there in almost 40 years. McGrath had hoped to return to cricket via the Commonwealth Games tournament, which saw Australia, the hot favourites, reduced to Silver Medal status in the final against South Africa. However, an 11th-hour soft tissue injury forced him to delay his comeback for a month.

Warne, unavailable for both Kuala Lumpur and Pakistan, had admitted his insecurities about his future. Initially he'd hoped his rehabilitation would allow him to be ready for the start of the Ashes campaign. Now he wasn't sure if he'd be able to play before the autumn tour of the West Indies. He'd made himself available for Victoria, but purely as a batsman. The only other net work he was doing was as an adviser, and he found he couldn't complete all of the aerobic work.

McGrath's presence was a comfort. Like Taylor, he was superbly fit again and had bowled with good pace at the trials. Since the premature retirement of Craig McDermott, McGrath had been a magnificent leader for Australia, his intimidating on-field presence integral to Australia's buoyant record. No player had been missed more than McGrath in India.

While he'd played 96 Tests and was due to play his 100th match in Brisbane come the start of the Ashes campaign, Taylor refused to commit himself past Pakistan, saying that players his age had no option but to look short-term.

'When you get to the age of 33, 34 and beyond, it's something you tend to review more regularly than you would at 22 or 23,' he said.

Asked how close he had come to standing down after the 1–2 reverse in India in March, he said: 'It's not something I'd throw in easily and I wouldn't like to put a figure or a percentage on how close I've been. It's something I think about.

'I think about my role as Australian captain regularly because I take it that seriously.'

Taylor admitted his form had been mediocre for much of 1997 and any repeated slumps could never again be tolerated. 'You've always got to perform as a player,' he said. 'Last year [1997] I got carried a little bit and didn't have a good year.

'This year I may have carried some other players. That's the way a team works. [But] no one has a right to hang on to the job until they get kicked out,' he said. 'You have to make sure you're doing the best thing you can for Australian cricket and that's what I've tried to do all the time I've had the job.'

A double-century by Slater coming off only a mediocre season of county cricket, and nine wickets to Stuart MacGill in the tour opener at Karachi, was a heartening start. MacGill remained relaxed about replacing the injured Warne. While he hadn't played a Test in India the previous March, he'd been a willing worker in the nets, spinning his leg-break sharply and fine-tuning his variety, including the perfecting of a second, harder-to-pick wrong'un.

All the batsmen (bar Taylor) got a start in the warm-up fixture at Karachi, and it was with high expectations that the Australians went to Rawalpindi for the first of the three Tests, looking for revenge after being so narrowly beaten four years earlier.

The resurfacing of cricket's betting scandal was a complicating factor, particularly for Mark Waugh, who was one of three players allegedly offered bribes by Pakistani captain Saleem Malik in 1994. Taylor urged each of his 14-man squad to remain tunnel-visioned and focused. As a precaution, a Brisbane security guard had joined Australia's touring entourage to provide protection, particularly for Taylor and Waugh, who were due to front Pakistan's match-fixing inquiry.

Asked about the bombardment of bribery publicity, Taylor told reporters: 'I really hope it just toughens "Junior" [Waugh] up. He's come over here to play cricket but unfortunately, that's not all that's surrounding him for the last week or two.'

The new-look Australian attack for the first Test consisted of McGrath, MacGill, Damien Fleming (playing his first Test for three years) and cricket journeyman Colin Miller, who in honour of his first Test at the age of 34, had his hair cut super short and dyed snowy blond. None of the quartet had figured in the Indian Tests earlier in the year.

From a first-day 8/147, Pakistan reached a respectable 269 with opener Saeed Anwar ninth out for 145. In his first overseas Test, MacGill, with 5/66, created an immediate presence, enjoying the conditions, tailor-made for spin.

Taylor had impressed on his players the need to win sessions, and having dominated much of the opening day's fortunes, the Australians fought back on the second after Taylor was out for 3 and Justin Langer and Mark Waugh for ducks.

Four years previously in Rawalpindi, Akram had bowled as furious an opening spell as in recent memory. He was similarly intimidating this time, even on the slowish wicket, being on a hat-trick after having Taylor caught behind and Langer lbw to consecutive deliveries.

Steve Waugh and Slater had been saviours at Rawalpindi in '94 and they again combined to lift the Australians when another key wicket would have exposed Ian Healy and the lower order.

Slater was typically adventurous, advancing fearlessly at the finger spinners, while Waugh showed commendable calm and punished the loose ball with ruthless authority. He could have been out at 81, at slip to the bowling of Saqlain, but deserved his luck and along with Slater reached his century as the Australians retrieved lost ground.

Slater punched the air, kissed his cap and generally showed all of his old delight on making his century, his eighth overall and first since 1995–96. Waugh's 100 inspired Test selector Allan Border to tell his Foxtel audience: 'They needed Steve Waugh on the *Titanic*. They'd probably have all survived if he'd been there.'

Thanks to Waugh's 157 and Darren Lehmann's 98, Australia reached 513 before bowling Pakistan out a second time for just 145 to give the Aussies a historic innings victory, their first in Pakistan for 39 years.

'Previously we've found too many reasons not to play well over here,' Taylor told pressmen. 'Over a long period of time, our thinking hasn't been right.'

He said the win, at the start of such an important campaign, was almost as crucial as Jamaica in 1995 and Johannesburg in 1997 when the Australians stamped their authority as Test cricket's No. 1-ranked side.

'We took some punts in this game,' he said. 'We sat down two days before the Test and after about an hour's deliberation, we still had 14 players to choose from.'

He said the Australian selectors – coach Geoff Marsh, deputy-captain Steve Waugh and himself – had eventually decided to play the conditions. The introduction of Miller, who took three wickets in a highly successful debut, may have been seen as a shock move, but as few of the Pakistanis knew much about him, it was a gamble worth taking.

Fresh from his annual off-season stint playing weekends with the

Harleon cricket club in Holland, Miller had seen his career blossom since adding orthodox off-spin to his arsenal. He took a wicket in his debut over of medium pace before reverting, in his fifth, to briskish off-spin. In the second innings he induced an edge from Akram which gave Healy, standing up, his record 356th dismissal in Test cricket. 'It has been an amazing dream come true for me,' Miller said, 'one which I thought had passed me by until I started bowling spin. It has opened up my whole career.'

Taylor said the Australians had come to Pakistan aiming to win 66 per cent of their matches. 'Now we only have to win 50 per cent. If we win at Peshawar we're home.'

Pakistan's gamble of playing three spin specialists in Rawalpindi had backfired. Waqar Younis was still nursing an elbow injury which had shortened his English county season and much was made of Shoaib's first appearance, in Peshawar. Akram dropped out on the morning of the match with a throat infection and Shoaib, clocked at 156 km/h in South Africa earlier in the year, found himself heading a highly inexperienced attack. It was only his fifth Test. His new-ball partner, the open-chested seamer Muhammad Zahid, was in his fourth. He was quick, and, like Shoaib, had never previously opposed Australia.

Winning the toss and batting first, Taylor emerged with Slater in 90° heat, both sporting black armbands, as a mark of respect at the passing, in Melbourne, of 80-year-old ex-Test captain Ian Johnson, one of Don Bradman's famous Invincibles.

Having missed out in Rawalpindi, Taylor was almost out without scoring in the opening overs when he inside-edged a Shoaib express just wide of his leg stump to the fine-leg boundary. Soon afterwards, on 18, he lifted a half-strength drive at Mushtaq Ahmed to Saeed Anwar at short cover only to see the catch inexplicably grassed. Seven runs later, Anwar offended a second time, Taylor again the beneficiary.

Shoaib was as fast as anyone in the world on the first morning. Sprinting to the wicket energetically from almost 40 metres, he had all the Australians ducking. Not only was he quick, he was consistently quick and, despite the flatness of the wicket, commanded immediate respect.

He dismissed Slater early and could easily have had Langer lbw first ball, before losing a little of his sting when forced to operate around the wicket after being warned twice by umpire Steve Bucknor, in his second and fifth overs, for running up the line of the left-hander's off stump.

His target area, especially when operating to the left-handers from wide on the return crease, was so small he struggled to make either Taylor or Langer play as often as the great fast bowlers.

Taylor could have been run out at 55 when Zahid, snoozing at mid-off, missed the stumps with a rushed throw from close range. While Taylor was living dangerously, he was playing positively and with the determination of a captain wanting to cement his team's ascendancy.

Finally his innings blossomed when he greeted a new spell from Shoaib by twice pulling him to the midwicket boundary. Another pull shot cleared the fence at square leg and by stumps, when bad light brought a premature halt, Taylor was looking as commanding as he had for several years, having made 112 and added an unbeaten 206 with Langer (97).

'It's hard to take five months off and just jump straight back in where you left off,' Taylor told reporters. 'But then your confidence comes; you start hitting sixes and all sorts of things.'

Langer was equally satisfied. Recalled as Australia's No. 3, he'd rated being given the benefit of the doubt in the desperately close lbw appeal against Shoaib as a career turning point. Asked how he felt as the Pakistanis appealed as one, 'I thought, "Test career over for this young man",' he said. 'Two first ball ducks in a row. Where do you go from there?'

As well as Taylor had played, presenting the full blade to everything after lunch on day one, there was little hint of what was to come, especially as his last truly-mammoth score, 219 at Trent Bridge, had come almost a decade earlier. However, he was feeling surprisingly fresh and keen to further consolidate Australia's formidable position.

After Langer's early demise for 116, he dominated a third-wicket stand of 123 with Mark Waugh, scoring at a ratio of 2 to 1 and at lunch, after the opening session had extended to three full hours because of the opening day's early finish, Taylor was 215, having scored 103 for the session, another career first.

Shoaib and Zahid were not nearly as menacing as on the first day, Zahid being used sparingly after complaining of a groin strain.

Having passed 7000 Test runs and his highest Test and first-class score, Taylor's monumental knock saw Australia to 500 and a potential declaration.

Resorting to a floppy hat after tea, his concentration hardly flagged. He could have been run out at 257 and 270 by Saleem Malik, but the Pakistani's attempted direct hits both narrowly missed.

His triple-century, via a fierce square cut against a near-exhausted Mushtaq, was greeted generously, the Australian players regularly ferrying Taylor drinks and urging him to maintain his focus.

'During my innings there were several occasions when I felt tired,' Taylor said in his foreword to Chevell's book, *Rebuilding Your Body, Your Mind and Your Life*. 'But, just when I was about to give it away I'd think to myself: "Hang on. I don't feel as tired as I did when I was in the gym with Kev. I'm going to keep going."'

He passed Bob Cowper's 307 as the biggest Australian Test score in more than 30 years and Bob Simpson's 311 as the highest by an Australian captain. Not since 1989 in England had he played with such command.

The Pakistanis were wilting, bowling to defensive, restrictive fields, willing for stumps to come.

In the final over, Taylor joined Don Bradman on his all-time high 334 and a firm clip to midwicket from the last ball just failed to bypass Ijaz Ahmed, a notably suspect fieldsman, who this time was able to make a fine save. The Australians formed a guard of honour for Taylor as he walked off, still with spring in his step. Pakistani coach Javed Miandad offered a handshake and a cool drink. It had been an extraordinary 12-hour knock in which he'd faced 564 balls and hit 33 4s and a 6.

'I just kept on playing,' he told Australian pressmen. 'I kept telling myself I would be mad to throw it away. I remember Allan Border telling me when I made 219 nine years ago that I threw it away that day and he was right. I kept thinking about that and kept playing the ball.

'In the last over I knew I was on the same score as Sir Donald, but I didn't want to throw it away. The last couple of years I've had some tough times. Now the good times are here I wanted to make full use of it.'

The previous night, back home in Sydney, Mark's parents Tony and Judy Taylor were having a meal out at the Wentworthville leagues club and afterwards, as they were about to head home, had stopped to watch some of the cricket coming in via cable television. 'Here was this very recognisable face on a very large screen on about 80 or 90 at the time,' said Tony Taylor. 'We settled down and thought it would be nice if he could get a 100. When he did, we went home. We had no idea he was going to go on and on like he did.'

There was overwhelming support from within and outside the Australian team for Taylor to continue into a third day and try to make the 41 runs he needed to equal Brian Lara's all-time Test high of 375. That night he received several calls from India, with fans urging him to go on. One man who'd never even played cricket sent a fax from Australia telling Taylor that people would soon forget the result of the Test but would always remember his record knock. Test selector Border later wrote in *Inside Edge* magazine: 'If I'd been captain with a player on that score, I'd have said, "Look, you've got half an hour. See what you can do."'

The Pakistanis, who covet records, were also expectant, thousands being there for the start of the third day, only to see the Australian innings details taken from the scoreboard inside the hour before the resumption. Taylor had declared, wanting to win the match first and foremost and believing that, with 599 runs on the board, the Australians had more than enough runs to maintain a high level of pressure on the Pakistanis for the rest of the match.

Explaining his decision to remain anchored on 334 with The Don, he said: 'It will be nice to be bracketed with Sir Donald. It will be

Ian Healy's quest to be the first wicketkeeper to 400 dismissals has seen him practise at all sorts of locations, including this common in St Vincent in the Caribbean in 1995.

*Ray Titus*

Curtly Ambrose's intimidating 'throat' ball sees Steve Waugh swaying for cover at Trinidad in 1994–95.

*Ray Titus*

Australia hold the Ashes yet again, after Devon Malcolm becomes Glenn McGrath's 36th victim in the series, via a Mark Waugh catch at Trent Bridge in 1997.

*Patrick Eager*

On the balcony at Trent Bridge, Shane Warne celebrates as only he can, after the 1997 Australians secure the series win against England.

*David Munden/Sportsline*

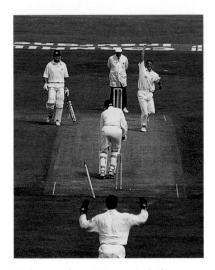

With more than 550 runs, including a Test-best 199 at Headingley, Matthew Elliott was Australia's most prolific batsman in the 1997 Ashes contests.

*David Munden/Sportsline*

Mark Taylor's return to form at Edgbaston was greeted with acclaim and almost turned the Test.

*David Munden/Sportsline*

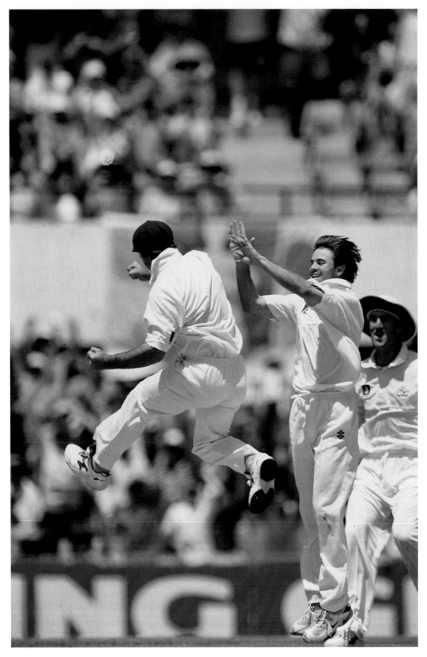

Ricky Ponting's fielding reached a new exalted level in 1997–98. One of four direct-hit run-outs in the internationals included this one, on Jacques Kallis, in the Sydney Test.

*Stephen Laffer*

Mark Taylor's diplomacy and ambassadorial skills with the media were never more needed than during the first section of the '97 tour when he and Australia struggled for form. He's pictured here with David Gower.

*Sergio Dionisio*/Australian Cricket *magazine*

Mark Taylor batting at the WACA Ground in what proved to be his farewell series, in 1998–99.

*Stephen Laffer*

Steve Waugh, Shane Warne and the Aussies enjoy holding the Frank Worrell Trophy again at Antigua, but it took a titanic fight. The Aussies had to come back from 1–2 down after the Brian Lara-inspired Windies recorded victories at Jamaica and Barbados.

*Ken Piesse*

After a debut Test in Adelaide the season before, Stuart MacGill played a frontline role in England's demise in 1998–99. In Sydney, when joined in the team by a fit-again Shane Warne, he claimed 12 wickets.

*Stephen Laffer*

The Australians herald Mark Taylor's fabulous triple century at Peshawar.

*Keith Beckley/Allsport*

Mark Taylor's 100th Test, 1998–99. Fifteen minutes later he was in the middle, on his way to 46 in his final appearance at the 'Gabba.

*Stephen Laffer*

Dropped late on the opening day of the first Ashes Test in Brisbane, Steve Waugh motored to 112 on the second, sharing a 187-run sixth-wicket stand with close mate Ian Healy.

*Stephen Laffer*

Hours before being officially inducted as Australia's new Test captain in 1999, Steve Waugh admitted to having done little all morning other than watch cartoons with his daughter Rosalie, an anecdote enjoyed by a packed press gallery gathered at VCA House in Jolimont.

*Ken Rainsbury*/Australian Cricket *magazine*

the only chance I have ever to be compared with him. It would have been nice to get one more run and the [Australian] record, but I already hold it with him and that will do me.'

Making an attempt at Lara's world record was not a genuine consideration, he believed, as it would have taken him too long for the required 41 runs and the Pakistanis would have deliberately slowed their over rate to the detriment of Australia's hopes to force a result.

The wicket, however, was to be the ultimate winner, Pakistan replying with 9/580 declared before Australia batted out the final day, Taylor again in rare form, with 92, giving himself 426 runs for the match in 15 extraordinary hours. Only one other player, England's Graham Gooch, had scored more runs in a Test and only one other, Pakistan's Hanif Mohammad, had batted longer.

'His effort was phenomenal,' said Steve Waugh. 'To concentrate for such an extended time was fantastic, but I thought the aggressive way in which he batted made the knock even better. He was back to his best form of 1989, always looking for runs and always taking to the bowlers with a very straight bat.'

Given his appearance in court only days before the Test, it had been an extraordinary knock of skill and focus, bringing to mind the famous Courtney Walsh T-shirt inscription, 'Form is temporary, class is permanent'. While the game was drawn, he had no regrets about his declaration, instead preferring to concentrate on the third Test and clinching the win or draw that Australia needed to complete his team's first success in Pakistan and 10th series win in 11 since he first became captain in 1994.

The National Stadium at Karachi had long been a stronghold for Pakistani Test cricket. In 33 matches there, Pakistan had won 17 and drawn 16. Since 1956–57, it had beaten Australia five times in seven starts.

A fit-again Akram counteracted the withdrawal of Mushtaq, who had struggled all summer with a knee problem. The veteran left-arm paceman struck both Taylor and Slater during his furious opening spell, before Aamir Sohail reverted to spin after just seven overs. Taylor, with 16, was first out, but Slater, looking as convincing as at any other time in the series, held the innings together on a difficult wicket which saw one leg-break take off and strike Pakistani wicketkeeper Moin Khan in the side of the face.

Slater had deserved a century, but at 96 fell to the flight of Arshad Khan, being stranded looking for a lofted off-drive down the ground. While criticised by some for poor shot selection, Slater's adventure had been instrumental in Australia reaching 6/207 at stumps. An all-out score of 280 was enough to allow a 28-run first-innings lead, thanks to McGrath's 5/66 and MacGill's 3/64.

Akram again bowled superbly, without luck, in the Australian second innings. Taylor's 64 and Langer's 51 were sturdy contributions in heatwave conditions.

The wicket had baked into a batting paradise and after initial problems with Akram, Mark Waugh accelerated to his 15th Test century, with Akram off the ground suffering heat exhaustion.

By batting more than four sessions, including the entire fourth day's play, the Australians had established an unassailable 419-run lead.

'I'm very pleased. Today was going to be a tough day, but we didn't have a bad session,' said Taylor.

Miller's three quick wickets on the fifth morning ended any slim chance Pakistan had of forcing a win. Had Taylor been able to hang on to a sharp chance at slip from the bowling of McGrath, centurion Ijaz Ahmed snr would also have been back in the pavilion cheaply. He was missed again at 60, a rare stumping blemish by Healy shortly before tea, but the miss was inconsequential, the game being called off early. Pakistan had defended their proud Karachi record and forced a draw – but without being able to square the series.

The first Australian captain to win in Pakistan since Richie Benaud in 1959–60, Taylor said the Australians would have liked to finish 2–0, given their series dominance, but the Pakistanis, when cornered, had showed grit and courage in emerging with a draw. At one stage McGrath sent down six maiden overs in a row as the locals desperately tried to keep their wickets intact.

'One of the big things about the amount of cricket being played is that it emphasises the good and bad aspects of form,' said ex-coach

Bob Simpson on ABC Radio. 'It accentuates a bad run, but once you're on a roll, you can do almost anything. The way Mark came back not only took a lot of courage and skill, but also a tremendous amount of endurance and concentration.'

Taylor said any Australian win without Warne had to be rated highly. The bowlers had come through and the top-order batting, a weakness in India, had been far more stable. 'Usually you say that your bowlers win you the series, but our batsmen won this,' Taylor told Ron Reed of the *Herald Sun*. 'After 39 years of picking players who deserve to be included and being wrong all the time, we decided to go for horses for courses. We picked the best players for the conditions and it worked.'

Having seen their mantle questioned as unofficial world champions after their loss in India seven months earlier, the Australians could again claim, without hesitation, to be the No. 1 Test team in the world. Coach Geoff Marsh had wanted others to step up and share some of the responsibility the veterans had been carrying for years. Slater at the head of the order and MacGill, substituting for Warne, had been particularly effective. And Taylor, with a spectacular series average of 128.25, had reignited his career in spectacular style. As always, his captaincy was almost impossible to fault in sometimes difficult circumstances. There would be a 100th Test match to play after all.

**MARK TAYLOR'S BEST TEST SERIES**

| Runs | Ave | Opponent | Year |
| --- | --- | --- | --- |
| 839 | 83.90 | England | 1989 |
| 513 | 128.25 | Pakistan | 1998–99 |
| 479 | 59.88 | NZ & S. Af. | 1997–98 |
| 471 | 47.10 | England | 1994–95 |
| 441 | 49.00 | West Indies | 1990–91 |
| 428 | 42.80 | England | 1993 |
| 422 | 46.88 | India | 1991–92 |

# EIGHTEEN

## A PROUD FAREWELL

*BRW magazine had listed Taylor's income
in 1997 as $990 000.
And that was expected to increase markedly
given his new star status.*

ONE OF MARK TAYLOR'S FEARS approaching what proved to be his
Australian farewell was that the team might have peaked in Pakistan
and might not play as well on their return home against a re-energised
opposition clearly stronger than in the immediate past. Alec Stewart
was a world-rated new captain and had led a come-from-behind 2–1
victory against the South Africans, his gritty second innings century
at Old Trafford in mid-series central in England's storming finish. Ex-
captain Mike Atherton remained resolute and committed at the head
of the order, strike bowler Darren Gough had regained his form and
fitness and deputy-captain Nasser Hussain was one of the batting
newcomers undaunted by reputation or the prospect of an old-
fashioned scrap.

Australia's one-day commitments on the subcontinent meant that
many of the potential first Test team, including the Waugh twins and
Glenn McGrath, did not return to Australia until just a week before
Brisbane. Publicly Taylor was unconcerned. Privately he would have

far preferred for the players to have had access to first-class matchplay and their normal home routines, rather than again being subject to the exhausting one-day round-robin of travelling and playing with little time off in foreign parts.

He reacted warily to reports of Shane Warne's first bowling stint since April – six overs in an early-October Melbourne club match. He urged caution, saying Australian cricket needed a fit Warne rather than one who risked breaking down attempting a premature return, no matter how enticing the prospect of seeing him return in time for the final Ashes Tests in Melbourne and Sydney. Representing St Kilda, Warne had taken a wicket during the first over of his comeback – Geelong's Rohan Sadler, who was stumped third ball by Saints' wicketkeeper Jason Jacoby at the Junction Oval. He was to repeat his success in Victoria's Mercantile Mutual game against a Taylor-led New South Wales, bowling a first-up maiden before all-rounder Scott Thompson was caught going for a big shot down the ground. His spin coach Terry Jenner refused to rule Warne out of the Ashes summer, but said he needed to work like he'd done in the past and put the work into his shoulder all over again, just as if he were a rookie taking his first steps in the major leagues.

'What's holding him back is now more of a mental thing than anything else,' Jenner said. 'Bowling 30 or so balls in the nets or a couple of five- and six-over spells in a one-day game is a start. But if he wants to play in a Test, he needs to be capable of bowling 30 overs and come back the next day ready to go again. Even for Shane, right now that's a very hard ask.'

Having won five Ashes series in a row since 1989 and coming off its Pakistan triumph, Australia was an odds-on favourite for the first Test. It was Taylor's 100th in his 11 years as an international, and only 18 others, including six opening batsmen, had achieved the feat. Four were Australian: Allan Border, David Boon, Ian Healy and Steve Waugh.

To mark the occasion, Taylor had his family join him in Brisbane. His parents and many of his oldest mates were also present. Several tour parties from interstate also shared in the moment, including 20 of the most ardent Taylor fans travelling with Melbourne cricket buff Kevin Dale's National Network Travel group. They considered it a highlight of their Test week to dine in mid-match in the same restaurant as Taylor, his family and friends.

Despite being either captain or an important member of the side throughout the first 10 years of his international career, Taylor did not enjoy the same high profile as other leading Australian sportsmen. But Pakistan changed everything. Everywhere he went, from cricketing places to milk bars and even his son's school, he was stopped and warmly congratulated for Australia's outstanding achievements and in particular, for his 334. 'I didn't realise how special it was making a Test 300 until I got back home,' he told reporters.

He was honoured by Channel Nine via its *This Is Your Life* program and featured on the front cover of *Time* magazine. He was the centre of frenetic marketing activity from personal sponsors such as Melbourne bat makers Puma/Millichamp who planned a top-grade '334' bat, all bearing the Taylor signature, through to those producing limited-edition posters and wine releases. *BRW* magazine had listed his income in 1997 as $990 000 and that was expected to increase markedly given his new star status.

Just 18 months before, coming into the opening Test in Birmingham, his career was meandering. Even Taylor had wondered when it would finish. Now he was being feted like a pop star.

Asked what was the foundation of his success, he said, 'I think I've been able to play badly and make runs and that's probably what I forgot about before England last year. I've never been a super graceful player, but I've been able to make runs whether I'm hitting them in the middle every time or squirting them past gully. There have been days when I've walked out, feeling magnificent, hit two or three shots in the middle and then got out caught spectacularly somewhere. And you think: "Gee, I've been unlucky today." Other days I walk out there and look terrible for an hour, two, even three or four hours, but it's never worried me. I've just thought my job is to make runs and I'm still out here. That's what the game is all about.'

Taylor admitted to some nerves. But that was only natural. 'If you're not nervous, you're probably not thinking enough about it. You probably don't care enough about it.'

England was unbeaten on tour coming to Brisbane, with batting specialists Hussain, Graham Thorpe and Mark Ramprakash all having made 100s in the lead-ups. Gough had 10 wickets in two initial first-class games while the responsibility accorded left-armer Alan Mullally, who'd figured years earlier in a Sheffield Shield final for Western Australia as a teenager, was an indicator of his position of importance in England's pace plans.

Taylor's milestone had cornered much of the publicity and even 15 minutes before opening the batting, he was involved in a presentation from ACB chief Denis Rogers.

It was a relief when the cricket started, and only after padding up fifth ball to Gough and being fortunate to survive the thunderous lbw appeal did Taylor appear to truly focus and start to move his feet with any purpose.

Just as in 1994–95 and again in 1997, he'd reinforced at the team dinner the importance of a good start to the series. Teams which won first-up were rarely headed. While he was to make only 46 in three hours, he held out England's four-pronged pace attack when the pitch was at its most helpful. Australia was to make almost 500, Steve Waugh and Ian Healy both scoring 100s and Damien Fleming a breezy 71. Only a thunderstorm of a severity rarely seen, even in tropical Brisbane, saved the Englishmen. Stuart MacGill threatened to run through the lower order in Warne-like fashion after trapping Hussain lbw with a pearler of a googly. Taylor's second innings duck, his very first in Test cricket on home soil, was the only other downer as Australia stamped an immediate authority.

Following successive victories in Perth and Adelaide, by mid-December the Ashes had been retained, Fleming and the recalled Jason Gillespie sharing 16 wickets at the WACA Ground and Fleming and McGrath 11 in Adelaide.

MacGill, controversially omitted for an extra paceman in Perth, had returned for the third Test and formed an effective dual spin attack with Miller, who captured five wickets for the game, operating off his short run.

Perth was a low-scoring game on a typically pacy wicket. Adelaide was more batsman-friendly and produced two centuries, an unbeaten 179 from Justin Langer in the first innings and 103 from Michael Slater in the second.

With 198 runs in six hits, including two half-centuries, Taylor hadn't been as prolific as in Pakistan, but was still playing with assurance. Significantly, he hadn't once been dismissed by Gough, England's No. 1 strike bowler.

Leading into the fourth Test, Taylor announced he'd be making himself available for the autumn tour of the West Indies. 'I'm still enjoying myself, the team is playing well with me as captain and provided those things are maintained I'll keep going,' he told reporters after Australia had completed its fielding training on Christmas Eve.

He wasn't prepared to predict if Melbourne would be his last Boxing Day Test match. 'A year is too long,' he said. 'There's West Indies, Sri Lanka, Zimbabwe and then India and Pakistan next year. There's too many games between now and then. I'll just see what happens over the next six months.'

Part of the motivation, he said, was to improve his career average of just 28 against the West Indies, compared with 44 overall. 'I was picked to play for Australia in 1989 because everyone assumed I was going to be a very good player of fast bowling. I think I've proved that throughout my career, yet the one side I haven't played well against has been the West Indies. They've been my one bogey side . . . I'll be going over there just trying to relax and trying to play the way I have played against every other side.'

Taylor's decision was a boost for team stability and was greeted with relief, especially by the Australian Cricket Board chiefs, who had been embarrassed earlier in the month by the ongoing Pakistan bribery affair which saw high-profile pair Warne and Mark Waugh apologise for their involvement with an Indian bookmaker.

Until his Melbourne press conference, there had been increasing speculation that the final Test in Sydney would be his last. He'd conceded years earlier that ideally he'd like to finish in Australia – and on his terms. However, by extending his career past the immediate Australian season and into autumn, it could be that he was committing for another 12 months, rather than just three.

The Melbourne Test, his 49th as captain, saw him move into outright second place among Australian Test leaders, behind Allan Border with 93 games as skipper. He also equalled Border's world record of 156 catches when he caught Dean Headley from the bowling of McGrath.

Again he won the toss, for the ninth time in 10 Ashes Tests. There was no elaborate plan to his good fortune. He'd used a different coin each time and Stewart insisted on again calling 'heads'.

Australia's 70-run first innings lead was set up by Steve Waugh's unbeaten 122, his 17th Test century. Fifteen of these had come in the first innings of the match. He was 77 not out when joined by Australian No. 10 MacGill, who survived some early luck to make an invaluable 43, matching his senior partner virtually run for run.

Waugh's was a chanceless knock, one of his best in Australia, and it even saw him reach his 100 with a hook shot, skied high over square leg against Darren Gough, who had been timed earlier in the day at 143 km/h (more than 90 mph).

Waugh was particularly delighted and showed rare elation as he responded to an outstanding reception. Upstairs in the Legends Stand, many of Don Bradman's Invincibles were gathered, enjoying the moment as much as everyone else.

Waugh said afterwards he had been inspired by the presence of eight of the greatest team of all. 'In 50 years this team wants to be remembered as a great team as well,' he said.

McGrath's suspended $2000 fine for sledging Mullally at the conclusion of England's second innings was a rare occasion when a Taylor-led player had overstepped the mark and commanded an official rebuke. Referee John Reid considered that the sometimes-volatile Australian had brought the game into disrepute after his mid-pitch outburst.

Coming off five ducks in six innings, Mullally swung lustily for an invaluable 16 before being caught and bowled by McGrath, his 199th Test wicket.

The fourth-innings target of 175, after England had been bowled out a second time for 244, seemed comfortable enough. The wicket was benign and there was still a day and a half to play.

But once again, as so often has happened when chasing seemingly moderate fourth-innings scores, the Australians faltered. After Slater virtually walked when struck in front by Headley, and Taylor skied a hook shot to fine-leg, England suddenly looked dangerous. The resolute Langer and the Waugh twins helped regain the momentum before the last 7 wickets fell for just 32 runs in an amazing collapse inspired by Headley (6/60) and Gough, who took the final two wickets (MacGill and McGrath) in three deliveries. The last session had gone almost four hours, Australia being bowled out for 162, 12 runs short.

It had been one of the greatest Ashes Test matches, and restored some of the bite into the Bulldog. It was also the longest day in Australian Test cricket history, play not finishing until 7.33 p.m. Many had wondered what could happen if England held their catches – and other than Langer, who was dropped in the slips at 1, this time even the half chances had been taken. THE CHOKE'S ON US headlined the *Age*. HOW'S THAT FOR A MIRACLE? ENGLAND WIN A CRICKET TEST said the *Sydney Morning Herald*. ASHES REVIVED IN TWILIGHT said the *Australian*.

Taylor said the game should never have been lost with just 45 runs needed and seven wickets in hand. 'It just shows that when you give a team a sniff they can go all the way,' he said. 'We probably thought we were unbeatable. All of a sudden you do lose and you start realising there is another side out there playing and giving it their best shot.'

Taylor believed the unexpected loss would act as a spur, as the Australians looked to clinch the series 3–1 and continue their mastery over the Englishmen which had started during Taylor's first overseas tour, in 1989.

The return of Shane Warne into the Australian team for his first Test of the summer after shoulder surgery was a bonus, even though his form at state level had been indifferent and included only eight expensive wickets in four Sheffield Shield games.

Warne had bowled in tandem with MacGill only once before, in the final Test against the South Africans in Adelaide in 1997–98, where Warne took 3 wickets and MacGill 5 on debut. Since then MacGill, looking more mature and comfortable at every appearance, had taken 30 wickets in six Tests, and Warne hastened his comeback accordingly. It had been 277 days since he had last played a Test. He'd still commanded the headlines, mainly through the elongated bookmaking scandal, but also having signed a $200 000 sponsorship deal with the Nicorette company to stop smoking for a minimum of four months.

Australia's selection chairman Trevor Hohns said Warne had virtually picked himself, after giving his personal 'all-clear' that he was once again ready for international cricket. After Victoria's Shield game against NSW in Sydney when he bowled more than 50 overs, his old Test team-mates including Slater and the Waugh brothers told Warne his lengthy spells were among the best he'd ever bowled. It wasn't until six months later that Warne was to show anything like his best form, with consecutive man of the match awards in the World Cup play-offs in London.

Australia's Ashes success had revolved around pace pair McGrath and Fleming, with back-up from MacGill and, in mid-series, the versatile Tasmanian Miller. Sydney was considered the ultimate wicket for spinners and Taylor was not only to be given access to two leggies, but Miller played as well, opening the bowling with his medium pace before later reverting to off-breaks.

A 190-run stand by the Waugh twins, their highest partnership in Tests since Jamaica '95 and Gough's hat-trick, only the fourth by an Englishman in Anglo-Australian Test cricket this century, were among the opening day highlights. Great interest also surrounded the reception Warne was to receive in his first appearance for Australia since he'd admitted to a liaison in 1994 and 1995 with 'John' the Indian bookmaker. Weeks before in Adelaide, Mark Waugh, who had also been fined heavily for providing pitch and weather reports, was openly booed by sections of the crowd, including several South Australian Cricket Association members, as he skipped down the concrete steps onto the arena. Commentating on ABC Radio, Peter Roebuck said it was the worst reception he could remember accorded an Australian player.

Warne, too, was subject to boos, but unlike in Adelaide, they were by far outweighed by applause. It seemed the Australian sporting public were prepared to forgive and forget, despite the furore and undoubted tainting of their golden boy's reputation.

Mark Waugh had also been subjected to another mixed reception. After being dropped at short leg before scoring, he played with commanding polish in scoring his first 100 of the summer and second in a row in New Year Tests in Sydney. Brother Steve fell just four runs short of his ton. It was the ninth time he'd been out in the 90s.

Gough's hat-trick, featuring late out-swing at high pace, was as high in quality as any ever achieved. He had Ian Healy caught at the wicket before dismissing MacGill first ball with a swinging yorker and hitting Miller's off stump with a repeat which the Australians later claimed would have knocked anyone over. England's new-found competitiveness had seen the last seven Australian wickets fall for 80, but hopes of a series-squaring victory soon vanished on the second day when MacGill took 5 wickets, and the tourists conceded a 102-run lead. Introduced for five overs before lunch from the Randwick end, Warne took a wicket with his fourth ball, Mark Butcher lbw to a quicker leg-break which fizzed through. While upstaged by MacGill, he was to repeat his success in the first over against Butcher in the second innings, too.

Set 287 to win after an extraordinary century from Slater, England was bowled out for 188, Hussain's 53 the top score. Man of the match MacGill took seven more wickets to give him 12 for the match, the best haul ever recorded in Taylor's 50 Tests as captain.

McGrath also claimed his 200th Test wicket, continuing his path towards joining Dennis Lillee as the greatest of all Australian pacemen.

Taylor felt the 3–1 scoreline adequately reflected the gulf between the teams, especially after the wash-out at the 'Gabba which effectively cost the Australians victory. He believed Australia's depth would allow it to stay at or around world Test championship standard for many years to come. 'Our love of the game is probably second to none, so there's no reason why we can't remain at the top,' he said.

With four consecutive failures in the final two Tests, he'd finished poorly, but reinforced his decision to be available for the West Indies. Within weeks, however, everything was to change irrevocably . . .

### MOST CATCHES, BOWLER–FIELDSMAN COMBINATION

| | |
|----|-------------------------|
| 51 | c Taylor b Warne |
| 39 | c Sobers b Gibbs |
| 27 | c Coney b Hadlee |
| 26 | c Lara b Walsh |
| 25 | c Azharuddin b Kumble |

'One of Mark's great assets, and he has many, is that he can take criticism, accept it and on occasions, thank you for it. He is also willing to take a chance. Most people don't, because they are afraid that if it goes wrong, they'll be blamed. Mark takes a chance because he wants to win. He doesn't think of failure.'
– *Neil Marks*

### PROFILE: STUART MacGILL

STUART MacGILL'S EMERGENCE as Australia's newest spin bowling star was critical in Australia's Ashes defence. Just when England thought it was headed for a Warne-free zone, the unearthing of sandy-headed Stuart Charles Glyndwr MacGill provided captain Mark Taylor with new strikepower he thought he'd forfeited with Warne's wintertime surgery.

Instead of long-time tormentor Warne stepping up the pressure after McGrath and Co. had attacked with the new ball, it was the Perth-born MacGill's big-spinning leg-breaks which fizzed, ducked and ultimately embarrassed the slow-footed Englishmen.

In an incredible 48-hour period in the 1999 New Year Test when he snared 5/57 and 7/50 in his adopted home town, MacGill stamped his name on the international scene in an even more authoritative manner than a young Warne had. It took him only nine Test matches in a fairytale first 12 months to reach 50 wickets. By comparison, Warne took 14 Tests and Richie Benaud 13.

His rapid advancement was a shock to most, except for his NSW team-mates and his long-time coach Peter Philpott, who believed MacGill only needed regular opportunity to make his mark. Ever since he first saw him bowl, as a 14-year-old in Perth, Philpott has believed that he had potential to play and eventually turn a Test, as occurred at the Sydney Cricket Ground in 1998–99.

Luring him away from the pace havens of Perth was a priority for the amenable kid Philpott has treated as an adopted son since his mid-teens. 'When I first saw Stewie he used to bowl very much out of the front of his hand and fairly flat,' Philpott said. 'But he showed a tremendous desire to learn and a great deal of intelligence in listening and wanting to do things.

'Very rapidly he moved from a front-of-the-hand flat-spinner into somebody who really gave them a rip. As soon as you get the kid who can really give them a twist and has the intelligence and physical capacity, all the potential is there.

'At first the biggest problem was that he had to deal with his own enthusiasm and ambition, which at times got him into a bit of strife with people here and there.'

Philpott admits MacGill's colourful past may have previously shunted him into the background. 'He could go off a bit,' he says. However, traits which may have offended, most notably one of his old Sydney grade captains, were mostly to do with wanting to make up ground, given his lost years in an environment which had seen many Perth-born spin specialists tread water before disappearing altogether.

'The West Australians don't favour the leg-spinners the way we do here in New South Wales, in particular,' said Philpott. 'Stewie was being held back by the WA attitude that favours seam and finger-spin. He had picked up an unfortunate reputation for volatility and it was holding him back a wee bit. We spoke about it and I suggested a move to the eastern states was the best way to go. I've no doubt at all that Melbourne, Sydney and Brisbane are the best places to be for a young wrist-spinner.'

One nets session, soon after MacGill's arrival in Sydney, convinced Philpott that his protégé would play for Australia, with or without Shane Warne. 'Stewie was bowling to Mark Waugh and not only did he beat him a couple of times, he also knocked him over twice. Mark came out, walked over to me and said, "This kid can really bowl." To me that was fairly significant.'

As a kid growing up in a town which had produced some of the all-time greats of fast bowling, including Dennis Lillee, Graham McKenzie and Terry Alderman, MacGill, too, wanted to sprint in and bowl as fast as he could. But he found he wasn't strong or quick enough, so instead experimented with the wrist-spinners his father, Terry, a former Shield-standard leggie, had shown him.

MacGill admits his frustration at playing just one game in three years with Western Australia, and after having been overlooked so often, he's only now convincing himself of his right to a regular international place.

'I wouldn't be disappointed to be a very good Shield player forever, but I want to develop at the next level,' he says. 'I want to be a very good Test cricketer, too.

'I count myself really lucky to have the opportunity to find out if I'm good enough.'

In an outstanding summer in 1997–98, his first full year in Sheffield Shield ranks, he took 50 first-class wickets, including five on his Test debut for Australia against South Africa in Adelaide, when he bowled in tandem with Warne. 'It was a case of "Hang on, I can actually do this,"' he said.

His 'signature' ball, the big-spinning leg-break, was a feature of back-to-back hauls of 6/99 against Victoria in Melbourne and 6/64 against the Tasmanians at Bellerive Oval.

'The leg-spinner has always been my best delivery,' he said. 'It's how Shane [Warne] has got most of his wickets. It's so difficult to play a very good leg-spinner. People concentrate so much on that particular ball, when they do come up against something different, they're not ready for it. I try and use my leg-spinner as much as I can and try and get as much turn and bounce as I can.'

His performances helped him gain a berth on the autumn tour of India and the pre-Ashes tour to Pakistan where he helped win the first Test at Rawalpindi with some superb deliveries. While he used his variety deliveries such as his googly and back-spinner only sparingly, he was gathering more belief in his right to be playing international cricket.

He is thankful to have the support of Philpott, with whom he lived as a 20-year-old Cricket Academy inductee in Adelaide in 1991. The pair worked together for hours in the nets, discussing mechanics and working on technique. 'Peter is always available to me whenever I need him,' MacGill says. 'Always the concentration is to make sure my action remains as consistent as possible throughout a year.'

Asked how daunting he is finding the challenge of filling in for Warne, the best-performed spin bowler in Test history, MacGill said, 'My goal has never been to *replace* Shane Warne. I'd like to be in a position where I can be selected to play *with* Shane. I'd love it if we could regularly bowl in tandem together; him bowling like he bowls and me bowling as well as I can. I reckon that would be pretty good fun. Hard work for the batsmen, too.'

### STUART MACGILL'S RECORD (TO 20 AUGUST 1999)

| | Mts | Runs | HS | Ave | 100s | Wicks | Ave | BB |
|---|---|---|---|---|---|---|---|---|
| Tests | 12 | 165 | 43 | 9.70 | – | 59 | 23.32 | 7/50 |

Yet to play one-day international cricket

Stuart MacGill says his career has had more downs than ups, ever since his grade debut with the West Perth fourth XI when he was struck for 12 6s at Wanneroo Oval.

'Young leg-spinners can worry too much about doing different balls, instead of bowling their natural leg-break time and time again,' he said. 'Dad helped put it all into perspective. He said there'd be plenty of days like that. But there'd also be a lot of good times. The following match I got 6/40 and was promoted to third grade.'

Just as important an essential in Stuart MacGill's kitbag as his bowling boots and equipment is a tiny tube of healing balm, anhydrous wool fat, used most notably previously by shearers to warm their fingers on particularly cold mornings.

'I came back from the Pakistan tour with wear-and-tear problems with my spinning finger and a shearer out in the back blocks recommended it,' he said. 'It's a lanolin substance and it has done the trick.'

# NINETEEN

## AUSTRALIAN OF THE YEAR

*'I don't think it would have been Mark Taylor to
walk off there saying, "This is going to be my last
Test." I've never been much into grandstanding.'*

MANY OF THE HUGE holiday crowd revelling in the drama-packed
Sydney Test hadn't even made it to their seats on the third morning
when Mark Taylor shaped at Darren Gough and was caught at first
slip in the opening over. It was one of those have-to-play-at deliveries,
pitched right in the corridor of uncertainty. At Gough's speed, there
was no time for a readjustment. The nick travelled at good pace
through to Alec Stewart and Taylor, having not added to his overnight
score of 2, was on his way – for the final time.

That night he rang his manager John Fordham. Something was
amiss. He wasn't his normal relaxed self. Fordham arrived at the
cricket the next morning with a clear premonition that this would be
Taylor's last hurrah. England had begun its chase as an 8/1 outsider
before some brave hitting by Stewart, including a lofted drive to the
cover boundary from the very first ball he faced from Glenn McGrath.
England reached 50 for no wicket for the first time all summer,
causing the bookmakers to shorten their winning odds to 7/2.

Stuart MacGill changed everything when he had Stewart stumped late on the penultimate night and from an overnight 2/104, the Englishmen cracked on the final day, losing 8/84, including six wickets to the rampant MacGill. The variable bounce forced wicketkeeper Ian Healy to use a mouthguard, MacGill operating to a cordon of close-in catchers, both in front of the wicket and in the slips. Taylor was delighted to share in an early wicket and take his record 157th catch when Mark Ramprakash, one of England's batsmen of the summer, fanned at McGrath and could only get an edge.

After the victory ceremony, Taylor seemed reluctant to leave the ground and spoke with Fordham again just inside the members' gate. Something was definitely evolving. He'd played his very first Test in Sydney. And maybe his last.

By mid-week, Taylor, his wife Judi, and sons William and Jack were on the north coast on holiday, lapping up the free time which previously had not been available because of Taylor's one-day commitments.

By mid-January, having also dabbled in some commentary for Channel 9, Taylor had formalised his thinking. Mates had told him why he should go to the West Indies, but he wasn't so sure. He remembered what Ian Chappell and others had said about retiring. You'd wake up one morning and know that you'd played your last game. He repeated to himself a question which had been occupying his mind ever since Australia had retained the Ashes in Adelaide before Christmas: 'Do you still have the urge to play?'

Back in Sydney and midway through a domestic fixture with NSW, he rang Fordham and said he was retiring. First, however, was his priority commitment as the Australia Day Council's Australian of the Year, his greatest-ever honour, which was to be bestowed by Prime Minister John Howard. Before the celebratory dinner at Brisbane's Sheraton hotel, Taylor joined Mr Howard, by invitation, in his suite for a beer. He told the PM of his intentions. He would be retiring but wouldn't make an announcement until the appropriate moment.

The next day he carried out his duties in consummate fashion, observing protocol and the dignity of the position. It was a long and demanding day and almost every interview included at least one question about his immediate playing future. 'Nice Australia Day, isn't it,' said Taylor with a grin.

That night, after all his duties had been completed, he joined his family and 20 of his closest friends at Sydney's Star City Casino for a private party, hosted by Fordham, at which he announced his decision. Most cricketers had no option when to go. He had had a magnificent innings. Now there were other priorities in his life to address; especially Judi and his boys. His wife had been a cricket widow for a decade, ever since Taylor left for England just weeks into their marriage in 1989.

Before accepting the award the previous night, he said, 'I've always considered myself to be a proud Australian and one who does what he can to the best of my ability. It goes to show you that if you hang in there long enough you can turn things around. Just 18 months ago, I could have been out of the Australian side.'

He said sport was a great teacher of social skills, communication and team work. He'd always be in the game's debt for what it had allowed him and the friends he'd made from it.

He informed the Australian Cricket Board and a press conference was arranged for early the following week, where Taylor's retirement letter to Board chairman Denis Rogers was circulated. In the letter, Taylor made some key points:

- He was proud to have represented Australia, and particularly to have captained such a successful team over a five-year period;
- He'd achieved his goals, set in 1994, of consolidating Australia's standing in world cricket and making his own satisfying contribution;
- His time away from the game in January had been a timely reminder of his family responsibilities. Basically he needed – and wanted – to spend more time with his sons, William and Jack.

He also thanked the ACB directors for their support and encouragement and said he'd be there, in spirit, with the team in the West Indies.

Rogers had asked him to consider continuing for a further 12 months, but respected his decision. 'Once he made up his mind to retire, we accepted it,' he said. 'We made it abundantly clear we wanted him to go on, but he would ultimately be the one who chose when he was to retire. I would not dare challenge the intellectual rigour he has put into this decision.'

Unlike his immediate predecessors Kim Hughes, who had departed in tears in '84, and Allan Border, who was clearly miffed at being made to hurry his decision in '94, Taylor had gone quietly in the manner of the easygoing country kid, unwilling to cause a fuss. Simply, he'd lost his desire to play at the highest level.

'I've enjoyed what I've done,' he said at his press conference. 'I don't see myself as anything too special. I've enjoyed my time in a game that has given me so much. I don't think it would have been Mark Taylor to walk off there saying, "This is going to be my last Test." I've never been much into grandstanding.

'As it turned out, Sydney was my last Test and I'm glad I played my first and last Test in Sydney at my home ground.'

He intended to finish his season with NSW, but with four failures in his last five innings, the option of retiring to the commentary box (where he displayed an undoubted skill) as well as pursuing his other family and business interests seemed more appealing. Before leading a supporters' tour to the World Cup in June, he also announced his decision to step down from all playing duties with NSW.

An unforgettable chapter had closed, but dozens of other opportunities were surfacing, in the short term in his key role promoting the Sydney Olympics and longer term, with Channel 9.

The best days of his life may have been over, but life after cricket shaped as being every bit as rewarding.

### RETIREMENT TRIBUTES

'I'd like, on behalf of all Australians, to thank Mark Taylor for a magnificent innings as captain of Australia. He has been a very great captain.'

*– Prime Minister John Howard*

'When Mark came into the Australian cricket team it started to win. A slips cordon which had extremely difficult times in the mid-1980s suddenly started to take catches. From his first full series against England in 1989, Taylor scored big runs and seemed to drag the side along with him.'

*– Allan Border*

'Mark's captaincy will be the thing he's most remembered for. He got the best out of players. He gave you room to be yourself and play your own way out on the field. He'd also like to be remembered for being a top-quality batsman. He scored 19 Test hundreds and, at his best, was the safest opening bat going around.'

*– Steve Waugh*

'He's the best captain I've ever played against. Tactically he is outstanding. Australia is a top side and I'm sure it will remain so.'

*– Alec Stewart*

'It is a sad day for Australian cricket. I congratulate Mark on a wonderful career and hope he's just as successful in his post-cricket life.'

*– Kieren Perkins*

'When he scored that 334, that was very impressive. It was like shooting a 58 in golf.'

*– Greg Norman*

'He will be remembered as a man who brought dignity back into what has become a professional and commercial sport.'

*– Kim Hughes*

## PROFILE: STEVE WAUGH

WHEN MARK TAYLOR DECLARED his captaincy reign over, there was only one truly worthy candidate, Steve Waugh. As an ambassador and icon of the game, his approval was virtually unanimous. He may not have been as outwardly dynamic as Shane Warne, but he was tough and shrewd and, with the fall-out from the much-publicised book-making scandals, the conservative powerbrokers dominant on the Australian Cricket Board felt they had no other option.

Waugh represented everything the ACB wanted in its captain: dignity, diligence, calmness and an undisputed standing as a Test and limited-overs topliner.

Waugh's popularity and standing within the Australian team had remained at a consistent high ever since the West Indies in 1995, when he averaged 106.

He may have been only 10 months younger than Taylor and increasingly susceptible to wear and tear, but his focus, strength and steely commitment to Australian cricket was undeniable. What's more, he was the natural leader for both five- and one-day cricket, an important factor given the conflict of dual leadership in 1997–98. Not for him the form fluctuations which ultimately forced Taylor's re-think. Ever since he'd fine-tuned his technique, refocused his ambitions and sacrificed his cavalier counter-punching in the pursuit of a 50-plus Test average, Waugh became the hardest-to-dismiss batsman in the world, a player opponents roused only at their own peril. Certainly his wicket was the most cherished, the uninhibited joy of the passionate Barbados fans after Neremiah Perry had trapped Waugh lbw on day two in Bridgetown in 1999 reflecting the unanimous respect the cricket world reserves for Waugh. The only trouble was that he'd made 199!

As a match-winning performer and tormentor of all bowlers, fast and slow, Waugh has had no postwar Australian parallel, not even the great Neil Harvey, the most nimble-footed of left-handers who should have been wearing glasses from mid-career because his eyesight was so poor. All but one of Waugh's first 15 Test centuries were scored in Tests in which Australia went on to win. Thirteen came in the first innings, when runs traditionally count the most.

No one dominated the Taylor years as decisively or cast as formidable a presence. Waugh made more runs, more frequently and at more critical times than gifted brother Mark, his captain or any of the young guns from the Academy.

Australia could not possibly have won the world championship in the Caribbean in 1995 without Waugh's heroics. Even Don Bradman would have been proud to play a set of innings as distinguished against such quality opposition. In four series in five in the mid-90s, Waugh topped Australia's batting averages, his defence impregnable, his manner imperious. While Waugh was at the crease, Australia was safe. No other postwar Australian, not even street-fighters Ian Chappell and Allan Border, had been as consistently reliable. While many may have preferred watching brother Mark in full flight, there was a fascination in Steve's authoritative displays which were the very essence of Test cricket at its most competitive. At Bridgetown in 1999, with Australia 3/36, Waugh fairly skipped out of the Sir Garfield Sobers Pavilion, being halfway to the wicket before passing his brother who had been castled by Curtly Ambrose second ball. Here was a player impatient to be in the cauldron, yearning for the battle to begin.

Jamaica '95, Manchester '97 and Barbados '99 are among three of his most remembered 100s. All were distinguished. But almost as memorable, both for Waugh and the small contingent of Australians fortunate enough to be witness, was his 63 on a Port-of-Spain green-top in 1995 when he broke a golden rule and swore at a fired-up Ambrose. It was a David and Goliath act, not unlike basketballer Shane Heal taking on Charles Barkley at the Olympics, and served to show, once and for all, that the Australians wouldn't back off, no matter what. He finished that innings black and blue, having been struck 10 times. But not even the intimidating Ambrose, who won the game in three days, could take his wicket. 'He was the rock which held the team together,' said Ian Healy. 'That tour was the Steve Waugh show. He dominated it from start to finish.'

Never before had Waugh batted so effectively, felt as strong or in so much control. Before his Bobby Simpson-inspired technical changes against the short ball, he'd been unsure how he could consistently adapt to facing the bevy of West Indian fast bowlers, peppering their bouncers at him for hours on end. But so assured had he become that he found himself in a 'zone' highlighted by a unique self-belief and unwavering concentration. 'It was a big series for me,' he said. 'I'd always struggled against the West Indies and had a reputation for not being able to handle the quicks. There was a lot of incentive.'

His batting secret was simple: stop the good balls and hit the bad ones. It was no coincidence that his best-ever series coincided with his return as a bowler. A back injury had forced him to play purely as a specialist batsman during the Ashes series. He'd always been happiest and at his most successful when he had been a frontline all-rounder, involved in the game at every turning.

While only used sparingly by Taylor in the Caribbean in '95, he did take five key wickets at just 12 runs apiece, pushing him closer to his ambition of 100 Test wickets.

His team ethic was so strong that he advanced first-time tourist Ricky Ponting money after Ponting, known as 'Punter' to his team-mates, had spent most of his initial tour allowance at the race track.

The amazing factor in Waugh's rise to prominence is that he took 27 Tests and more than 40 innings to make his maiden Test century. Rarely had a batting all-rounder been persevered with for so long for so little return, especially in the Australian environment where boy wonders have to stand up immediately or face a firing squad. He'd been thrust into the spotlight early, helping to fill a gap left by the defection of more senior players on two rebel tours of South Africa, and privately wondered whether he had what it takes.

Except for a period in 1990–91 (when his spot was taken by his brother), Waugh was rarely under pressure for his spot again. From the mid-1990s he has been the international game's outstanding batsman, an unflawed genius ranking ahead even of the subcontinent's superman Sachin Tendulkar and the Caribbean king, Brian Lara.

Waugh's tunnel-vision has been as important in Australia's rise to world championship status as any other player, Shane Warne included. With 18 more centuries since his breakthrough ton at Leeds in 1989, he has become Australia's leading batsman in an all-star team which is in demand all around the world.

His feats on three English tours have been particularly remarkable and have seen him average 70-plus, with hundreds aplenty, including two (108 & 116) in Australia's famous win on a Manchester green-top in 1997. Only two others had made twin centuries for Australia in an Ashes Test, Warren Bardsley (in 1909) and Arthur Morris (1946–47).

Ever since his hesitant beginnings, when as a 20-year-old he didn't know if he was going to come off or not and was shunted up and down Australia's Test match order before being dropped altogether at 26, he has displayed rare focus and inner fire. His axing in the New Year of 1991 in favour of brother Mark proved to be a watershed in his career. Before being axed, he'd made four 100s in 42 Tests; on recall he amassed another 15 in the next 73.

Integral to his transformation was his self-assessment in reappraising his technique when facing short-pitched deliveries. His dislike of fast bowling, especially his early habit of turning his back on the ball, was well documented. But, in association with coach Simpson, he analysed his problems and worked tirelessly at improving. He began to edge inside the line, loosened his grip on the bottom hand and worked at letting deliveries go. He was also realistic about his own game. In the classic Bridgetown Test in '99 he declared that Ambrose had simply been too good for him in the pre-lunch period on day one. Never before had a quality player played and missed so often in a single period. Yet he refused to lose focus, kept playing shots and went within one run of a double century. Even the Bajans, as loyal a set of cricket fans as any in the world, stood as one and applauded him off Kensington Oval. It had been yet another epic from the consummate big-match performer in the world.

**STEVE WAUGH'S RECORD (TO 20 AUGUST 1999)**

|  | Mts | Runs | HS | Ave | 100s | Wicks | Ave | BB |
|---|---|---|---|---|---|---|---|---|
| Tests | 115 | 7622 | 200 | 50.81 | 19 | 89 | 35.10 | 5/28 |
| One-day Int. | 268 | 6239 | 120* | 31.99 | 2 | 190 | 34.37 | 4/33 |

● Asked the difference between the Waugh twins, one of the family's oldest friends, Bankstown-Canterbury president Brian Freedman, said: 'Mark was very dedicated and Steve super dedicated. I've never seen a person more focused or able to simplify everything. He won't use three words if two will do.'

● Fast bowlers love nothing more than making runs. Ask Glenn McGrath.

As part of a running joke about McGrath's questionable batting abilities, one of team-mate Mark Waugh's New Year resolutions for 1999 was to outscore McGrath in every Test they played.

To McGrath's delight, in two of the first three Tests in the West Indies, he defied the odds and outdid Waugh, his Test-best 39 at Port-of-Spain being third top-score in a low-scoring game.

# FINAL OVER

JOLLY HARBOUR ON THE FAMED Antiguan coastline just outside St John's is the most idyllic of locations for an adventure in paradise. The 1999 touring Australians thought so. While the newly in-charge Steve Waugh led his team through its first decent nets session all tour, three players, Glenn McGrath, Jason Gillespie and Matthew Elliott, did nothing more physical than a short swim in the milky-green waters off Club Antigua, one of 365 beaches highlighting the most picturesque of all West Indian islands.

McGrath was resting after his superhuman efforts in the classic modern-day Test of them all at Bridgetown, Gillespie was talking about demons which had once again entered his injury-prone body and an out-of-form Elliott was nursing a back complaint, knowing that his tour and immediate international career was over.

Having to come from behind to square the series and retain the Frank Worrell Trophy, so brilliantly won in their previous campaign under Mark Taylor in 1995, Waugh and his men were displaying a new urgency in their training. The casual, almost cavalier attitude on a solitary centre wicket at the Wanderers Cricket Club in Bridgetown had been replaced by a fresh air of determination. Among the invited net bowlers were former Testmen Merv Hughes and Carl Rackemann. Even team manager Steve Bernard, 49, a former Sheffield Shield opening bowler, borrowed some boots and ran in off a short run.

Shane Warne had noticeably not bowled more than a dozen deliveries, and then only to wicketkeeper Ian Healy at the conclusion of training at Wanderers. Here, with his place in question, he was operating in an adjacent net to leg-spin rival Stuart MacGill, stern-faced, and at full bore, looking to power through the crease and turn his leg-break with its old venom.

It hadn't seemed possible that the Australians could have been challenged as boldly as they had after bowling the Windies out for just 51 in the second innings of the first Test at Port-of-Spain. Yet thanks to Brian Lara, who defied incredible personal pressure to score memorable back-to-back centuries, the Windies had won the next two Tests to grab a 2–1 lead. They only had to draw at Antigua to wrest back one of the most famous trophies of all.

Supporter groups, several of which had paid $US25 per person for the privilege of attending the Australian training, were asked to keep back from the players and save their autograph and picture requests for the end of the session. The Australian team was glad to have their support so far from home, but there was a Test match to be won.

It had been a rocky investiture for Waugh. Despite back-to-back centuries, at Sabina Park and Bridgetown, his captaincy had, not unnaturally, lacked Taylor's spark and imagination. And when his leggies struggled to make an impression at Barbados, Gillespie broke down with back spasms and the fielding and catching subsided, he'd been powerless to repel the Windies charge.

With 153 not out, Lara had played one of the innings of his life, lifting the Windies to a 300-run last day target which had seemed insurmountable on the final morning.

The passion of the Bajans, especially those drinking their triple rums in the Kensington and Banks beer enclosures, had to be seen to be believed. Not only were they knowledgeable, they were fervent in their support. Steve Waugh said he'd never played in a match quite like it – and probably never will again.

The urgency of Australia's position coming into the decider was highlighted by the axing of Warne, against his wishes.

It had been 20 years since the Australians had played two leg-spinners in the same XI in the Caribbean and the ploy, while successful on occasions in Australia, had backfired on the unyielding island wickets. Australia's Bridgetown mix of two leg-spinners and two pacemen hadn't worked, with the leggies, in particular, struggling against the West Indian left-handers.

Since his comeback Test in Sydney in January, Warne had taken 4/378 in four Tests. He had long been below peak fitness – on one notable occasion being unable to complete one of Victoria's pre-season aquatic sessions. His work-rate in the nets had also dropped off.

But it was still an incredibly bold call, especially as Warne was a member of the selection panel. No more celebrated Australian had ever been dropped. Don Bradman was just 20 and had played only one Test when he was omitted from the Sydney Test in 1928–29. As vice-captain, Warne voted for himself, but was overruled by coach Geoff Marsh and captain Waugh in consultation with Australia's selection chairman Trevor Hohns back in Australia. He was clearly miffed and very publicly wore his disappointment, even talking of retirement.

The balance for Antigua was to radically change, with seamster Adam Dale being belatedly included for his first Test of the tour and Colin Miller promoted ahead of Warne to bowl his combinations of swing and spin.

As tour groups took off to the beach or the spectacular sights of English Harbour, the Australians completed their net work and stopped off at St John's for some fielding practice before finally returning to their hotel for a compulsory swimming session of stretching and cool-downs.

With Adam Gilchrist having arrived early, speculation was rife that veteran wicketkeeper Ian Healy might also be dropped. He'd strained both calf muscles and dropped matchwinner Lara at a critical time in Barbados. However, he'd completed both net sessions at Jolly Harbour and moved so impressively that he had to be told to stop.

While some team members took a dip and others surfed the internet, Healy slept most of the afternoon. He'd told the selection hierarchy that his legs had improved and he'd be right, but he knew the axe was raised. Some thought he should have followed Taylor's lead after Sydney and retired while on top. But it had never been his way to open doors for others. Like Steve Waugh, he had a come-and-get-me mentality about his cricket. Gilchrist was to watch on, yet again.

ANTIGUA'S RECREATION GROUND boasts a unique atmosphere with cow-bells, cross-dressers and Chickie's non-stop disco all a highlight. Just as in Barbados, or at The Wanderers in Johannesburg, barbecues dot the back of the stands, and at noon the coastal breezes waft the delicious aromas of the cooked chicken breasts and burgers across the square, reminding the players of the upcoming lunch break.

It seemed strange to see two right-handers walk out, in Slater and Greg Blewett, who had missed the Barbados Test with a badly bruised hand after being struck twice in two days in the lead-ups in Bridgetown. Mark Taylor had opened the batting in each of his 50 Tests as captain. The last time he'd missed a game was in South Africa in 1993–94 when he woke up ill on the morning of the Johannesburg Test. And even then, Slater's partner had been another left-hander in Queensland's Matthew Hayden.

Just as the Australians had sought to dominate the game in Barbados, only to be railroaded by the brilliance of Lara, it seemed the West Indian captain was on another one-man show of destruction.

Australia's 303 was a drawn-out affair, featured at the close by newcomer Miller's cavalier 43, which included one mighty smite at first-gamer Cory Collymore in which he lost grip of his bat altogether and watched it sail 15 metres away toward the square-leg umpire!

Continuing the most magical moments of his career, Miller captured the wickets of both openers and at 2/20, the Windies were under immediate pressure. But Lara changed the game again, playing a stunning, carefree knock, taking on the bowling like he was in a Super 8s slogathon.

In the first 40 minutes after tea, Lara made 68 and partner Dave Joseph 8. When Waugh brought back Dale to restrict the scoring, Lara smashed him for 22 in the over, including several into the midwicket bleachers adjacent to the new Richie Richardson Stand. It was the most extraordinary innings of the summer and Waugh and the Australians could only hope that he'd make a mistake. Having made 100 from 82 balls, his third 100 in a row, Lara fell to the big-hearted McGrath, having tickled a rising leg-side delivery through to Healy.

Despite the best endeavours of home town hero Curtly Ambrose and fellow veteran Courtney Walsh to control the Australians, Justin Langer made a century and the West Indies' fourth innings target was 388 in four and a half sessions.

Even Lara couldn't repeat his blistering run of centuries and when McGrath's off-cutter induced a nick, umpire David Orchard was up almost with the Australians. Opener Adrian Griffith fought hard and was ninth out at 209, having retired hurt earlier in his innings at 10.

McGrath, Australia's man of the series, finished proceedings by having West Indian No. 10 Collymore, protecting life and limb, easily taken in the slips. The Australians had been tested, but had been good enough to play at close to their best when it counted. In winning by 176 runs, they'd squared the series 2–2. With 30 wickets in four Tests, McGrath had been simply outstanding. Some of the Australians were peeved that he wasn't made the man of the series, but it wouldn't have been as competitive a series without Lara, the enigmatic genius, who could be seen one night vehemently complaining to match referee Raman Subba Row about McGrath's mid-pitch behaviour and on another, inviting the Australians home for tea!

Australia's reward after the incident-packed one-day series which followed – in which Steve Waugh went within inches of having his head split by a bottle thrower at Kensington Oval – was to enjoy a week's break, many with their partners on the beachfront at Barbados, before heading to England, where they were to win cricket's seventh World Cup.

It had been a dramatic, extended summer, in which the Ashes battles with Gough and Co. seemed lost in the haze. Back home in Sydney, where he was completing his new luxurious house, Taylor was preparing for yet another cricket trip, this time as one of Channel 9's frontline commentators for the tournament finale. The station was seeking an eventual replacement for 68-year-old Richie Benaud, the long-time voice of Australian cricket.

While the careers of the Waugh twins and Healy were also gradually winding down, it seemed Australian sport's love affair with the knockabout kid from Wagga, known across the country as 'Tubby', was just beginning.

# TAYLOR TRIBUTES

ALLAN BORDER (Australian captain, 1984–94)
'Mark has been outstanding. He has taken a good side when I left to a great side. He doesn't let the game drift. He's a very good communicator and he's had a big influence on the team. They've always played positively to win right from the first ball.'

WAYNE CAREY (Champion AFL footballer, originally from Wagga Wagga)
'When you're born and raised in the country, you play every sport and glory in the deeds of the guys who make it, whether they be champions of rugby league, Aussie rules or cricket. Everyone in Wagga and surrounds is proud of Mark Taylor and what he has achieved.

'Just like a Michael Slater who wanted to emulate the deeds of Test cricketers like Geoff Lawson, Steve Rixon and Mark, all guys from the southern Riverina, I'm sure there are a host of Wagga teenagers now all playing their backyard tests and fighting over the right to call themselves "Mark Taylor".

'The way Mark came into Test cricket, did well and came back again after that bad patch, speaks of his great tenacity as well as his undoubted skill.

'He'll be remembered of course for declaring on the same score as Don Bradman. Not many would have done that. But then again, not many have ever had the same leadership qualities as Mark. He's a champion on and off the field.'

GREG CHAPPELL (Australian captain 1975–77 & 1979–82)
'Mark's personal and captaincy records stand up with the very best. He was a very astute leader who tactically was very good and who communicated well.

'Always there was a sense of calmness about him. It didn't matter what was going on around him or the team.

'His career kicked again after England '97 when I frankly felt it was time for him to step aside. But in true Mark Taylor back-to-the-wall fashion, he pulled out one of the amazing comeback innings which will always be remembered.'

ALAN CROMPTON (The immediate past chairman of the Australian Cricket Board)
'Mark is first and foremost a gentleman and courteous to the extreme. He sees the big picture in terms of cricket administration. He understands the needs of sponsors, the media and the public, especially children. He has been a magnificent all-rounder for Australia. He batted, he captained and he was the world's best slips fieldsman.

'He also has the ability to adapt to many off-field roles, too. During the Nauru Cup tournament in 1989, the ABC's Neville Oliver was doing a ball-by-ball virtually by himself and several of the players not involved in the immediate games took turns at helping out. Mark was superb and tremendously deep in his comments. Even then he was showing himself to be captaincy and media material.'

JOHN FORDHAM (Mark Taylor's manager since 1994)
'Mark is a very intelligent man, capable of sizing up situations. He shows an extraordinary balance when making important judgements and is so alert and well organised.

'It's a pleasure dealing with him in a business sense. He knows exactly where's he's going and people queue to have an association with him. He's very much in demand when it comes to leadership and motivation at the corporate level.

'Even when the media had him dead in the water, Mark never thought he was dead in the water. He had faith in his abilities to get back and he never gave up. The nation embraced his courage and commitment and also his steel in not publicly showing it was getting to him.

'He's also very active when it comes to charity work, from being a benefactor of the leukemia ward at the Sydney Children's Hospital through to his work as patron of the Parramatta City Mission and a founding director with the Sporting Chance Cancer Foundation. People like Bobby Skilton, Gai Waterhouse, Raelene Boyle and Reg Gasnier are also involved. Leading into the Pakistan tour they raised more than $200 000 for the kids at a golf day. Greg Blewett came over from Adelaide. Glenn McGrath played. It was great. Nothing was too much trouble for Mark.'

GRAHAM HALBISH (Australian Cricket Board chief executive 1993–97)
'A captain like Mark Taylor comes along only once every 40 years. When I went to the Caribbean in '95 and saw the Barbados and Antigua Test matches, apart from the cricket being the most compelling I'd ever witnessed at close quarters – you felt something was going to happen almost every delivery – Taylor's demeanour and body language on the field emphasised the control he was in.

'He was dynamic with his leadership and tactics. It confirmed in my mind in absolute terms that he was an outstanding leader. He didn't let a game run its course.

'Australia would not have been successful if Taylor hadn't been captain. It's a fantastic team but there have been vital times in games where Mark has made the right decision, got the best out of his players and summed up situations in a way which very few people are able to do consistently.'

BILL LAWRY (A former Test captain, inducted into the MCG Media Hall of Fame in 1999)
'Mark is going to be remembered as the best captain of his era, not necessarily in Ian Chappell or Richie Benaud's class as I felt England was far stronger then than they have been since Mark has been captain.

'He did inherit a very good side, too, when Shane Warne was at his best and that has been a factor in his fantastic record. But you can only beat the teams as they turn up and there have been some particularly wonderful victories where his captaincy has been superb.

'He's also been a very determined batsman. Anyone who can hold their average in the mid-40s is a very good player. Mark's reflex catching at slip is again not far short of the best of my time.

'It is a tremendous effort to have lasted so long. Like Steve Waugh, he's been very professional in hanging in. He has always had a certain dignity about him and played with great purpose and courage.

'If you play long enough, the opposition will sort you out and since the 1989 tour, when he really was magic, I don't think he got any better. But he showed great resolve and was a very fine ambassador for the game.'

STUART MACGILL (Australian Test leg-spinner)
'My first eight Tests were under Mark and he remains the single most important figure in my first-class playing career to date.

'When I first played for New South Wales alongside him, he quickly assessed what I had to do in order to reach a level which could take me to Test cricket – and made no secret of his thoughts.

'Right through until his retirement, he continued to assist me. He has probably seen me bowl in first-class and Test cricket more than anybody else, so knows my bowling inside and out.

'I would love to have seen him bat on and take Brian Lara's record in Peshawar in 1998. He doesn't always receive the accolades that he deserves for his own on-field performances, as everyone tends to remember the slump. To me he had a fantastic career, full stop.'

DENIS ROGERS (Australian Cricket Board chairman)
'Mark did so many things which had an influence on society which were not publicly recognised. He influenced even people who may not have been terribly interested in cricket.

'A captain needs to have an ability to cope with all those different aspects of life, and Mark did.'

PETER TAYLOR (Club, state and Test team-mate)

'Mark never lost his perspective or his normality, through good times and bad. He's probably up in the clouds in terms of earnings. You could almost forgive him for getting a bit blasé about his mates, but he's not. He's one of those blokes happy to go and rough it and go to somebody's place for a barbie.

'Maybe he could have gone on, but a good decision often is one taken a bit earlier than necessary. There's nothing worse than watching a fellow hang on when he's past it. Mark being comfortable with the decision is the main thing.'

TONY TAYLOR (Mark's father)

'You dream of your son playing Test cricket, but you also dream of having a good relationship with him. I'm proud to call Mark a good friend and a good mate of mine, even if I reckon I have to make an appointment to see him!'

# STATISTICS

## THE AUSTRALIAN TEST TEAM UNDER MARK TAYLOR 1994–99

Captain: Mark Taylor (50 Tests) Vice-captains: Ian Healy 1994–97 (26 Tests), Steve Waugh (22 Tests, 1997–99), David Boon (1 Test, 1994–95), Mark Waugh (1 Test, 1997–98)

### SERIES RESULTS

| Season | Opponent | Venue | Played | Won | Lost | Drawn |
|--------|----------|-------|--------|-----|------|-------|
| 1994–95 | Pakistan | Pakistan | 3 | 0 | 1 | 2 |
| | England | Australia | 5 | 3 | 1 | 1 |
| | West Indies | West Indies | 4 | 2 | 1 | 1 |
| 1995–96 | Pakistan | Australia | 3 | 2 | 1 | 0 |
| | Sri Lanka | Australia | 3 | 3 | 0 | 0 |
| 1996–97 | India | India | 1 | 0 | 1 | 0 |
| | West Indies | Australia | 5 | 3 | 2 | 0 |
| | South Africa | South Africa | 3 | 2 | 1 | 0 |
| 1997 | England | England | 6 | 3 | 2 | 1 |
| 1997–98 | New Zealand | Australia | 3 | 2 | 0 | 1 |
| | South Africa | Australia | 3 | 1 | 0 | 2 |
| | India | India | 3 | 1 | 2 | 0 |
| 1998–99 | Pakistan | Pakistan | 3 | 1 | 0 | 2 |
| | England | Australia | 5 | 3 | 1 | 1 |
| Total | | | 50 | 26 | 13 | 11 |

## RECORDS VERSUS EACH COUNTRY

| Opponent | Tests | Won | Lost | Drawn |
|---|---|---|---|---|
| England | 16 | 9 | 4 | 3 |
| India | 4 | 1 | 3 | 0 |
| New Zealand | 3 | 2 | 0 | 1 |
| Pakistan | 9 | 3 | 2 | 4 |
| South Africa | 6 | 3 | 1 | 2 |
| Sri Lanka | 3 | 3 | 0 | 0 |
| West Indies | 9 | 5 | 3 | 1 |
| Total | 50 | 26 | 13 | 11 |

## HOME & AWAY RECORD

| Opponent | Played | Won | Lost | Drawn |
|---|---|---|---|---|
| Home | 27 | 17 | 5 | 5 |
| Away | 23 | 9 | 8 | 6 |
| Total | 50 | 26 | 13 | 11 |

## RUNS & WICKETS FOR AND AGAINST

| | Runs | Wickets | Average |
|---|---|---|---|
| For | 26 623 | 759 | 35.07 |
| Against | 23 990 | 873 | 27.47 |

## NARROW MARGINS OF VICTORY

*By Australia:*

Two wickets v South Africa at Port Elizabeth 1996–97

Note – Australia's closest win by a runs margin was by 98 runs at Sydney in 1998–99 (Taylor's last Test)

*Against Australia:*

One wicket by Pakistan at Karachi 1994–95 (Taylor's first Test as captain)

12 runs by England at Melbourne 1998–99

19 runs by England at the Oval 1997

## LARGEST MARGINS OF VICTORY

*By Australia:*

| | |
|---|---|
| Innings & 196 runs | v South Africa at Johannesburg 1996–97 |
| Innings & 183 runs | v West Indies at Adelaide 1996–97 |
| Innings & 126 runs | v Pakistan at Brisbane 1995–96 |
| 329 runs | v England at Perth 1994–95 |
| 295 runs | v England at Melbourne 1994–95 |
| 264 runs | v England at Nottingham 1997 |

*Against Australia:*

| | |
|---|---|
| Innings & 219 runs | by India at Calcutta 1997–98 |
| 179 runs | by India at Chennai 1997–98 |

## THE TOSS

Taylor won the toss 26 times (52 per cent) in his 50 Tests as captain. His best series for winning the toss were in 1997 against England when he called correctly in each of the first five Tests in the six-Test series, and in his last series, also against England, in 1998–99, when won the toss in all five Tests (other Australian captains to win the toss in all five Tests were M. A. [Monty] Noble in 1909 v England and Lindsay Hassett in 1953 v England). Taylor lost the toss in all four Tests in the West Indies in 1994–95. Prior to the 1997 series against England, Taylor had won the toss only 11 times in 27 Tests (40.7 per cent), but thereafter he called correctly 15 times in 23 Tests (65.2 per cent). The result of the toss made little impact on Australia's results, as demonstrated below:

| | Tests | Won | Lost | Drawn |
|---|---|---|---|---|
| Won toss | 26 | 13 | 7 | 6 |
| Lost toss | 24 | 13 | 6 | 5 |

## INSTANCES WHERE MARK TAYLOR SENT THE OPPOSITION IN TO BAT

| | | |
|---|---|---|
| 1996–97 | Port Elizabeth | Australia won by 2 wickets |
| 1997 | Lord's | Match drawn |
| 1997 | Leeds | Australia won by an innings & 61 runs |
| 1998–99 | Perth | Australia won by 7 wickets |
| 1998–99 | Melbourne | England won by 12 runs |

## HIGHEST INNINGS TOTALS

*For Australia:*

628/8 dec.   v South Africa at Johannesburg 1996–97

617/5 d      v Sri Lanka at Perth 1995–96

599/4 d      v Pakistan at Peshawar 1998–99

531          v West Indies at Kingston 1994–95

521/9 d      v Pakistan at Rawalpindi 1994–95

517          v West Indies at Adelaide 1996–97

513          v Pakistan at Rawalpindi 1998–99

502/9 d      v Sri Lanka at Adelaide 1995–96

501/9 d      v England at Leeds 1997

500/6 d      v Sri Lanka at Melbourne 1995–96

*Against Australia:*

633/5 d      by India at Calcutta 1997–98

580/9 d      by Pakistan at Peshawar 1998–99

537          by Pakistan at Rawalpindi 1994–95 (2nd innings)

517          by South Africa at Adelaide 1997–98

## COMPLETED INNINGS OF UNDER 100 RUNS

*By Australia:*

No instance. Australia's lowest totals are as follows:

104          v England at the Oval 1997 (2nd innings)

105          v West Indies at Port-of-Spain 1994–95 (2nd innings)

108          v South Africa at Port Elizabeth 1996–97

*Against Australia:*

77           by England at Lord's 1997

92           by England at Melbourne 1994–95 (2nd innings)

97           by Pakistan at Brisbane 1995–96 (one batsman absent)

## THE PLAYERS

Australia used 36 players during Taylor's captaincy, 20 who were newcomers to Test cricket. Apart from Taylor himself, the only player to appear in every Test during this period was Mark Waugh. Ian Healy missed only one Test, at Lahore in 1994–95, through injury.

*Tests*

| | |
|---|---|
| 50 | M. A. Taylor, M. E. Waugh |
| 49 | I. A. Healy |
| 46 | S. R. Waugh |
| 42 | S. K. Warne |
| 40 | G. D. McGrath |
| 31 | G. S. Blewett* |
| 30 | M. J. Slater |
| 23 | P. R. Reiffel |
| 22 | R. T. Ponting* |
| 18 | M. G. Bevan, D. C. Boon |
| 17 | M. T. G. Elliott* |
| 14 | M. S. Kasprowicz* |
| 13 | C. J. McDermott |
| 13 | J. L. Langer |
| 10 | D. W. Fleming*, J. N. Gillespie* |
| 8 | S. C. G. MacGill* |
| 6 | M. L. Hayden, C. R. Miller* |
| 5 | B. P. Julian, D. S. Lehmann*, T. B. A. May |
| 4 | G. R. Robertson* |
| 3 | J. Angel, A. J. Bichel* |
| 2 | S. H. Cook*, P. E. McIntyre* |
| 1 | A. C. Dale*, P. A. Emery*, G. B. Hogg*, S. G. Law*, M. J. Nicholson*, P. Wilson*, S. Young* |

\* Indicates Test debut occurred during Taylor's term of captaincy

## BATTING RECORDS (IN ORDER OF RUNS SCORED)

*For Australia:*

| | Inns | NO | Runs | HS | Avge | 100 | 50 |
|---|---|---|---|---|---|---|---|
| S. R. Waugh | 79 | 16 | 3718 | 200 | 59.01 | 10 | 21 |
| M. E. Waugh | 86 | 6 | 3663 | 153* | 45.78 | 10 | 21 |

**Batting Records** (continued)

*For Australia:*

|  | Inns | NO | Runs | HS | Avge | 100 | 50 |
|---|---|---|---|---|---|---|---|
| M. A. Taylor | 89 | 7 | 3250 | 334* | 39.63 | 7 | 16 |
| M. J. Slater | 55 | 2 | 2358 | 219 | 44.49 | 9 | 6 |
| I. A. Healy | 79 | 13 | 2216 | 161* | 33.57 | 2 | 11 |
| G. S. Blewett | 53 | 2 | 1843 | 214 | 36.13 | 4 | 10 |
| R. T. Ponting | 35 | 2 | 1209 | 127 | 36.63 | 2 | 7 |
| M. T. G. Elliott | 28 | 1 | 1102 | 199 | 40.81 | 3 | 4 |
| D. C. Boon | 31 | 2 | 858 | 131 | 29.58 | 3 | 2 |
| S. K. Warne | 61 | 4 | 800 | 53 | 14.03 | – | 1 |
| M. G. Bevan | 30 | 3 | 785 | 91 | 29.07 | – | 6 |
| J. L. Langer | 19 | 1 | 747 | 179* | 41.50 | 2 | 4 |
| P. R. Reiffel | 37 | 11 | 728 | 79* | 28.00 | – | 5 |
| M. L. Hayden | 10 | 0 | 241 | 125 | 24.10 | 1 | – |
| D. S. Lehmann | 8 | 0 | 228 | 98 | 28.50 | – | 2 |
| M. S. Kasprowicz | 18 | 2 | 180 | 25 | 11.25 | – | – |
| G. D. McGrath | 49 | 14 | 159 | 24 | 4.54 | – | – |
| D. W. Fleming | 10 | 1 | 143 | 71* | 15.88 | – | 1 |
| G. R. Robertson | 7 | 0 | 140 | 57 | 20.00 | – | 1 |
| S. C. G. MacGill | 10 | 1 | 134 | 43 | 14.88 | – | – |
| C. J. McDermott | 16 | 4 | 123 | 29 | 10.25 | – | – |
| J. N. Gillespie | 15 | 7 | 97 | 28* | 12.12 | – | – |
| B. P. Julian | 6 | 0 | 67 | 31 | 11.16 | – | – |
| S. G. Law | 1 | 1 | 54 | 54* | – | – | 1 |
| A. J. Bichel | 5 | 0 | 47 | 18 | 9.40 | – | – |
| T. B. A. May | 8 | 4 | 43 | 10* | 10.75 | – | – |
| J. Angel | 5 | 0 | 31 | 11 | 6.20 | – | – |
| P. E. McIntyre | 4 | 1 | 22 | 16 | 7.33 | – | – |
| C. R. Miller | 7 | 2 | 20 | 11 | 4.00 | – | – |
| M. J. Nicholson | 2 | 0 | 14 | 9 | 7.00 | – | – |
| P. A. Emery | 1 | 1 | 8 | 8* | – | – | – |
| A. C. Dale | 1 | 0 | 5 | 5 | 5.00 | – | – |
| G. B. Hogg | 2 | 0 | 5 | 4 | 2.50 | – | – |
| S. Young | 2 | 1 | 4 | 4* | 4.00 | – | – |
| S. H. Cook | 2 | 2 | 3 | 3* | – | – | – |
| P. Wilson | 2 | 2 | 0 | 0* | – | – | – |

*Against Australia:* (Minimum 600 runs)

|  | Inns | NO | Runs | HS | Avge | 100 | 50 |
|---|---|---|---|---|---|---|---|
| G. P. Thorpe (Eng) | 25 | 3 | 983 | 138 | 44.68 | 2 | 7 |
| N. Hussain (Eng) | 21 | 1 | 838 | 207 | 41.90 | 2 | 4 |
| M. A. Atherton (Eng) | 30 | 1 | 774 | 88 | 26.68 | – | 6 |
| Aamir Sohail (Pak) | 17 | 0 | 767 | 133 | 45.11 | 2 | 4 |
| Saleem Malik (Pak) | 14 | 1 | 749 | 237 | 57.61 | 2 | 2 |
| A. J. Stewart (Eng) | 26 | 3 | 657 | 107 | 28.56 | 1 | 3 |
| Saeed Anwar (Pak) | 9 | 0 | 604 | 145 | 67.11 | 2 | 3 |
| B. C. Lara (WI) | 17 | 1 | 604 | 132 | 37.75 | 1 | 4 |
| *(Leading runscorers for countries not represented above:)* | | | | | | | |
| S. R. Tendulkar (Ind) | 7 | 1 | 456 | 177 | 76.00 | 2 | 1 |
| W. J. Cronje (SA) | 11 | 1 | 445 | 88 | 44.50 | – | 5 |
| H. P. Tillekeratne (SL) | 6 | 0 | 245 | 119 | 40.83 | 1 | 1 |
| A. C. Parore (NZ) | 6 | 1 | 229 | 63 | 45.80 | – | 1 |

## CENTURIES

*For Australia* (53):

| | |
|---|---|
| 10 | M. E. Waugh, S. R. Waugh. |
| 9 | M. J. Slater. |
| 7 | M. A. Taylor. |
| 4 | G. S. Blewett. |
| 3 | D. C. Boon, M. T. G. Elliott. |
| 2 | I. A. Healy, J. L. Langer, R. T. Ponting. |
| 1 | M. L. Hayden. |

*Against Australia* (31):

3     Ijaz Ahmed (Pak)

2     Aamir Sohail (Pak); N. Hussain (Eng), Saeed Anwar (Pak); Saleem Malik (Pak); S. R. Tendulkar (Ind); G. P. Thorpe (Eng).

1     M. Azharuddin (Ind); M. A. Butcher (Eng); S. L. Campbell (WI); M. W. Gatting (Eng); A. P. Gurusinha (SL); C. L. Hooper (WI); M. J. Horne (NZ); S. T. Jayasuriya (SL); J. H. Kallis (SA); G. Kirsten (SA); B. C. Lara (WI); Moin Khan (Pak); N. R. Mongia (Ind); R. B. Richardson (WI); A. J. Stewart (Eng); H. P. Tillekeratne (SL).

## CARRYING BAT THROUGH COMPLETED INNINGS

M. A. Taylor 169 not out, out of 350 v South Africa at Adelaide 1997–98 (only instance by either side).

## HIGHEST INDIVIDUAL SCORES

*For Australia:*

| | |
|---|---|
| 334 not out | M. A. Taylor v Pakistan at Peshawar 1998–99 |
| 219 | M. J. Slater v Sri Lanka at Perth 1995–96 |
| 214 | G. S. Blewett v South Africa at Johannesburg 1996–97 |
| 200 | S. R. Waugh v West Indies at Kingston 1994–95 |
| 199 | M. T. G. Elliott v England at Leeds 1997 |
| 179 not out | J. L. Langer v England at Adelaide 1998–99 |
| 176 | M. J. Slater v England at Brisbane 1994–95 |
| 170 | S. R. Waugh v Sri Lanka at Adelaide 1995–96 |
| 169 not out | M. A. Taylor v South Africa at Adelaide 1997–98 (carried bat) |
| 161 not out | I. A. Healy v West Indies at Brisbane 1996–97 |
| 160 | S. R. Waugh v South Africa at Johannesburg 1996–97 |
| 157 | S. R. Waugh v Pakistan at Rawalpindi 1998–99 |
| 153 not out | M. E. Waugh v India at Bangalore 1997–98 |

*Against Australia:*

| | |
|---|---|
| 237 | Saleem Malik for Pakistan at Rawalpindi 1994–95 |
| 207 | N. Hussain for England at Birmingham 1997 |
| 177 | S. R. Tendulkar for India at Bangalore 1997–98 |
| 163 not out | M. Azharuddin for India at Calcutta 1997–98 |
| 155 not out | S. R. Tendulkar for India at Chennai 1997–98 |
| 155 | Ijaz Ahmed for Pakistan at Peshawar 1998–99 |
| 152 | N. R. Mongia for India at Delhi 1996–97 |

## PARTNERSHIPS OF 200 AND MORE

*For Australia:*

| | | | |
|---|---|---|---|
| 385 | 5th | S. R. Waugh & G. S. Blewett v South Africa at Johannesburg | 1996–97 |
| 279 | 2nd | M. A. Taylor & J. L. Langer v Pakistan at Peshawar | 1998–99 |
| 268 | 5th | M. T. G. Elliott & R. T. Ponting v England at Leeds | 1997 |

*For Australia:* (continued)

| 231 | 4th | M. E. Waugh & S. R. Waugh v West Indies at Kingston | 1994–95 |
| 228 | 1st | M. J. Slater & M. A. Taylor v Sri Lanka at Perth | 1995–96 |
| 208 | 1st | M. A. Taylor & M. J. Slater v England at Sydney* | 1994–95 |
| 204 | 2nd | M. A. Taylor & G. S. Blewett v England at Birmingham* | 1997 |
| 203 | 6th | *S. R. Waugh & G. S. Blewett v England at Perth* | 1994–95 |

*Against Australia:*

| 288 | 4th | N. Hussain & G. P. Thorpe for England at Birmingham | 1997 |
| 211 | 2nd | Saeed Anwar & Ijaz Ahmed for Pakistan at Peshawar | 1998–99 |
| 208 | 3rd | R. G. Samuels & B. C. Lara for West Indies at Perth | 1996–97 |

* indicates second innings

## PARTNERSHIP RECORDS FOR EACH WICKET

*For Australia:*

| 1st | 208 | M. A. Taylor & M. J. Slater v England at Sydney* | 1994–95 |
| 2nd | 279 | M. A. Taylor & J. L. Langer v Pakistan at Peshawar | 1998–99 |
| 3rd | 183 | M. J. Slater & M. E. Waugh v England at Perth | 1994–95 |
| 4th | 231 | M. E. Waugh & S. R. Waugh v West Indies at Kingston | 1994–95 |
| 5th | 385 | S. R. Waugh & G. S. Blewett v South Africa at Johannesburg | 1996–97 |
| 6th | 203 | S. R. Waugh & G. S. Blewett v England at Perth* | 1994–95 |
| 7th | 117 | S. R. Waugh & P. R. Reiffel v Sri Lanka at Adelaide | 1995–96 |
| 8th | 74 | S. R. Waugh & P. R. Reiffel v West Indies at Kingston | 1994–95 |
| 9th | 96 | I. A. Healy & G. R. Robertson v India at Chennai | 1997–98 |
| 10th | 49 | P. R. Reiffel & G. D. McGrath v South Africa at Melbourne | 1997–98 |

*Against Australia:*

| 1st | 191 | V. V. S. Laxman & N. S. Sidhu for India at Calcutta | 1997–98 |
| 2nd | 211 | Saeed Anwar & Ijaz Ahmed for Pakistan at Peshawar | 1998–99 |
| 3rd | 208 | R. G. Samuels & B. C. Lara for West Indies at Perth | 1996–97 |
| 4th | 288 | N. Hussain & G. P. Thorpe for England at Birmingham | 1997 |
| 5th | 158 | G. P. Thorpe & M. R. Ramprakash for England at Perth | 1994–95 |

*Against Australia:* (continued)

|      |     |                                                                                                    |         |
|------|-----|----------------------------------------------------------------------------------------------------|---------|
|      |     | M. Azharuddin & S. C. Ganguly for India at Calcutta                                                 | 1997–98 |
| 6th  | 196 | Saleem Malik & Saeed Anwar for Pakistan at Lahore*                                                  | 1994–95 |
| 7th  | 98  | Aamir Sohail & Wasim Akram for Pakistan at Karachi                                                  | 1998–99 |
| 8th  | 85  | B. M. McMillan & D. J. Richardson for South Africa at Port Elizabeth                                | 1996–97 |
| 9th  | 120 | Saeed Anwar & Mushtaq Ahmed for Pakistan at Rawalpindi                                              | 1998–99 |
| 10th | 74  | B. M. McMillan & P. L. Symcox for South Africa at Adelaide                                          | 1997–98 |

* indicates second innings

## Bowling Records (in order of most wickets captured)

*For Australia:*

|                   | Overs  | Mdns | Runs | Wkts | Avge  | Best  | 5wI | 10wM |
|-------------------|--------|------|------|------|-------|-------|-----|------|
| S. K. Warne       | 2006.4 | 570  | 5086 | 199  | 25.55 | 9/71  | 9   | 3    |
| G. D. McGrath     | 1580.5 | 428  | 4252 | 190  | 22.37 | 8/38  | 11  | –    |
| P. R. Reiffel     | 670.3  | 184  | 1754 | 73   | 24.02 | 5/39  | 3   | –    |
| C. J. McDermott   | 531    | 117  | 1638 | 60   | 27.30 | 6/38  | 5   | –    |
| S. C. G. MacGill  | 348    | 65   | 1024 | 47   | 21.78 | 7/50  | 3   | 1    |
| J. N. Gillespie   | 250.4  | 68   | 824  | 39   | 21.12 | 7/37  | 3   | –    |
| M. S. Kasprowicz  | 463.2  | 105  | 1344 | 38   | 35.36 | 7/36  | 2   | –    |
| D. W. Fleming     | 355.2  | 77   | 1007 | 37   | 27.21 | 5/46  | 1   | –    |
| M. G. Bevan       | 214.1  | 30   | 703  | 29   | 24.24 | 6/82  | 1   | 1    |
| M. E. Waugh       | 343.1  | 58   | 1053 | 25   | 42.12 | 5/40  | 1   | –    |
| S. R. Waugh       | 244.4  | 64   | 609  | 23   | 26.47 | 4/34  | –   | –    |
| C. R. Miller      | 220    | 49   | 567  | 17   | 33.35 | 3/57  | –   | –    |
| G. R. Robertson   | 149.4  | 20   | 515  | 13   | 39.61 | 4/72  | –   | –    |
| B. P. Julian      | 101    | 27   | 308  | 10   | 30.80 | 4/36  | –   | –    |
| J. Angel          | 105.4  | 20   | 391  | 9    | 43.44 | 3/54  | –   | –    |
| G. S. Blewett     | 178.2  | 48   | 520  | 9    | 57.77 | 2/25  | –   | –    |
| S. H. Cook        | 37.2   | 10   | 142  | 7    | 20.28 | 5/39  | 1   | –    |
| T. B. A. May      | 193    | 50   | 470  | 7    | 67.14 | 3/69  | –   | –    |
| P. E. McIntyre    | 65.3   | 10   | 194  | 5    | 38.80 | 3/103 | –   | –    |
| M. J. Nicholson   | 25     | 4    | 115  | 4    | 28.75 | 3/56  | –   | –    |

*For Australia:* (continued)

| | Overs | Mdns | Runs | Wkts | Avge | Best | 5wI | 10wM |
|---|---|---|---|---|---|---|---|---|
| R. T. Ponting | 14.5 | 5 | 31 | 3 | 10.33 | 1/0 | – | – |
| A. C. Dale | 28 | 7 | 92 | 3 | 30.66 | 3/71 | – | – |
| D. S. Lehmann | 17 | 4 | 45 | 2 | 22.50 | 1/6 | – | – |
| A. J. Bichel | 86.2 | 18 | 297 | 2 | 148.50 | 1/31 | – | – |
| M. J. Slater | 1.1 | 0 | 4 | 1 | 4.00 | 1/4 | – | – |
| M. A. Taylor | 3 | 1 | 11 | 1 | 11.00 | 1/11 | – | – |
| G. B. Hogg | 17 | 3 | 69 | 1 | 69.00 | 1/69 | – | – |
| M. T. G. Elliott | 2 | 1 | 4 | 0 | – | – | – | – |
| D. C. Boon | 3 | 0 | 9 | 0 | – | – | – | – |
| S. G. Law | 3 | 0 | 9 | 0 | – | – | – | – |
| S. Young | 8 | 3 | 13 | 0 | – | – | – | – |
| P. Wilson | 12 | 2 | 50 | 0 | – | – | – | – |

*Against Australia:* (minimum 30 wickets)

| | Overs | Mdns | Runs | Wkts | Avge | Best | 5wI | 10wM |
|---|---|---|---|---|---|---|---|---|
| D. Gough (Eng) | 497 | 100 | 1623 | 57 | 28.47 | 6/49 | 3 | – |
| C. A. Walsh (WI) | 341 | 66 | 1023 | 39 | 26.23 | 6/54 | 3 | – |
| D. W. Headley (Eng) | 252.5 | 40 | 867 | 35 | 24.77 | 6/60 | 1 | – |
| A. Kumble (Ind) | 256 | 70 | 546 | 32 | 17.06 | 6/98 | 3 | – |
| C. E. L. Ambrose (WI) | 261 | 56 | 702 | 32 | 21.93 | 5/43 | 3 | – |
| Mushtaq Ahmed (Pak) | 368.3 | 50 | 1126 | 31 | 36.32 | 5/95 | 2 | – |

*(Leading wicket-takers for countries not represented above:)*

| | Overs | Mdns | Runs | Wkts | Avge | Best | 5wI | 10wM |
|---|---|---|---|---|---|---|---|---|
| A. A. Donald (SA) | 208.4 | 55 | 539 | 23 | 23.43 | 6/59 | 2 | – |
| C. L. Cairns (NZ) | 103.1 | 31 | 325 | 13 | 25.00 | 4/90 | – | – |
| W. P. U. J. C. Vaas (SL) | 137.4 | 33 | 371 | 9 | 41.22 | 3/44 | – | – |

## TEN WICKETS IN A MATCH

*For Australia:*

12/107    S. C. G. MacGill (5/57 & 7/50) v England at Sydney 1998–99

11/77    S. K. Warne (7/23 & 4/54) v Pakistan at Brisbane 1995–96

11/109    S. K. Warne (5/75 & 6/34) v South Africa at Sydney 1997–98

*For Australia:* (continued)

11/110    S. K. Warne (3/39 & 8/71) v England at Brisbane 1994–95

10/113    M. G. Bevan (4/31 & 6/82) v West Indies at Adelaide 1996–97

*Against Australia:*

11/93     P. C. R. Tufnell (7/66 & 4/27) for England at the Oval 1997

## SIX OR MORE WICKETS IN AN INNINGS

*For Australia:*

8/38     G. D. McGrath v England at Lord's 1997

8/71     S. K. Warne v England at Brisbane 1994–95

7/23     S. K. Warne v Pakistan at Brisbane 1995–96

7/36     M. S. Kasprowicz v England at the Oval 1997

7/37     J. N. Gillespie v England at Leeds 1997

7/50     S. C. G. MacGill v England at Sydney 1998–99

7/76     G. D. McGrath v England at the Oval 1997

6/34     S. K. Warne v South Africa at Sydney 1997–98

6/38     C. J. McDermott v England at Perth 1994–95

6/47     G. D. McGrath v West Indies at Port-of-Spain 1994–95

6/48     S. K. Warne v England at Manchester 1997

6/53     C. J. McDermott v England at Brisbane 1994–95

6/64     S. K. Warne v England at Melbourne 1994–95

6/82     M. G. Bevan v West Indies at Adelaide 1996–97

6/85     G. D. McGrath v England at Brisbane 1998–99

6/86     G. D. McGrath v South Africa at Centurion Park 1996–97

6/136    S. K. Warne v Pakistan at Lahore 1994–95

*Against Australia:*

7/66     P. C. R. Tufnell for England at the Oval 1997

7/87     S. M. Pollock for South Africa at Adelaide 1997–98

6/49     D. Gough for England at Sydney 1994–95

6/54     C. A. Walsh for West Indies at St John's 1994–95

6/59     A. A. Donald for South Africa at Melbourne 1997–98

6/60     D. W. Headley for England at Melbourne 1998–99

6/98     A. Kumble for India at Bangalore 1997–98

## FIVE WICKETS IN AN INNINGS

*For Australia* (40):

| | |
|---|---|
| 11 | G. D. McGrath. |
| 9 | S. K. Warne. |
| 5 | C. J. McDermott. |
| 3 | J. N. Gillespie; S. C. G. MacGill; P. R. Reiffel. |
| 2 | M. S. Kasprowicz. |
| 1 | M. G. Bevan; S. H. Cook; D. W. Fleming; M. E. Waugh. |

*Against Australia* (25):

| | |
|---|---|
| 3 | C. E. L. Ambrose (WI); D. Gough (Eng); A. Kumble (Ind); C. A. Walsh (WI) |
| 2 | A. A. Donald (SA); Mushtaq Ahmed (Pak). |
| 1 | A. R. Caddick (Eng); A. R. C. Fraser (Eng); D. W. Headley (Eng); A. D. Mullally (Eng); S. M. Pollock (SA); Shahid Afridi (Pak); P. M. Such (Eng); P. C. R. Tufnell (Eng); Wasim Akram (Pak). |

## HAT-TRICKS

*For Australia* (2):

D. W. Fleming v Pakistan at Rawalpindi 1994–95 (Aamer Malik c M. G. Bevan 65, Inzamam-ul-Haq lbw 0, Saleem Malik c I. A. Healy 237).

S. K. Warne v England at Melbourne 1994–95 (P. A. J. DeFreitas lbw 0, D. Gough c I. A. Healy 0, D. E. Malcolm c D. C. Boon 0).

*Against Australia* (1):

D. Gough for England at Sydney 1998-99 (I. A. Healy c W. K. Hegg 14; S. C. G. MacGill b 0; C. R. Miller b 0).

## WICKETKEEPING DISMISSALS (FOR AUSTRALIA)

| | |
|---|---|
| 176 | I. A. Healy (162 ct & 14 st) |
| 6 | P. A. Emery (5 ct, 1 st) |

## CATCHES IN THE FIELD (FOR AUSTRALIA)

*(excludes catches taken by substitute fieldsmen)*

| | |
|---|---|
| 84 | M. A. Taylor |
| 52 | M. E. Waugh |

| 36 | G. S. Blewett |
|----|----|
| 32 | S. K. Warne |
| 30 | S. R. Waugh |
| 21 | R. T. Ponting |
| 14 | D. C. Boon; M. J. Slater |
| 13 | G. D. McGrath |
| 11 | M. T. G. Elliott |
| 10 | J. L. Langer; P. R. Reiffel |
| 8 | M. G. Bevan; C. J. McDermott |
| 7 | D. W. Fleming; M. L. Hayden; S. C. G. MacGill |
| 5 | M. S. Kasprowicz |
| 3 | J. N. Gillespie; D. S. Lehmann |
| 2 | B. P. Julian |
| 1 | J. Angel; A. J. Bichel; S. G. Law; C. R. Miller; G. R. Robertson |

## ALL TESTS: AUSTRALIANS SHARING IN MOST CENTURY PARTNERSHIPS

|  | Total | 1st | 2nd | 3rd | 4th | 5th | 6th | 7th | 8th | 9th | 10th |
|---|---|---|---|---|---|---|---|---|---|---|---|
| Allan Border | 62 | – | 2 | 14 | 20 | 16 | 8 | 1 | 1 | – | – |
| Greg Chappell | 44 | – | 2 | 15 | 13 | 11 | 2 | 1 | – | – | – |
| David Boon | 42 | 6 | 13 | 16 | 5 | 1 | 1 | – | – | – | – |
| Mark Taylor | 40 | 17 | 13 | 5 | 3 | 1 | 1 | – | – | – | – |
| Steve Waugh | 39 | – | 1 | – | 8 | 16 | 10 | 3 | – | 1 | – |
| Don Bradman | 35 | – | 14 | 11 | 3 | 6 | 1 | – | – | – | – |
| Mark Waugh | 35 | – | – | 18 | 10 | 5 | 1 | 1 | – | – | – |
| Neil Harvey | 32 | – | 6 | 13 | 9 | 3 | 1 | – | – | – | – |
| Ian Chappell | 30 | – | 18 | 8 | 1 | 1 | 2 | – | – | – | – |

## AUSTRALIA'S LEADING TEST CAPTAINS

(qualification: 20 Tests as captain)

|  | Tests | Won | Lost | Drawn | Tied | % won |
|---|---|---|---|---|---|---|
| D. G. Bradman | 24 | 15 | 3 | 6 | – | 62.5 |
| A. L. Hassett | 24 | 14 | 4 | 6 | – | 58.3 |
| W. M. Woodfull | 25 | 14 | 7 | 4 | – | 56.0 |
| M. A. Taylor | 50 | 26 | 13 | 11 | – | 52.0 |

**Australia's leading Test captains** (continued)

| | Tests | Won | Lost | Drawn | Tied | % won |
|---|---|---|---|---|---|---|
| I. M. Chappell | 30 | 15 | 5 | 10 | – | 50.0 |
| R. Benaud | 28 | 12 | 4 | 11 | 1 | 44.6 |
| G. S. Chappell | 48 | 21 | 13 | 14 | – | 43.7 |
| W. M. Lawry | 25 | 9 | 8 | 8 | – | 36.0 |
| A. R. Border | 93 | 32 | 22 | 38 | 1 | 34.9 |
| J. Darling | 21 | 7 | 4 | 10 | – | 33.3 |
| R. B. Simpson | 39 | 12 | 12 | 15 | – | 30.7 |
| K. J. Hughes | 28 | 4 | 13 | 11 | – | 14.3 |

(Tied Tests counted as 0.5 of a win for calculating percentage)

## BATTING RECORDS OF AUSTRALIAN CAPTAINS FROM BRADMAN TO TAYLOR

before and during captaincy

(qualification: minimum 10 Tests as captain, specialist batsmen only)

| | Tests | Inns | NO | Runs | HS | Avge | 100 | 50 |
|---|---|---|---|---|---|---|---|---|
| **D. G. Bradman** | | | | | | | | |
| non-captain | 28 | 42 | 3 | 3849 | 334 | 98.69 | 15 | 6 |
| as captain | 24 | 38 | 7 | 3147 | 270 | 101.51 | 14 | 7 |
| Total | 52 | 80 | 10 | 6996 | 334 | 99.94 | 29 | 13 |
| **A. L. Hassett** | | | | | | | | |
| non-captain | 19 | 28 | 2 | 1192 | 198 * | 45.84 | 3 | 3 |
| as captain | 24 | 41 | 1 | 1881 | 167 | 47.02 | 7 | 8 |
| Total | 43 | 69 | 3 | 3073 | 198 * | 46.56 | 10 | 11 |
| **R. B. Simpson** | | | | | | | | |
| non-captain | 23 | 40 | 3 | 1246 | 92 | 33.67 | – | 11 |
| as captain | 39 | 71 | 4 | 3623 | 311 | 54.07 | 10 | 16 |
| Total | 62 | 111 | 7 | 4869 | 311 | 46.81 | 10 | 27 |
| **W. M. Lawry** | | | | | | | | |
| non-captain | 42 | 76 | 6 | 3314 | 210 | 47.34 | 9 | 16 |
| as captain | 25 | 47 | 6 | 1920 | 205 | 46.82 | 4 | 11 |
| Total | 67 | 123 | 12 | 5234 | 210 | 47.15 | 13 | 27 |

| | Tests | Inns | NO | Runs | HS | Avge | 100 | 50 |
|---|---|---|---|---|---|---|---|---|
| **I. M. Chappell** | | | | | | | | |
| non-captain | 45 | 82 | 7 | 2795 | 165 | 37.26 | 7 | 12 |
| as captain | 30 | 54 | 3 | 2550 | 196 | 50.00 | 7 | 14 |
| Total | 75 | 136 | 10 | 5345 | 196 | 42.42 | 14 | 26 |
| **G. S. Chappell** | | | | | | | | |
| non-captain | 39 | 65 | 9 | 2901 | 247 * | 51.80 | 11 | 12 |
| as captain | 48 | 86 | 10 | 4209 | 235 | 55.38 | 13 | 19 |
| Total | 87 | 151 | 19 | 7110 | 247 * | 53.86 | 24 | 31 |
| **K. J. Hughes** | | | | | | | | |
| non-captain | 42 | 73 | 4 | 2689 | 213 | 38.97 | 7 | 12 |
| as captain | 28 | 51 | 2 | 1726 | 106 | 35.22 | 2 | 10 |
| Total | 70 | 124 | 6 | 4415 | 213 | 37.41 | 9 | 22 |
| **A. R. Border** | | | | | | | | |
| non-captain | 63 | 111 | 20 | 4551 | 162 | 50.06 | 12 | 27 |
| as captain | 93 | 154 | 24 | 6623 | 205 | 50.94 | 15 | 36 |
| Total | 156 | 265 | 44 | 11174 | 205 | 50.56 | 27 | 63 |
| **M. A. Taylor** | | | | | | | | |
| non-captain | 54 | 97 | 6 | 4275 | 219 | 46.97 | 12 | 24 |
| as captain | 50 | 89 | 7 | 3250 | 334 * | 39.63 | 7 | 16 |
| Total | 104 | 186 | 13 | 7525 | 334 * | 43.49 | 19 | 40 |

Note: I. W. Johnson (17 Tests as captain) and R. Benaud (28 Tests as captain) are not listed as both were selected primarily as bowlers. *Indicates not out.

## MARK TAYLOR'S FIFTY TESTS AS CAPTAIN

### 1994–95 v Pakistan in Pakistan

1: v PAKISTAN–1st Test (Karachi), 28 September–2 October 1994. Lost by one wicket. AUSTRALIA 337 (M. G. Bevan 82, S. R. Waugh 73, I. A. Healy 57) and 232 (D. C. Boon 114 not out; Wasim Akram 5/64, Waqar Younis 4/69); PAKISTAN 256 (Saeed Anwar 85) and 9/315 (Saeed Anwar 77, Inzamam-ul-Haq 58 not out; S. K. Warne 5/89).

2: v PAKISTAN–2nd Test (Rawalpindi), 5–9 October 1994. Drawn. AUSTRALIA 9/521 dec. (M. J. Slater 110, S. R. Waugh 98, M. G. Bevan 70, M. A. Taylor 69,

M. E. Waugh 68, I. A. Healy 58) and 1/14; PAKISTAN 260 (Aamir Sohail 80; C. J. McDermott 4/74, D. W. Fleming 4/75) and 537 (Saleem Malik 237, Saeed Anwar 75, Aamir Sohail 72, Aamer Malik 65).

3: v PAKISTAN–3rd Test (Lahore), 1–5 November 1994. Drawn.
PAKISTAN 373 (Moin Khan 115 not out, Saleem Malik 75, Inzamam-ul-Haq 66; S. K. Warne 6/136) and 404 (Saleem Malik 143, Aamir Sohail 105; G. D. McGrath 4/92); AUSTRALIA 455 (M. G. Bevan 91, M. J. Slater 74, M. E. Waugh 71, J. L. Langer 69; Mohsin Kamal 4/116, Mushtaq Ahmed 4/121).

## 1994–95 v England in Australia

4: v ENGLAND–1st Test (Brisbane), 25–29 November 1994. Won by 184 runs.
AUSTRALIA 426 (M. J. Slater 176, M. E. Waugh 140, M. A. Taylor 59; D. Gough 4/107) and 8/248 dec. (M. A. Taylor 58; P. C. R. Tufnell 4/79); ENGLAND 167 (M. A. Atherton 54; C. J. McDermott 6/53) and 323 (G. A. Hick 80, G. P. Thorpe 67, G. A. Gooch 56; S. K. Warne 8/71).

5: v ENGLAND–2nd Test (Melbourne), 24–29 December 1994. Won by 295 runs.
AUSTRALIA 279 (S. R. Waugh 94 not out, M. E. Waugh 71; D. Gough 4/60) and 7/320 dec. (D. C. Boon 131); ENGLAND 212 (G. P. Thorpe 51; S. K. Warne 6/64) and 92 (C. J. McDermott 5/42, S. K. Warne 3/16 inc. hat-trick).

6: v ENGLAND–3rd Test (Sydney), 1–5 January 1995. Drawn.
ENGLAND 309 (M. A. Atherton 88, J. P. Crawley 72, D. Gough 51; C. J. McDermott 5/101) and 2/255 dec. (G. A. Hick 98 not out, M. A. Atherton 67); AUSTRALIA 116 (D. Gough 6/49) and 7/344 (M. A. Taylor 113, M. J. Slater 103; A. R. C. Fraser 5/73).

7: v ENGLAND–4th Test (Adelaide), 26–30 January 1995. Lost by 106 runs.
ENGLAND 353 (M. W. Gatting 117, M. A. Atherton 80) and 328 (P. A. J. DeFreitas 88, G. P. Thorpe 83, J. P. Crawley 71; M. E. Waugh 5/40); AUSTRALIA 419 (G. S. Blewett 102 not out, M. A. Taylor 90, I. A. Healy 74, M. J. Slater 67) and 156 (I. A. Healy 51 not out; C. C. Lewis 4/24, D. E. Malcolm 4/39).

8: v ENGLAND–5th Test (Perth), 3–7 February 1995. Won by 329 runs.
AUSTRALIA 402 (M. J. Slater 124, S. R. Waugh 99 not out, M. E. Waugh 88) and 8/345 dec. (G. S. Blewett 115, S. R. Waugh 80, M. A. Taylor 52); ENGLAND 295 (G. P. Thorpe 123, M. R. Ramprakash 72) and 123 (C. J. McDermott 6/38).

## 1994–95 v West Indies in West Indies

9: v WEST INDIES–1st Test (Bridgetown), 31 March–2 April 1995. Won by 10 wickets.
WEST INDIES 195 (B. C. Lara 65, C. L. Hooper 60; B. P. Julian 4/36) and 189 (G. D. McGrath 5/68); AUSTRALIA 346 (I. A. Healy 74 not out, S. R. Waugh 65, M. A. Taylor 55) and 0/39.

10: v WEST INDIES–2nd Test (St John's), 8–13 April 1995. Drawn.
AUSTRALIA 216 (C. A. Walsh 6/54) and 7/300 dec. (D. C. Boon 67, S. R. Waugh 65 not out, M. E. Waugh 61); WEST INDIES 260 (B. C. Lara 88) and 2/80.

11: v WEST INDIES–3rd Test (Port-of-Spain), 21–23 April 1995. Lost by nine wickets.
AUSTRALIA 128 (S. R. Waugh 63 not out; C. E. L. Ambrose 5/45) and 105 (C. E. L. Ambrose 4/20); WEST INDIES 136 (G. D. McGrath 6/47) and 1/98.

12: v WEST INDIES–4th Test (Kingston), 29 April–3 May 1995. Won by an innings & 53 runs.
WEST INDIES 265 (R. B. Richardson 100, B. C. Lara 65) and 213 (W. K. M. Benjamin 51; P. R. Reiffel 4/47, S. K. Warne 4/70); AUSTRALIA 531 (S. R. Waugh 200, M. E. Waugh 126, G. S. Blewett 69).

---

## 1995–96 v Pakistan in Australia

13: v PAKISTAN–1st Test (Brisbane), 9–13 November 1995. Won by an innings & 126 runs.
AUSTRALIA 463 (S. R. Waugh 112 not out, M. A. Taylor 69, M. E. Waugh 59, G. S. Blewett 57, D. C. Boon 54); PAKISTAN 97 (S. K. Warne 7/23) and 240 (Aamir Sohail 99, Inzamam-ul-Haq 62; S. K. Warne 4/54, G. D. McGrath 4/76).

14: v PAKISTAN–2nd Test (Hobart), 17–20 November 1995. Won by 155 runs.
AUSTRALIA 267 (M. E. Waugh 88; Mushtaq Ahmed 5/115) and 306 (M. A. Taylor 123, M. J. Slater 73; Mushtaq Ahmed 4/83); PAKISTAN 198 (Rameez Raja 59; P. R. Reiffel 4/38) and 220 (Aamir Sohail 57; G. D. McGrath 5/61).

15: v PAKISTAN–3rd Test (Sydney), 30 November–4 December 1995. Lost by 74 runs.
PAKISTAN 299 (Ijaz Ahmed 137; S. K. Warne 4/55) and 204 (Inzamam-ul-Haq 59; C. J. McDermott 5/49, S. K. Warne 4/66); AUSTRALIA 257 (M. E. Waugh 116; Mushtaq Ahmed 5/95, Wasim Akram 4/50) and 172 (M. A. Taylor 59; Mushtaq Ahmed 4/91).

---

## 1995–96 v Sri Lanka in Australia

16: v SRI LANKA–1st Test (Perth), 8–11 December 1995. Won by an innings & 36 runs. SRI LANKA 251 (R. S. Kaluwitharana 50; G. D. McGrath 4/81) and 330 (H. P. Tillekeratne 119); AUSTRALIA 5/617 dec. (M. J. Slater 219, M. E. Waugh 111, R. T. Ponting 96, M. A. Taylor 96, S. G. Law 54 not out).

17: v SRI LANKA–2nd Test (Melbourne), 26–30 December 1995. Won by 10 wickets. AUSTRALIA 6/500 dec. (S. R. Waugh 131 not out, D. C. Boon 110, R. T. Ponting 71, M. J. Slater 62, M. E. Waugh 61) and 0/41; SRI LANKA 233 (A. Ranatunga 51, R. S. Kaluwitharana 50; G. D. McGrath 5/40) and 307 (A. P. Gurusinha 143; S. K. Warne 4/71).

18: v SRI LANKA–3rd Test (Adelaide), 25–29 January 1996. Won by 148 runs. AUSTRALIA 9/502 dec. (S. R. Waugh 170, M. E. Waugh 71, I. A. Healy 70, P. R. Reiffel 56) and 6/215 dec. (S. R. Waugh 61 not out); SRI LANKA 317 (H. P. Tillekeratne 65, S. Ranatunga 60; P. R. Reiffel 5/39, G. D. McGrath 4/91) and 252 (S. T. Jayasuriya 112, S. Ranatunga 65; S. R. Waugh 4/34).

## 1996–97 v India in India

19: v INDIA–Only Test (Delhi), 10–13 October 1996. Lost by seven wickets. AUSTRALIA 182 (A. Kumble 4/63) and 234 (S. R. Waugh 67 not out; A. Kumble 5/67); INDIA 361 (N. R. Mongia 152, S. C. Ganguly 66) and 3/58.

## 1996–97 v West Indies in Australia

20: v WEST INDIES–1st Test (Brisbane), 22–26 November 1996. Won by 123 runs. AUSTRALIA 479 (I. A. Healy 161 not out, R. T. Ponting 88, S. R. Waugh 66; C. A. Walsh 4/112) and 6/217 dec. (M. E. Waugh 57); WEST INDIES 277 (C. L. Hooper 102, S. Chanderpaul 82; P. R. Reiffel 4/58) and 296 (S. L. Campbell 113; G. D. McGrath 4/60).

21: v WEST INDIES–2nd Test (Sydney), 29 November–3 December 1996. Won by 124 runs.
AUSTRALIA 331 (G. S. Blewett 69; C. A. Walsh 5/98) and 4/312 dec. (M. T. G. Elliott 78 r.h., M. E. Waugh 67, M. G. Bevan 52); WEST INDIES 304 (S. L. Campbell 77; G. D. McGrath 4/82) and 215 (S. Chanderpaul 71, C. L. Hooper 57; S. K. Warne 4/95).

22: v WEST INDIES–3rd Test (Melbourne), 26–28 December 1996. Lost by six wickets. AUSTRALIA 219 (G. S. Blewett 62, S. R. Waugh 58; C. E. L. Ambrose 5/55) and 122

(C. E. L. Ambrose 4/17); WEST INDIES 255 (J. C. Adams 74 not out, S. Chanderpaul 58, J. R. Murray 53; G. D. McGrath 5/50) and 4/87.

23: v WEST INDIES–4th Test (Adelaide), 25–28 January 1997. Won by an innings & 183 runs.
WEST INDIES 130 (M. G. Bevan 4/31) and 204 (B. C. Lara 78; M. G. Bevan 6/82); AUSTRALIA 517 (M. L. Hayden 125, G. S. Blewett 99, M. G. Bevan 85 not out, M. E. Waugh 82).

24: v WEST INDIES–5th Test (Perth), 1–3 February 1997. Lost by 10 wickets.
AUSTRALIA 243 (M. G. Bevan 87 not out, M. E. Waugh 79; C. E. L. Ambrose 5/43) and 194 (C. A. Walsh 5/74); WEST INDIES 384 (B. C. Lara 132, R. G. Samuels 76, C. L. Hooper 57; P. R. Reiffel 5/73).

---

## 1996–97 v South Africa in South Africa

25: v SOUTH AFRICA–1st Test (Johannesburg), 28 February–4 March 1997. Won by an innings & 196 runs.
SOUTH AFRICA 302 (W. J. Cronje 76, D. J. Richardson 72 not out; G. D. McGrath 4/77) and 130 (M. G. Bevan 4/32, S. K. Warne 4/43); AUSTRALIA 8/628 dec. (G. S. Blewett 214, S. R. Waugh 160, M. T. G. Elliott 85).

26: v SOUTH AFRICA–2nd Test (Port Elizabeth), 14–17 March 1997. Won by two wickets.
SOUTH AFRICA 209 (B. M. McMillan 55; J. N. Gillespie 5/54) and 168; AUSTRALIA 108 and 8/271 (M. E. Waugh 116).

27: v SOUTH AFRICA–3rd Test (Centurion), 21–24 March 1997. Lost by eight wickets.
AUSTRALIA 227 (S. R. Waugh 67; B. N. Schultz 4/52) and 185 (S. R. Waugh 60 not out; A. A. Donald 5/36); SOUTH AFRICA 384 (A. M. Bacher 96, W. J. Cronje 79 not out, B. M. McMillan 55; G. D. McGrath 6/86) and 2/32.

---

## 1997 v England in England

28: v ENGLAND–1st Test (Birmingham), 5–8 June 1997. Lost by nine wickets.
AUSTRALIA 118 (A. R. Caddick 5/50) and 477 (M. A. Taylor 129, G. S. Blewett 125, M. T. G. Elliott 66); ENGLAND 9/478 dec. (N. Hussain 207, G. P. Thorpe 138, M. A. Ealham 53 not out; M. S. Kasprowicz 4/113) and 1/119 (M. A. Atherton 57 not out).

29: v ENGLAND–2nd Test (Lord's), 19–23 June 1997. Drawn.

ENGLAND 77 (G. D. McGrath 8/38) and 4/266 dec. (M. A. Butcher 87, M. A. Atherton 77); AUSTRALIA 7/213 dec. (M. T. G. Elliott 112; A. R. Caddick 4/71).

30: v ENGLAND–3rd Test (Manchester), 3–7 July 1997. Won by 268 runs.

AUSTRALIA 235 (S. R. Waugh 108; D. W. Headley 4/72) and 8/395 dec. (S. R. Waugh 116, M. E. Waugh 55, S. K. Warne 53; D. W. Headley 4/104); ENGLAND 162 (M. A. Butcher 51; S. K. Warne 6/48) and 200 (J. P. Crawley 83; G. D. McGrath 4/46).

31: v ENGLAND–4th Test (Leeds), 24–28 July 1997. Won by an innings & 61 runs.

ENGLAND 172 (J. N. Gillespie 7/37) and 268 (N. Hussain 105, J. P. Crawley 72; P. R. Reiffel 5/49); AUSTRALIA 9/501 dec. (M. T. G. Elliott 199, R. T. Ponting 127, P. R. Reiffel 54 not out; D. Gough 5/149).

32: v ENGLAND–5th Test (Nottingham), 7–10 August 1997. Won by 264 runs.

AUSTRALIA 427 (M. A. Taylor 76, S. R. Waugh 75, M. T. G. Elliott 69, M. E. Waugh 68, G. S. Blewett 50; D. W. Headley 4/87) and 336 (I. A. Healy 63, G. S. Blewett 60); ENGLAND 313 (A. J. Stewart 87, G. P. Thorpe 53; G. D. McGrath 4/71, S. K. Warne 4/86) and 186 (G. P. Thorpe 82 not out).

33: v ENGLAND–6th Test (Kennington Oval), 21–23 August 1997. Lost by 19 runs.

ENGLAND 180 (G. D. McGrath 7/76) and 163 (G. P. Thorpe 62; M. S. Kasprowicz 7/36); AUSTRALIA 220 (P. C. R. Tufnell 7/66) and 104 (A. R. Caddick 5/42, P. C. R. Tufnell 4/27).

---

## 1997–98 v New Zealand in Australia

34: v NEW ZEALAND–1st Test (Brisbane), 7–11 November 1997. Won by 186 runs.

AUSTRALIA 373 (M. A. Taylor 112, P. R. Reiffel 77, I. A. Healy 68; S. B. Doull 4/70, C. L. Cairns 4/90) and 6/294 dec. (G. S. Blewett 91, R. T. Ponting 73 not out); NEW ZEALAND 349 (S. P. Fleming 91, C. L. Cairns 64, B. A. Pocock 57, C. D. McMillan 54; S. K. Warne 4/106) and 132 (G. D. McGrath 5/32).

35: v NEW ZEALAND–2nd Test (Perth), 20–23 November 1997. Won by an innings & 70 runs.

NEW ZEALAND 217 (C. D. McMillan 54, C. L. Cairns 52; S. K. Warne 4/83) and 174 (A. C. Parore 63; S. H. Cook 5/39); AUSTRALIA 461 (S. R. Waugh 96, M. E. Waugh 86, I. A. Healy 85, P. R. Reiffel 54; C. L. Cairns 4/95).

36: v NEW ZEALAND–3rd Test (Hobart), 27 November–1 December 1997. Drawn.

AUSTRALIA 400 (M. T. G. Elliott 114, G. S. Blewett 99, M. E. Waugh 81) and 2/138 dec.

(M. A. Taylor 66 not out, G. S. Blewett 56); NEW ZEALAND 6/251 dec. (M. J. Horne 133) and 9/223 (S. K. Warne 5/88).

## 1997–98 v South Africa in Australia

37: v SOUTH AFRICA–1st Test (Melbourne), 26–30 December 1997. Drawn.
AUSTRALIA 309 (R. T. Ponting 105, S. R. Waugh 96; P. L. Symcox 4/69) and 257 (P. R. Reiffel 79 not out, M. A. Taylor 59; A. A. Donald 6/59); SOUTH AFRICA 186 (G. Kirsten 83) and 7/273 (J. H. Kallis 101, W. J. Cronje 70).

38: v SOUTH AFRICA–2nd Test (Sydney), 2–5 January 1998. Won by an innings & 21 runs.
SOUTH AFRICA 287 (W. J. Cronje 88, H. H. Gibbs 54; S. K. Warne 5/75) and 113 (S. K. Warne 6/34); AUSTRALIA 421 (M. E. Waugh 100, S. R. Waugh 85, R. T. Ponting 62).

39: v SOUTH AFRICA–3rd Test (Adelaide), 30 January–3 February 1998. Drawn.
SOUTH AFRICA 517 (B. M. McMillan 87 not out, G. Kirsten 77, W. J. Cronje 73, A. M. Bacher 64, P. L. Symcox 54) and 6/193 dec. (G. Kirsten 108 not out); AUSTRALIA 350 (M. A. Taylor 169 not out, M. E. Waugh 63; S. M. Pollock 7/87) and 7/227 (M. E. Waugh 115 not out; L. Klusener 4/67).

## 1997–98 v India in India

40: v INDIA–1st Test (Chennai), 6–10 March 1998. Lost by 179 runs.
INDIA 257 (N. S. Sidhu 62, N. R. Mongia 58, R. S. Dravid 52; G. R. Robertson 4/72, S. K. Warne 4/85) and 4/418 dec. (S. R. Tendulkar 155 not out, M. Azharuddin 64, N. S. Sidhu 64, R. S. Dravid 56); AUSTRALIA 328 (I. A. Healy 90, M. E. Waugh 66, G. R. Robertson 57; A. Kumble 4/103) and 168 (A. Kumble 4/46).

41: v INDIA–2nd Test (Calcutta), on 18–21 March 1998. Lost by an innings & 219 runs.
AUSTRALIA 233 (S. R. Waugh 80, R. T. Ponting 60) and 181 (A. Kumble 5/62); INDIA 5/633 dec. (M. Azharuddin 163 not out, N. S. Sidhu 97, V. V. S. Laxman 95, R. S. Dravid 86, S. R. Tendulkar 79, S. C. Ganguly 65).

42: v INDIA–3rd Test (Bangalore), 25–28 March 1998. Won by eight wickets.
INDIA 424 (S. R. Tendulkar 177, N. S. Sidhu 74) and 169 (M. S. Kasprowicz 5/28); AUSTRALIA 400 (M. E. Waugh 153 not out, M. J. Slater 91, D. S. Lehmann 52; A. Kumble 6/98) and 2/195 (M. A. Taylor 102 not out).

### 1998–99 v Pakistan in Pakistan

43: v PAKISTAN (Rawalpindi), 1–5 October 1998. Won by an innings & 99 runs.
PAKISTAN 269 (Saeed Anwar 145; S. C. G. MacGill 5/66) and 145 (Saleem Malik 52 not out; S. C. G. MacGill 4/47); AUSTRALIA 513 (S. R. Waugh 157 M. J. Slater 108, D. S. Lehmann 98, I. A. Healy 82).

44: v PAKISTAN (Peshawar), 16–20 October 1998. Drawn.
AUSTRALIA 4/599 dec. (M. A. Taylor 334 not out, J. L. Langer 116, R. T. Ponting 76 not out) and 5/289 (M. A. Taylor 92); PAKISTAN 9/580 dec. (Ijaz Ahmed 155, Saeed Anwar 126, Inzamam-ul-Haq 97).

45: v PAKISTAN (Karachi), 22–26 October 1998. Drawn.
AUSTRALIA 280 (M. J. Slater 96; Shahid Afridi 5/52) and 390 (M. E. Waugh 117, M. A. Taylor 68, J. L. Langer 51; Shakeel Ahmed 4/91); PAKISTAN 252 (Aamir Sohail 133; G. D. McGrath 5/66) and 5/262 (Ijaz Ahmed 120 not out, Moin Khan 75).

---

### 1998–99 v England in Australia

46: v ENGLAND (Brisbane), 20–24 November 1998. Drawn.
AUSTRALIA 485 (I. A. Healy 134, S. R. Waugh 112, D. W. Fleming 71 not out; A. D. Mullally 5/105) and 3/237 dec. (M. J. Slater 113, J. L. Langer 74); ENGLAND 375 (M. A. Butcher 116, G. P. Thorpe 77, M. R. Ramprakash 69 not out, N. Hussain 59; G. D. McGrath 6/85) and 6/179.

47: v ENGLAND (Perth), 28–30 November 1998. Won by seven wickets.
ENGLAND 112 (D. W. Fleming 5/46) and 191 (G. A. Hick 68; J. N. Gillespie 5/88, D. W. Fleming 4/45); AUSTRALIA 240 (M. A. Taylor 61; A. J. Tudor 4/89) and 3/64.

48: v ENGLAND (Adelaide), 11–15 December 1998. Won by 205 runs.
AUSTRALIA 391 (J. L. Langer 179 not out, M. A. Taylor 59, S. R. Waugh 59; D. W. Headley 4/97) and 5/278 dec. (M. J. Slater 103, J. L. Langer 52, M. E. Waugh 51 not out); ENGLAND 227 (N. Hussain 89 not out, M. R. Ramprakash 61; S. C. G. MacGill 4/53) and 237 (A. J. Stewart 63 not out, M. R. Ramprakash 57; G. D. McGrath 4/50).

49: v ENGLAND (Melbourne), 26–29 December 1998. Lost by 12 runs.
ENGLAND 270 (A. J. Stewart 107, M. R. Ramprakash 63; S. C. G. MacGill 4/61) and 244 (G. A. Hick 60, A. J. Stewart 52, N. Hussain 50); AUSTRALIA 340 (S. R. Waugh 122 not out; D. Gough 5/96) and 162 (D. W. Headley 6/60).

50: v ENGLAND (Sydney), 2–5 January 1999. Won by 98 runs.

AUSTRALIA 322 (M. E. Waugh 121, S. R. Waugh 96; D. W. Headley 4/62, D. Gough 3/61 (inc. hat-trick) and 184 (M. J. Slater 123; P. M. Such 5/81, D. W. Headley 4/40); ENGLAND 220 (S. C. G. MacGill 5/57) and 188 (N. Hussain 53; S. C. G. MacGill 7/50).

Statistics: Ken Williams

# FURTHER READING

*Allan's Australian Cricket Annual.*

*Australian Cricket* magazine.

Benaud, John. *Matters of Choice*. Swan Publishing, 1997.

Boon, David and Thomas, Mark. *Under the Southern Cross: The Autobiography of David Boon*. HarperCollins, 1997.

Chevell, Kevin. *Rebuilding Your Body, Your Mind and Your Life*. Information Australia, 1998.

*Cricketer* magazine.

Frindall, Bill, ed./compiler. *The Wisden Book of Test Cricket*, Volume 2, 1977–94. Headline, 1995.

Hair, Darrell. *Decision Maker: An Umpire's Story*. Random House, 1998.

Healy, Ian, as told to Craddock, Robert. *Playing for Keeps: The Ian Healy Story*. Swan Publishing, 1996.

*Inside Edge* magazine.

Marks, Neil. *Tales for All Seasons*. HarperSports, 1997.

—— *Tales from the Locker Room*. Ironbark, 1993.

Maxwell, Jim, ed. *The ABC Cricket Book*. 1997.

McGrath, Glenn, with Lane, Daniel. *Pacemaker: The Inner Thoughts of Glenn McGrath*. Ironbark, 1998.

Perry, Roland. *Bold Warnie*. Random House, 1999.

Piesse, Ken, ed. *Australian Cricket Tour Guide*.

—— *Warne: Sultan of Spin*. Modern Publishing, 1995.

Ray, Mark. *Border & Beyond*. ABC Books, 1995.

Reiffel, Paul, with Baum, Greg. *Reiffel Inside Out*. HarperSports, 1998.

Simpson, Bob. *The Reasons Why*. HarperSports, 1996.

*Talking Cricket with Frank Crook*. ABC, 1989.

Taylor, Mark. *A Captain's Year*. Ironbark, 1997.

—— *Taylor Made: A Year in the Life of Australia's Cricket Captain*. Ironbark, 1995.

Warne, Shane. *My Own Story*. Swan Publishing, 1997.

Waugh, Stephen. *Steve Waugh's 1997 Ashes Diary*. HarperSports, 1997.

—— *Steve Waugh's West Indian Tour Diary*. HarperSports, 1995.

Waugh, Mark, with Keiza, Grantlee. *A Year to Remember*. Random House, 1997.

*Wisden Australia*. Hardie Grant Books.

*Wisden Cricketers' Almanack*. John Wisden & Co.

# INDEX

Numbers in **bold** indicate profile.

Aamir Malik 29
Aamir Sohail 30, 78, 85, 171
Adams, Jimmy 65, 71, 106–7, 149
Adams, Paul 119
Alcott, Errol 79, 147
Alderman, Terry 62, 185
Allom, Maurice 29
Ambrose, Curtly 11, 39, 64, 68, 69, 99,
    106, 107, 114, 150, 194, 202
  confrontation with Steve Waugh 70–1
  sleeping giant awakes 111–12
Angel, Jo 3, 26, 29
Armstrong, Warwick 4
Arshad Khan 172
Astle, Nathan 143
Atherton, Mike 38, 42, 43, 48, 57, 78, 174
Australian Cricket Academy 22
Azharuddin, Mohammad 156, 157

Bardsley, Warren 196
Barker, Lloyd 89
Barkley, Charles 194
Barlow, Eddie 126
Barnes, Sid 20
Basit Ali 86
Bedi, Bishen 156
Benaud, John 35
Benaud, Richie 26, 36, 98, 131, 202, 205
Benjamin, Joey 43
Benjamin, Kenny 64, 67, 72

Benjamin, Winston 64, 72
Bernard, Steve 198
Berry, Darren 140
Bevan, Michael 26, 28, 61, 111, 119, 120,
    122, 158
  game of his life 114–15
Bichel, Andy 113, 118, 136, 141
Bird, Dickie 26
Bishop, Ian 114
Blazey, John 15
Blewett family 61
Blewett, Greg 3, 57, **61–2**, 71, 73, 84, 86,
    112, 115, 121, 133, 143, 155, 201, 205
  bats through day's play 118–19
Bodyline 68, 143
Boon, David 3, 7, 8, 11, 21, 26, 36, 43,
    44–5, 46, 49, 50, 62, 67, 74, 76, 88,
    89, **90–3**, 104, 126, 148, 175
  all-time favourite memory 91
  farewell Test 89
  Geoff Marsh's tribute 93
  one-hundredth Test 69
Boon, Lesley 93
Border, Allan 6, 11, 18, 19, 25, 26, 36, 39,
    40, 65, 76, 90–1, 111, 125, 126, 139,
    166, 170, 175, 179, 191, 192, 194
  denied his finest moment 10
  leadership style compared with Mark
    Taylor's 7
  tribute to Taylor 203

Botham, Ian 146
Bower, Rod 16
Boyle, Raelene 205
Bradman, Don 2, 50, 61, 62, 105, 131, 133,
    138, 152, 169, 170–1, 200, 203
  Bradman's Invincibles 11, 52, 144, 167,
    179
  captaincy record 113
Brayshaw, James 57
Browne, Courtney 72
Bucknor, Steve 45, 168
Butcher, Mark 182

Cairns, Chris 141
Callahan, Simone 80
Campbell, Sherwin 65, 106
Carey, Wayne
  tribute to Mark Taylor 203
Chanderpaul, Shivnarine 106–7, 110, 114
Chappell brothers
  family record surpassed 116
Chappell, Greg 4, 91, 99–100, 125,
    129–30, 146
  advocates Warne for captaincy 146
  tribute to Mark Taylor 204
Chappell, Ian 4, 40, 87, 131, 189, 194,
    205
Chevell, Kevin 103, 161–3, 169
Cleese, John 136
Collymore, Corey 79, 201, 202
Conn, Malcolm 87, 120, 144, 156
Cook, Simon 141, 142, 143
Cowper, Bob 169
Cozier, Tony 110
Craddock, Robert 66, 156
Craig, Ian 61
Crawley, John 57
Croft, Colin 34
Crompton, Alan 8, 133
  tribute to Mark Taylor 204
Cronje, Hansie 119, 120, 122, 123
  Adelaide anger 144
Crook, Frank 18
Cullinan, Daryll 119

Dale, Adam 139, 153, 200
  concedes 22 in one over 201
Dale, Kevin 176
Darling, Joe 4, 26
Davis, Steve 144
DeFreitas, Phil 41, 43, 44, 57, 58, 59, 130
De Silva, Aravinda 87–8, 90, 96
Donald, Allan 96, 124
Done, Richard 21
Doull, Simon 142
Dowling, Graham 87
Dyson, John 16

Ealham, Alan 136
Eastwood, Clint 59, 70
Edwards, Jack 80–1
Elliott, Matthew 107, 108–10, 119, 135,
    143, 198
  maiden Test century 134
  mix-up with Hayden 122
  operations to both knees 141

Fleming, Damien 20, 27, 29, 42, 44, 48, 58,
    60, 64, 181
  first Test in three years 165
  highest Test score 177
Fordham, John 188, 189, 190
  tribute to Mark Taylor 204
Fraser, Angus 49, 58
Freedman, Brian 128, 196

Garner, Joel 33
Gasnier, Reg 205
Gatting, Mike 34, 58, 59, 110
Gibbs, Lance 36, 146, 156
Gilchrist, Adam 139, 140, 146, 147, 149,
    200
Gillespie, Jason 'Dizzy' 96, 117, 118,
    121–2, 141, 177, 198, 199
  fastest spell of his life 135
Gooch, Graham 43, 49, 59, 126, 171
Gough, Darren 38, 39, 41, 43, 44, 47, 49,
    58, 174, 177, 178, 179, 180, 188, 202
  Melbourne hat-trick 181–2
Gower, David 126

Greenidge, Gordon & Haynes, Desmond 46
Gregory, Jack 4
Griffith, Adrian 79, 202
Grimmett, Clarrie 34
Gurusinha, Asanka 87, 90

Hadlee, Richard 92
Hagdorn, Kim 40
Hair, Darrell 10, 115
  no-balling of Muralitharan 87, 89
Halbish, Graham
  tribute to Mark Taylor 205
Hammer, M.C. 135
Hammond, Jeff 64
Hanif Mohammad 171
Harvey, Neil 193
Hassett, Lindsay 113
Hayden, Matthew 47, 51, 109, 112, 115,
    201
  mix-up with Elliott 122
Haynes, Desmond 10
Headley, Dean 179, 180
Heal, Shane 194
Healy, Ian 1, 3, 4, 7–8, 20, 21, 28, 29, 30,
    41, 43, 44, 54, 58, 59, 65, 74–5, 81,
    86, 97, 118, 136, 138, 140, **146–9**,
    154, 155, 172, 175, 177, 182, 189,
    194, 198, 200, 201, 202
  accused by Lara 111
  advocates Steve Waugh as Australia's next
    captain 120–1
  captain of Australia 103
  confrontation with Ranatunga 88
  fastest bowling spell of his time 135
  mimicking a cross-dresser at St John's 149
  missed catch off Lara 147, 200
  missed stumping off Inzamam 26, 147
  record score by a wicketkeeper 108
  record 356th victim 167
  remarkable run-out of Ambrose 150
  removed as vice-captain 124
  Shane Warne's tribute 150
  South African suspension 124
  twenty-seven byes in a match 30
  winning six at Port Elizabeth 122

Healy, Laura 140
Hendy, Trevor 99
Hick, Graeme 48
Hobbs, Jack & Sutcliffe, Herbert 46
Hogg, Brad 84, 104
Hohns, Trevor 35, 107, 108, 146, 181, 200
Holdsworth, Wayne 162
Hookes, David 76
Hooper, Carl 64, 65, 66, 71, 72, 110
Horne, Matthew 143
Howard, John 132, 138, 146, 189, 191
Hoy, Greg 102–3
Hudson, Andrew 36, 120
Hughes, Austin 14, 15
Hughes, Kim 87, 191, 192
Hughes, Merv 11, 51, 75, 79, 98, 118, 135,
    147, 198
  weight problems 144–5
Hussain, Nasser 174, 177, 182
Hussey, Mike 84
Hutton, Len 43
Hayat, Khizer 88

Ijaz Ahmed (snr) 169, 172
Illingworth, Ray 47
Imran Khan 29, 85
Intikhab Alam 82, 85
Inzamam-ul-Haq 26, 27, 29

Jackson, Michael 110
Jacoby, Jason 175
Jarman, Barry 8
Javed Miandad 169
Jayasuriya, Sanath 88, 89, 90, 96
Jenner, Terry 35, 36, 82–3, 108, 145, 175
Johnson, David 54
Johnson, Ian 167
Jones, Dean 53, 73, 147, 148
  dropping of Mark Taylor 130, 131
Joseph, Dave 201
Joshi, Sunil 104
Julian, Brendon 64, 65, 67, 71

Kallis, Jacques 119–20, 121, 122, 123
  becomes Warne's 300th victim 145

Kaluwitharana, Romesh 90
Kapil Dev 95, 146
Kapoor, Aashish 104
Kasprowicz, Michael 107, 109, 143, 153, 154, 155–6, 157–8
Keating, Paul 38
King, Len 10
Kippax, Alan 126
Kirsten, Gary 121
Knott, Alan 148
Kumble, Anil 75, 104, 105, 155

Lane, Tim 144
Langer, Justin 112, 130, 131, 160, 165, 166, 172, 178, 180, 202
  famous stand at Peshawar 168
Lara, Brian 64, 65, 66, 67, 69, 71, 72, 73, 79, 85, 106, 151, 170, 195, 199, 201, 202, 206
  accusations against M. Waugh 126
  blow-up at WACA 115–16
  dispute with Healy 111
Laver, Frank 78
Law, Stuart 88
Lawry, Bill 8, 48
  tribute to Mark Taylor 205–6
Lawson, Geoff 'Henry' 17, 18, 52, 72, 76, 203
Laxman, V.V.S. 156
Lees, Ellis 13–14
Lehmann, Darren 57, 84, 153, 160, 166
Lewis, Chris 58, 59
Liebenberg, Karl 28
Lillee, Dennis 4, 64, 77, 98–9, 100, 103, 157–8, 163, 182, 185
Lloyd, Clive 33, 106, 111, 115, 144
Lloyd, David 79

Macartney, Charlie 52
MacGill, Stuart 135, 159, 160, 164–5, 172, 173, 177, 179, 180, 181, 182, 183–6, 189, 199
  nine Tests for 50 wickets 184
  struck for 12 6s in an innings 187
  tribute to Mark Taylor 206

MacGill, Terry 185
Majid Khan 70
Malcolm, Devon 38, 39, 41, 44, 47–8, 49, 58, 59, 62
Marks, Neil 14–15, 16, 17
  captaincy prediction 18
  tribute to Mark Taylor 183
Marsh, Geoff 4, 104, 111, 144, 146, 166, 173, 200
  opening combination with Mark Taylor 46
  succeeds Bob Simpson as coach 96–8
  tribute to David Boon 93
  voices concerns about Taylor form slump 121
Marsh, Rod 21, 36, 48, 77, 147, 148
Marshall, Malcolm 33, 100, 106, 112
Martin, Ray 10
Massie, Bob 64, 78
Matthew, Chris 16
Maxwell, Jim 136
May, Tim 10, 27, 44, 49, 60, 97, 104, 147
  bribery scandal 32
  lead role in pay dispute 137, 138
McCabe, Stan 126
McCague, Martin 43
McDermott, Craig 'Billy' 3, 10, 11, 21, 26, 27, 35, 36, 39, 42, 58, 59, 61–2, 77, 78, 83, 84, 86, 90, 96, 97, **98–101**, 103, 104, 117, 118, 135, 147, 164
  bomb threat 95
  breakdown in West Indies 64
  concedes 22 from an over 58
  health scare in England 100
  two-hundredth Test wicket 44
McDonald, Ian 8–9
McDonald, Ted 4
McGrath, Glenn 1, 3, 11, 22, 27, 31, 50–1, 64, 69, 72, 75, **77–9**, 88, 90, 99, 100, 118, 135, 141, 142, 153, 159, 163, 164, 165, 172, 174, 177, 179, 180, 181, 188, 196, 198, 201, 202, 205
  ball of his career 67, 79
  best figures for 75 years 134
  fitness campaign (1998) 161–3
  mastery over Lara 113–14, 151

six maidens in a row 172
suspended $2000 fine for sledging 179
two-hundredth wicket 182
McKenzie, Graham 185
McIntyre, Peter 35, 58, 62, 104
Miller, Colin 149, 165, 172, 181, 182, 200, 201
three wickets on debut 166–7
Mohammad Akram 85
Mohsin Kamal 129
Moin Khan 172
Mongia, Nayan 105
Morris, Arthur 196
& Barnes, Sid 46
Mullally, Alan 79, 177, 179–80
Muhammad Zahid 167, 168, 169
Muralitharan, Muttiah 88, 96
no-balled for throwing 87, 89, 90
Murray, Junior 10, 114
Mushtaq Ahmed 26, 27, 32, 85–6, 167, 171

Nobes, Paul 57
Norman, Greg 192

O'Connor, Bernie 14
O'Connor, Shayne 142–3
Oliver, Neville 204
O'Neill, Norman 61
Orchard, David 202
O'Reilly, Bill 'Tiger' 34

Packer, Kerry 137
Parore, Adam 142
Pascoe, Len 16
Patterson, Patrick 92, 99
Perkins, Kieren 132, 192
Perry, Neremiah 52, 193
Petherick, Peter 29
Phillips, Wayne 46
Philpott, Peter 184–5, 186
Pilon, Laurie 12
Pilon, Rod 12, 13–14
player pay dispute 137–9
Pollock, Shaun 144

Ponting, Ricky 3, 74, 90, 104, 130, 135, 155, 195
unlucky to miss debut century 88
Potter, Jack 36, 114

Rackemann, Carl 198
Rafter, Pat 2
Ramprakash, Mark 177, 189
Ranatunga, Arjuna 88, 90
sour relations with Australians 94
World Cup triumph 96
Randell, Steve 45
Rashid Latif 30
Ray, Mark 31, 50, 87
Reed, Ron 173
Reid, John 51, 179
Reiffel, Paul 64, 65, 71, 73, 90, 118, 135, 136, 148, 160
forced to field when injured 156
shoulder operation 160–1
Rhodes, Steve 44
Richards, Viv 33, 53, 66, 91, 133, 153
only duck of his career in Caribbean 99
Richardson, Dave 121, 123
Richardson, Richie 64, 65, 69, 70, 71, 81, 95, 107
Ritchie, Greg 'Fat Cat' 73
Rixon, Steve 17, 141, 203
Roberts, Andy 67, 81
Robertson, Gavin 27, 153, 155, 156
ten runs from his first over in Tests 154
Roebuck, Peter 153, 154, 182
Rogers, Denis 8, 177, 190–1
tribute to Mark Taylor 206

Sadler, Rohan 175
Saeed Anwar 25, 84, 165, 167
Saleem Malik 20, 25, 29, 36, 42, 83–4, 169
Australian tour (1995–96) 84–6
bribery scandal 31–3, 82
mastery over Shane Warne 82
Samuels, Robert 106, 108, 115–16
Schultz, Brett 124
Shastri, Ravi 35

Shoaib Akhtar 161, 168, 169
  timed at 156 km/h 167
Siddons, Jamie 84
Sidhu, Navjot 154, 155, 157
Simmons, Phil 115
Simpson, Bob 21, 33, 42, 49, 52, 74, 91,
    92, 131–2, 169, 172–3, 195
  opening combination with Bill Lawry 46
  replaced by Geoff Marsh 96–8
  role under Taylor 40
Skilton, Bobby 205
Slater, Michael 7, 23, 28, 41, 42, 47,
    48–9, **51–6**, 59, 60, 63, 67, 72, 75,
    85, 108, 109, 130, 157, 160, 164, 166,
    167, 168, 171–2, 173, 178, 180, 181,
    182, 201, 203
  Bodyline revisited 68
  career-best double century 88
  first Tests in 18 months 153–5
Smith, Steve 16
Smith, Warren 53
Squires, Tony 11
Srinath, Javagal 155
statistical tables (in text)
  Australia's leading Ashes centurions 54
  Australia's Test resurrection 22
  Mark Taylor & Michael Slater in Test
    cricket 55, 56
  Mark Taylor's best Test series 173
  Mark Taylor's first 5000 runs 76
  Mark Taylor's Test opening partners 56
  most catches, bowler–fieldsman
    combination 183
Stewart, Alec 42, 43, 48, 174, 179, 188,
    192
Subba Row, Raman 202
Symcox, Pat 144

Taylor, Jack 59, 189, 190
Taylor, Judi 9, 25, 189, 190
Taylor, Judy 132, 170
Taylor, Lisa 13, 14
Taylor, Mark 7, 18, 19, 20–1, 33, 35, 36,
    78, 80, 86–7, 88, 89, 90, 95, 97, 137,
    195, 199, 200, 201, 202

ACB salary 138
accused by G. Chappell of not being fit to
    lead 129–30
accuses Lara of being 'immature' 111
appearance on *This Is Your Life* 176
Ashes summer (1994–95) 38–60
asks Warne to address team 120
attitude to sledging 9
attitude to West Indies 60, 69
back injury 103, 129
batsman of the summer (1997–98) 143
batting slump 112–13, 120–1, 129–32,
    136
best Test series 173
'biggest Test win I've played in' 123
captain of Australia 6, 8–10
captain of New South Wales 17
captain of Northern District 15
career lowpoint 132
century in a session 169
childhood 12–13
comeback century at Edgbaston 132–3
comparing his side with other great XIs
    1–2
dressing room discipline 40
dropped by Dean Jones 130, 131
double-century stand with Slater 88
equalling Don Bradman's record 167–70
farewell season 174–83
fiftieth catch off Warne 145
first century as Test captain 50
first five thousand runs 76
first nickname 17
first Test wicket 30
fitness campaign 1998 161–63
forfeits one-day captaincy 140
foundation of success 176
four hundred and twenty-six runs for the
    match 171
last Test 188–91
leadership style and temperament 2–4,
    20, 31
'Let's-Get-Tubby' campaign 124
New Zealand series (1997–98) 141–3
on-field philosophy 41, 87

one-off Test in India 104–5
one-hundredth Test catch 89
one-hundredth Test match 175–7
opening partners 56
opening combination with Geoff Marsh 46
opening combination with Michael Slater 55, 109
record 157th catch 189
selection that wasn't 17
sends opposition in for first time 121
slow hand-clapped in Perth 23
South African series (1997–98) 143–6
tour of England (1997) 127–36
tour of India (1998) 151–9
tour of Pakistan (1994) 24–33
tour of Pakistan (1998) 163–73
tour of South Africa (1997) 117–24
tour of West Indies (1995) 63–76
tribute from Neil Marks 183
vice-captain of Australia 19–20
West Indies series (1996–97) 106–16
winning run ends 153
World Cup (1996) 94–6
Taylor, Peter 8, 9, 16, 17
  tribute to Mark Taylor 207
Taylor, Tina 12
Taylor, Tony 12, 13, 14, 132, 170
  tribute to Mark Taylor 207
Taylor tributes 203–7
Taylor, William 189, 190
Tendulkar, Sachin 35, 96, 105, 151, 153, 154–5, 156–7, 158, 195
  preparation for duel with Warne 152
Thompson, Patterson 63
Thompson, Scott 175
Thomson, Jeff 4, 99, 100
Thorpe, Graham 44, 177
Trueman, Fred 98
Trumble, Hugh 78
Trumper, Victor 4
Tufnell, Phil 41, 42, 44, 49, 58
Turner, Ross 15–16, 20
Tyson, Frank 'Typhoon' 11

Vaas, Chaminda 88
Venkatapathy Raju 155
Vettori, Daniel 141
Vidler, Bob 16

Walker, Ken 14
Walker, Max 64
Walsh, Courtney 10, 34, 64, 68, 69, 72, 99, 106, 107, 115, 171, 202
Walters, Doug 61, 62, 77
Waqar Younis 24, 25, 28, 30, 78, 86, 161, 167
Warne, Brooke 135
Warne, Shane 2, 3, 4, 7, 11, 22, 27, 30, 31, 33–7, 38, 39, 40, 41, 42, 43, 49, 51, 54, 57, 58, 67, 71, 73, 75, 76, 78, 86, 95, 104, 105, 118, 122, 135, 141, 151, 152, 153, 154, 155–6, 158–9, 163–4, 173, 175, 180–1, 185, 186, 195, 198, 205
  'ball of the century' 110
  'Billy Bunter-type figure' 144
  bribery scandal 32–3
  captaincy support from G. Chappell 146
  criticism of Lara 116
  diet causing concern 144
  finger operation 102–3
  hat-trick 44–5
  inducement to stop smoking 181
  involvement with Indian bookmaker 178, 181–2
  mastery over Daryll Cullinan 119
  million-dollar home 160
  most wickets by a slow bowler 156
  nerves against Proteas 122
  pace of flipper 42
  popularity overseas 157
  remarkable Chanderpaul dismissal 110
  revenge on Saleem Malik 84
  series v West Indies (1996–97) 107–16
  shoulder operation 159
  stress on body 90, 156
  three-hundredth Test wicket 143–6
  tour of West Indies (1995) 65
  tribute to Healy 150

West Indian axing 198–201
working with Terry Jenner 82–3
World Cup (1996) 96
Wasim Akram 24, 25, 26, 30, 32, 78, 82,
    86, 161, 165–6, 167, 171, 172
fiery spell at Rawalpindi (1994) 28
Waterhouse, Gai 205
Waugh, Lynnette 80
Waugh, Mark 4, 16, 26, 36, 39, 41, 50, 52,
    58, 66, 69, 88, 90, 109, 112, **125–7**,
    130, 132, 134–5, 136, 143, 153, 165,
    169, 185, 194, 196
accused of being frightened 125–6
Adelaide heroics 125, 143–4, 165
bribery scandal 32, 33
career-best form 116
denies rivalry with Steve 127
famous stand in Jamaica 72–5
highest Test score, under duress 157
huge six in Perth 141
innings of life 123
involvement with Indian bookmaker 178,
    181–2
plays grade cricket ahead of Steve 128
ranked No. 2 batsman in world 125
rated finest all-round fieldsman 127
World Cup brilliance 95–6
Waugh, Steve 7–8, 18, 20, 23, 26, 27,
    28–9, 30, 35, 39, 41, 58, 60, 63–4,
    80–1, 85, 87, 89, 95–6, 104, 109, 112,
    116, 120, 123, 125, 136, 138, 151,
    152, 155, 158, 166, 171, 175, 177,
    179, 192, **193–7**, 206
bats through an entire day's play 118–19

'Bradman-like record in England' 135
captain of Australia for first time 135
captaincy recommendation from Healy
    120–1
confrontation with Curtly Ambrose 70–1
disputed catch of Lara 66–7
famous stand in Jamaica 72–5
first-grade seasons 128
gains one-day captaincy 140
'my best cricket ahead' 116
ninth time out in the 90s 182
Test average reaches 50 for first time
    89
'They needed Steve Waugh on the *Titanic*'
    166
twin centuries at Old Trafford 134–5
vice-captain of Australia 124
warning to administrators 105
West Indies tour (1999) 198
Waugh twins 1, 3, 16, 21, 28, 97, 122, 160,
    174, 180, 181, 196, 202
named best batsmen in world 123
record 44th Test together 116
Whatmore, Dav 90
Wilkins, Phil 16, 67, 81, 113
Willey, Peter 115
Williams, Stuart 65, 71
Wills, Roger 61
Wilson, Bruce 97–8
Wilson, Paul 153, 155, 156
Woodfull, Bill 143

Zarawani, Sultan 96
Zoehrer, Tim 98